Japan Sea

HOKKAIDO

TOHOKU

CHUBU

KANTO

Tokyo

Pacific Ocean

0   300 km

HIKING IN JAPAN

HIKING IN JAPAN

An Adventurer's Guide to the Mountain Trails

Paul Hunt

KODANSHA INTERNATIONAL
Tokyo • New York • London

JACKET PHOTOS

Front: Shirouma-dake photographed by Sōnosuke Sakagami
Back: Photos by Paul Hunt

Distributed in the United States by Kodansha America, Inc., 114
Fifth Avenue, New York, N.Y. 10011, and in the United Kingdom
and continental Europe by Kodansha Europe Ltd., 95 Aldwych,
London WC2B 4JF. Published by Kodansha International Ltd.,
17-14, Otowa 1-chome, Bunkyo-ku, Tokyo 112-8652, and Kodansha
America, Inc. Copyright © 1988 by Kodansha International Ltd.
All rights reserved. Printed in Japan.

LCC 88-80125
ISBN 0-87011-893-5
ISBN 4-7700-1393-0 (in Japan)

First edition 1988
98 99 00   12 11 10 9

CONTENTS

Kanto 116

Tohoku 158

Hokkaido 176

Introduction

Japan—land of people crowded wall to wall into small houses, narrow streets, and restricted spaces, with traffic jams, factories, office blocks, and concrete buildings in every direction you look. This is the only view seen by many visitors, and even residents, in the overcrowded cities of Japan, where the population and industry are squeezed into narrow coastal corridors. However, there is another, opposite view, which can sometimes be glimpsed from Tokyo on a fine day—a world of forested mountains, craggy ridges and snowy peaks hovering over the city roofs like a mirage. Take an elevator ride to the top of one of Tokyo's skyscrapers on a fine day in winter, and the breathtaking panorama across the concrete to the unmistakable white cone of Mt. Fuji, surrounding mountains, and the sea will convince you of the reality of this world.

Although many pilgrims and hikers struggle to the top of Mt. Fuji during its two-month open season in July and August, this is one of the least scenic mountains to climb in Japan, and very disappointing for many climbers. However, lying below Fuji's revered peak, three-quarters of the area of the Japanese islands is mountainous, and offers spectacular alpine scenery, shady forests, and rushing mountain streams in picturesque valleys. Japan's modern economic advances have not left this natural world untouched, as roads encroach further each year, and the numbers of tourists and hikers increases, but the contrast between Japan's ugly cities and its natural mountain scenery is startling.

There is a mountain of Japanese guidebooks to their mountains—more comprehensive than I have seen for any other country in the world—but there is a lack of information in any language other than Japanese. As I struggled with the Japanese guidebooks and maps while struggling over their mountains, I found I was gathering a wealth of information useful to other foreigners wishing to escape the infernal Japanese cities. The result is this guidebook, which contains descriptions and information of hikes done by me in the period since 1980, with details brought up-to-date as near as possible to the time of publishing. I have had some exhilarating, as well as gruelling, times in the Japanese mountains, and I would not have missed these adventures for anything. My wish is to share these experiences with other foreigners coming to these mountainous islands, so that they too may see what I consider to be the best part of Japan.

My priorities in choosing the mountains to be included in this book from the amazing array of possibilities were their scenic value, as well as their height, and special features of interest, such as temples, shrines, and active volcanic areas. As the hikes included stretch from Northern Hokkaido to Southern Kyushu, there is quite a diversity in the natural environments and scenery of the different areas.

Most Japanese mountains are crisscrossed with a comprehensive network of trails allowing several routes up and down, but my choice of trails was based on the objectives of reaching the summits, seeing the main points of interest in the area, ease of access to the trailhead, convenience of campsites or mountain huts on the route, and either a circular or an A to B route with no backtracking. All of these objectives usually cannot be achieved on one route, and so I have tried to indicate alternatives.

The hikes described are not all of the same scenic value or difficulty, and so two scales are included to give an indication of these based on my own subjective appraisal. These can only be used as a rough guide, as the season and weather conditions greatly influence both. Times given on the hiking routes should also be treated with caution, as they were subjectively calculated by me to give the hiking time needed by a reasonably fit person in reasonable weather conditions. Fit hikers with a light pack can easily beat these times, but unfit hikers with a heavy pack and taking many rest stops need to add extra time. The times were calculated for the direction indicated by the arrows. If you hike in the opposite direction, the times on the slopes will change. Six hours of actual hiking in one day is enough for most people, and so you need to plan the hike adding rest times and calculating for places to stay overnight on longer hikes. Alternative plans should be considered in cases of bad weather—a constant problem in Japan.

Some of my routes are long two- or three-day hikes, but they may be done in part by returning the same or a different way. The descriptions and maps should allow you to plan your own routes of either more or less difficulty and I have tried to indicate possible alternatives. However, it is best to keep to the more popular trails until you become familiar with hiking in the Japanese mountains. If a route becomes too difficult, or the weather turns bad, you should stop and re-evaluate your plans, and possibly return or take the easiest route back down the mountain. It is always better to be safe and live to make another attempt under better conditions.

The main trails are usually clearly marked by signposts, but there are many smaller forestry trails in the Japanese mountains, and so if you loose the trail or seem to be going in the wrong direction, it is best to go back to the last signpost or place you were sure was on the main trail and check you did not take a wrong turn. The microtexture and precipitous valley slopes in Japan mean that losing the trail can be disastrous, and attempting to go cross-country often impossible or extremely dangerous. Trails usually follow ridges or valleys and only occasionally climb the steep slopes between, where extra care should be taken. Modifications or closed trails, due to road or dam construction and occasional landslides, should be checked by asking the local people or other hikers before setting out. New, alternative trails are also occasionally opened up in the Japanese mountains.

Winter and spring hiking in most of the Japanese mountains is dangerous without the necessary equipment and experience. The trails are also likely to be covered with new snow, making routes difficult to follow, and should only be attempted by experienced hikers in an area they know well.

Hikers and climbers in the Japanese mountains should be aware of the many dangers they are exposing themselves to and not attempt anything beyond their ability, but with proper preparation and planning these dangers are greatly reduced. The challenge is its own motivation, and once you have breathed the heady air of the peaks and viewed the majestic scenery, it is hard to stay put in a suffocating, sedentary city life—especially the overcrowded Japanese variety.

Happy hiking!

EDITOR'S NOTE: Unlike English, Japanese does not have spaces between words. In *Hiking in Japan* we decided to break the names, using hyphens, into the basic name and its geographical component unless such a split resulted in an extremely short basic name.

For example: Mitake (Mi Peak), but Asahi-dake (Asahi Peak).

Please refer to the Japanese language guide for a list of geographical terms.

Hike Gradings

Scenic Value

*	No particularly striking scenery.
**	Mostly forest trails, but some good views and pleasant scenery.
***	Good mountain scenery with lakes, marshes or interesting fauna and flora.
****	Magnificent mountain scenery with panoramic views from ridges or peaks.
*****	Spectacular alpine mountain scenery with year-round snow fields and alpine flowers.

Difficulty

+	Easy hike suitable for children or those not used to hiking.
++	Fairly easy, but may be difficult for those out of shape.
+++	Moderately difficult—should be attempted by those with experience on easier hikes.
++++	Strenuous, with steep, rocky slopes and sometimes chains or ladders on the trail over difficult spots.
+++++	Very strenuous with some scrambling or rock climbing involved up steep, rocky crags.

Map Symbols

♠ Supervised Shelter	✳ Water	═══	Road
⌂ Unsupervised Hut	▲ Peak	--------	Trail
⬧ Campsite	♨ Fumarole	------	Hiking Route
YH Youth Hostel	── River		

Mountain Festivals

Mountain	Event	Date
Aso-san	Hifuri shinji (bad spirits' ordeal by fire)	March 18
Daisen	Opening Festival	First Sunday in June
Dewa Sanzan	Haguro-san Pilgrimage	August 24-30
Fuji-san	Opening Festival	July 1
Futago-yama	Opening Festival	April 29
Hakusan	Opening Festival	July 17-18
Ishizuchi-san	Pilgrimage	July 1-10
Kamikōchi	Opening and tribute to Walter Weston	First Sunday in June
Kujū-san	Opening Festival	Second Sunday in June
Kumotori-yama	Opening Festival	First Sunday in June
Kurodake	Opening Festival	June 1
Meakan-dake	Opening Festival	First Sunday in July
Mitake-san	Hinode Matsuri	May 8
Mitsumine	Matsuri	April 8
Nantai-san	Pilgrimage	First week of August
Ōmine-san	Pilgrimage	August 1
Osore-zan	Shamanistic Meet	July 20-24
Rausu-dake	Opening Festival	July 3
Rishiri-san	Opening Festival	July 2-3
Shari-dake	Opening Festival	June 26
Takao-san	Fire Walking Festival	Second Sunday in March
Tanzawa-san	Opening Festival	Third Sunday in April
Tateyama	Opening the Alpine Route	April 28
Tokachi-dake	Opening Festival	June 12
Yōtei-zan	Opening Festival	June 19

NOTE: Opening Festival dates mark the start of the official climbing season, when huts and shops along the trails are open. This does not mean that climbing at other times is forbidden, but it is not advised.

National Holidays

January 1	New Year's Day
January 15	Coming of Age Day
February 11	Foundation Day
March 21	Spring Equinox
April 29	Greenery Day
May 3	Constitution Day
May 5	Children's Day
September 15	Respect for the Aged Day
September 23	Autumn Equinox
October 10	National Sports Day
November 3	Culture Day
November 23	Labor Day
December 23	Emperor's Birthday

NOTE: Although January 1 is the only official New Year holiday, many businesses close down until January 4 or 5.

Japan's Highest Mountains

1. Fuji-san	3,776 m.	Yamanashi, Shizuoka
2. Shirane-san, Kita-dake (South Alps)	3,192 m.	Nagano, Shizuoka, Yamanashi
3. Hotaka-dake, Okuhotaka (North Alps)	3,190 m.	Nagano, Gifu
4. Yari-ga-take (North Alps)	3,180 m.	Nagano, Gifu
5. Arakawa-dake, Warusawa-dake (South Alps)	3,141 m.	Shizuoka
6. Akaishi-dake (South Alps)	3,120 m.	Nagano, Shizuoka
7. Ontake-san (North Alps)	3,063 m.	Nagano, Gifu
8. Shiomi-dake (South Alps)	3,047 m.	Nagano, Shizuoka
9. Senjō-ga-take (South Alps)	3,033 m.	Nagano, Yamanashi
10. Norikura-dake (North Alps)	3,026 m.	Nagano, Gifu
11. Tateyama, Ōnanji-yama (North Alps)	3,015 m.	Toyama
12. Hijiri-dake (South Alps)	3,010 m.	Nagano, Shizuoka

Getting Around

Japan is one of the most expensive countries in the world for transport, although for the high prices you pay you do also get one of the fastest and most efficient services. The public transport network in Japan is very comprehensive and provides access to all corners of the country, including many remote mountain areas and islands. Generally public transport is faster than private car, especially in the large cities. The only drawback apart from high prices is that public transport often gets very crowded, particularly in the morning and evening rush hours, on Sundays, and on national holidays.

There is often a choice between different modes of transport to reach a destination, and in these cases the private railway lines (*shitetsu*) are usually the cheapest and best, followed by the Japan Railways (JR), and finally the buses, which tend to be more expensive. Internal flights to major cities are not much more expensive than the bullet train (*shinkansen*) fares, but for longer distances to Hokkaido, Kyushu, or the southern islands, ferries are cheaper if you have the time.

Passes are often available for travel within certain areas and cover various modes of transport, with validity extending from one day to much longer periods. These are often issued by private railways, but include bus and sometimes boat and ropeway services too, and can save you a lot of money. Enquiries should be made at tourist, train station, or bus station offices before making a journey.

The Japanese plan their short vacations in minute detail, noting the exact minute of arrival, departure, and connections. Planning ahead can save a lot of time and trouble, with timetables available at travel offices, and transport usually running punctually to the exact minute. In most cases, to reach a national park or good area for hiking it is necessary to make the first part of the journey by train, and then change to bus for the remainder of the journey, so planning for good connections is advisable.

JR (JAPAN RAILWAYS) operates an efficient and punctual nationwide service which is usually the best way of getting around Japan, with direct services to the four main islands.

A Japan Rail Pass valid for seven-, fourteen-, or twenty-one-day periods can be purchased before coming to Japan at JAL offices or authorized agents overseas, but cannot be bought in Japan. If you plan to do a considerable amount of traveling by train in a short period of time, one of these passes can save you a lot of money. Several discount tickets are also available for journeys to designated areas and on certain routes, so this information should be checked out at the station before buying a regular ticket.

JR operates several types of passenger trains. The slowest, which stops at all stations, is the local train (*futsū*). The rapid train (*kaisoku*) stops at fewer stations and runs as a commuter service in urban areas. Both of these trains only require a basic-fare ticket. Express (*kyūkō*), limited express (*tokkyū*), and super express or bullet trains (*shinkansen*) require surcharges in addition to the basic fare. They also have reserved and unreserved seats, first-class coaches called green cars, and sleeping cars for overnight journeys. JR also operates bus services on some country routes.

If you are not pushed for time, the local trains are much cheaper, and stopovers may be made within the validity period of the ticket if the journey is more than 100 kilometers.

PRIVATE RAILWAYS (*shitetsu*) usually operate in urban areas but often have routes going out to mountains and National Parks. They are cheaper than JR trains, and special excursion tickets are usually available. From Tokyo four private lines are especially convenient for reaching mountains and hiking areas. They are the Odakyu Line from Shinjuku Station, which passes the Tanzawa Mountains and goes to Izu-Hakone National Park; the Keio Line, also from Shinjuku Station, goes to the base of Takao-san; the Seibu Ikebukuro Line from Ikebukuro Station passes a hilly area on its way to Chichibu, a gateway to the Chichibu-Tama National Park; and the Tobu Line from Asakusa goes to Nikko, gateway to the Nikko National Park.

SUBWAYS (*chikatetsu*) operate in the big cities of Tokyo, Osaka, Nagoya, Sendai, Sapporo, and Kyoto. They are a fast and convenient way of getting around these cities.

BUSES are usually convenient for access to remoter country areas and reaching the starting point of trails in the mountains. Bus terminals are often found outside railway stations, and connections can be made with proper planning. Bus services often run along country routes and through mountainous areas where there are no rail lines, but they tend to be rather expensive. One useful bus service, however, runs from Shinjuku to the Fifth Stage of Mt. Fuji, and is the most convenient way of getting to Fuji from Tokyo.

TAXIS should not be ruled out, and may actually be cheaper than taking a bus for groups of four or five people. Japan is well served with taxis, even in country districts, and they may be taken to places not served by public transport. It's not uncommon to see small groups of hikers arriving at the start of a trail by taxi.

CAR HIRE is another alternative which may work out as an economical and convenient alternative for small groups. There are several car hire companies in Japan with offices in all major towns and cities, so you should shop around for the best deal to meet your requirements. However, travel by road in Japan tends to be much slower than by train, and there are tolls on the expressways making this means of transport rather expensive.

FERRIES are an important means of transport, with private companies operating many ferry services connecting all of the main islands and many of the smaller islands of Japan. Kyushu and Hokkaido are connected to Honshu by tunnel, and Shikoku is connected to Honshu by bridge, so it is not necessary to take ferries to Japan's four main islands. However, if you are travelling from Tokyo or Osaka to Hokkaido, Shikoku or Kyushu, and you are not in a hurry, going by ferry can be cheaper than by train.

PLANES operate frequently on domestic routes to major cities and islands, and are convenient if you are pressed for time. Plane fares between Tokyo and Sapporo or Kagoshima are not much more than the Shinkansen and limited-express fares to those cities.

HITCHHIKING, although not practiced by the Japanese, is a good way of getting around Japan and meeting the people. It is recommended that you learn a little Japanese before putting your thumb out, as the people who stop don't always know what you are doing, and usually speak little or no English. However, the Japanese often go out of their way to help foreign travellers in their country. It is a useful way of travelling through country or mountain regions where there is no public transport, but travelling long distances by hitchhiking often has the disadvantage of leaving one stuck in big cities.

BICYCLES may often be hired at tourist resorts and national parks for cycling around local sights. Cycling longer distances in Japan has the disadvantages of narrow, busy roads and the law of not allowing cycles on the road. There's usually a section of the sidewalk marked out for cyclists, but this is often crowded with pedestrians in towns and cities. Cycling in the country and national parks is much more pleasant, and the northern island of Hokkaido has become a mecca for young cyclists in the summer because of its wide open spaces and wider roads. Cycles can be carried by train or ferry to areas of interest for cycling.

ROPEWAYS, cable cars, and chairlifts are found on many mountains in Japan and are a fast and painless way of reaching the high mountains to start a hike. Trails usually start from the top stations, go to the mountain summits, and continue on over the mountains. Many ropeways are used by skiers in winter, but are a blessing for lazy hikers and mountaineers for the rest of the year. Tanigawa-dake in Gumma Prefecture, and Asahi-dake in Daisetsu-zan National Park, Hokkaido, both have excellent ropeway services up to alpine pastures and trails across mountain peaks.

For up-to-date information on timetables and fares, you should contact the Tourist Information Center (TIC) either in Tokyo or Kyoto. Their addresses and phone numbers are as follows:

TIC Tokyo
Kotani Building
1-6-6 Yurakucho
Chiyoda-ku, Tokyo 100
Tel: 03-3502-1461

This office is near Yurakucho Station on the Yamanote Line.

TIC Kyoto
Kyoto Tower Building
Higashi Shiokojicho
Shimogyo-ku, Kyoto 600
Tel: 075-371-5649

This office is near Kyoto Station.

There is also a Tourist Office at Narita Airport—Tokyo's main international airport. Tel: 0476-32-8711

If you are out in the country, there is a nationwide, toll-free telephone service to aid tourists. Just dial 106 and ask the operator for TIC. They will help with all travel and accommodation enquiries. This service is not available in Tokyo and Kyoto. Please note that red phones cannot be used for the toll-free service, and service hours are 0900 to 1700.

Finding Shelter

Accommodation in Japan also tends to be rather expensive, but with a little planning, costs can be greatly reduced. There is a wide variety of accommodation, ranging from first-class hotels down to the more than two thousand campsites scattered throughout the country. In between there are many Western-style business hotels, Japanese inns, people's lodges, youth hostels, mountain huts, and the occasional temple offering accommodation to travellers. In Tokyo and Kyoto, there have recently appeared dormitory-type accommodations—called ''gaijin houses''—which are popular with foreign travellers.

CAMPSITES offer a tremendous reduction in travel expenses for backpackers, usually costing only a few hundred yen and sometimes free. Many campsites are owned by local authorities, but some are privately run. They usually have water supplies and basic washing facilities, and there are often barbecue grills for cooking. Some campsites hire out equipment for camping, and a few have chalet-type accommodation. However, facilities are not quite up to the standards you may be used to at American or European campsites. Camping is particularly popular with young Japanese during the summer months of July and August, and many campsites are only open during the summer season. Nevertheless, hardy types may be seen camping in the mountains and at ski resorts year-round. Campsites are usually located in national parks, where camping outside designated campsites is not really allowed. Because it is not always possible to travel from one campsite to another on a trip through Japan, other forms of accommodation are needed, especially in the towns and cities, where the cheapest accommodation is usually the youth hostel or minshuku.

MOUNTAIN HUTS are found on most of the mountains in Japan, and in the more popular hiking areas are often closely spaced. There are different grades of mountain hut, and some are very basic wooden or stone structures offering nothing more than shelter. Others are privately run, well-kept cottages with resident wardens, and offer sleeping quarters with supplied bedding, and meals. During the summer and holiday seasons these mountain huts can become very crowded, as they do not usually turn people away. The cost of a night's stay with two meals varies depending on the hut between about ¥4,000 and ¥6,000. Bookings can be made by phoning the mountain huts directly.

YOUTH HOSTELS are usually the most economical form of accommodation in Japan, and are favored by young Japanese and travellers from abroad. There are about 460 public and private youth hostels scattered throughout Japan in most of the main towns and places of interest. It is possible to stay in hostels without membership by paying an extra charge, but if you intend to stay in a hostel for several nights, it is best to become a member. The most convenient office for information and membership is just a two-minute walk from the Tourist Information Center near Yurakucho station in Tokyo, in the second level basement of the Sogo Department Store. Other convenient offices are located on the 4th Floor of the Keio Department Store in Shinjuku, and on the 7th Floor of the Seibu Department Store in Ikebukuro. The main office is Japan Youth Hostels, Hoken Kaikan, 1-2 Sadoharacho, Ichigaya, Shinjuku-ku, Tokyo 162. (Tel: 03-3269-5831). Accommodation with breakfast and dinner at a hostel usually costs between ¥3,000 and ¥4,000. Two of the disadvantages of staying at youth hostels are the strict rules and the large groups of noisy school children who often stay at them. Booking is necessary during the summer and holiday seasons, and is best at all times to be sure of a place. Youth hostels are subject to close without notice, so contact should be made before a visit.

MINSHUKU are private family inns, something like the Japanese equivalent of a British bed and breakfast, and are often about the same or only a little more expensive than youth hostels. An overnight stay with two meals usually costs between ¥5,000 and ¥7,000. Minshuku may be found throughout Japan in the country or towns, and there are usually many situated in tourist areas. They are often family-run and informal, in Japanese style homes, offering a glimpse into, and close contact with, everyday Japanese life. Bookings can be made before arriving through tourist offices. A useful address and phone number is:

> Japan Minshuku Center
> Tokyo Kotsu Kaikan Building
> 21 Yurakucho
> Chiyoda-ku, Tokyo 100
> Tel: 03-3216-6556

RYOKAN are traditional Japanese-style inns, which are more expensive than minshuku, but offer the experience of traditional Japanese culture and customs. There are usually many ryokan situated at hot spring resorts where natural hot spring water is piped to the ryokan for the traditional Japanese hot spring baths which can be enjoyed in communal bathrooms in the ryokan. Some ryokan have *rotenburo* or natural outdoor hot spring baths, where you may bathe outside amidst natural surroundings. A stay at a ryokan includes two traditional Japanese meals, which are usually very substantial. Some ryokan are a little wary of foreign travellers, but there is an organization of ryokan that welcomes foreign guests. For their pamphlet, contact:

> Japanese Inn Group
> Hiraiwa Ryokan, 314 Hayaocho
> Kaminoguchi-agaru
> Ninomiyacho-dori
> Shimogyo-ku, Kyoto 600
> Tel: 075-351-6748

BUSINESS HOTELS offer economical, Western-style accommodation in cities and are usually located close to railway stations. They are a relatively recent development, catering to the needs of travelling Japanese businessmen. Their costs are cut by doing away with some of the services of the large hotels, but they are clean, efficient, and convenient. Daily rates are usually about ¥7,000 for a single room without meals.

PEOPLE'S LODGES (*Kokumin Shukusha*) are government-owned, Japanese-style hotels, usually located in national parks or other tourist areas.

NATIONAL VACATION VILLAGES (*Kokumin Kyukamura*) are similar in being government-run accommodation for tourists. Their rates vary, but you can expect to pay upwards from ¥6,000 including dinner and breakfast.

PENSIONS are a recent development mostly catering to the needs of young travellers. They are found in areas popular with young Japanese holidaymakers, such as Karuizawa, and usually have a hybrid Japanese-Western style. Accommodation with breakfast and dinner costs upwards from ¥7,000.

TEMPLES may be found offering accommodation to travellers in a few places such as Kōya-san on the Kii Peninsula. The style is similar to a ryokan with meals included; the only difference is that the monks serve the meals and clean the rooms. Rates are upwards from about ¥6,000.

GAIJIN HOUSES cater to the increasing number of young foreign travellers coming to Japan and looking for inexpensive accommodation. They are usually houses or dormitories, with shared rooms and cooking facilities, allowing short- or long-term periods of stay. The rates vary according to the length of stay, and are often much cheaper for stays of one month or more, usually about ¥60,000 a month. This makes them the cheapest form of accommodation for travellers. There are many gaijin houses in Tokyo and a few in Kyoto. The best place to find their addresses and phone numbers is in the monthly *Tokyo Journal* magazine.

A Note on Customs

If you are staying in a Japanese-style inn such as a ryokan or minshuku for the first time, there are many customs to be aware of. On entering the hall you must take off your shoes before stepping onto the raised floor level. Slippers are usually ready for guests to slip into, and are used for walking in the corridors. When entering a room of tatami mats, you must take off the slippers and walk on the tatami only in stockinged or bare feet. When entering the toilet, you must change slippers, and use the special ones only for toilet use. Do not forget to change back when leaving. Overlooking any of these points can greatly annoy the Japanese innkeepers.

A traditional tatami mat room has sliding doors and sliding paper screens across the windows. Care must be taken not to put your foot or hand through them as this will also annoy your Japanese hosts. Furniture and decoration in a Japanese-style room is minimal but tasteful, and the room is multi-purpose, being used as a living room in the daytime, a dining room at meal times, and a bedroom at night. There are no chairs, so you must sit on the floor.

In a ryokan or minshuku, meals may be carried to your room by a maid and laid out on a low table for you to eat privately, otherwise there may be a dining room for all the guests to eat together. Meal times are usually restricted to certain hours, so you should check the times on arrival.

The Japanese bath is communal (usually separate for men and women), and shared by all the guests at the inn. First you must wash yourself under a shower before entering the large bath of hot water, which is not used for washing but only for soaking and relaxing. The water is changed each day, but at hot spring resorts there may be a continuous flow of natural hot spring water through the bath. After relaxing in the bath, you can shower yourself off before drying and slipping into the Japanese robe (*yukata*) provided in your room. Guests usually wear yukata during the evening and at meal times.

In the wall cupboards of the room are stored *futon*, or Japanese mattresses, which are laid out on the tatami mat floor at night. Sometimes a maid will lay out the futon for you. In the morning you are expected to fold up the futon and replace them in the wall cupboards.

Observing these Japanese customs will please the innkeepers and will greatly help the next foreigners to wander there after you.

Eating Adventures

Although Japanese eating habits are changing, and many Western foods are finding their way into the Japanese diet, the best and most economical way of surviving in Japan is to adjust to Japanese food and eating styles. This may be difficult at first, as Japanese food tends to taste rather bland and seems insubstantial to the foreigner raised on beefsteaks and apple pie. However, the Japanese diet, based on rice, seafood, vegetables, and soybeans, opens up a new world of delicate taste and is an important factor in the longevity of the Japanese people compared with Westerners. There is a wide variety of eating places, ranging from top-class restaurants down to fast-food chains and take-aways. Although prices tend to be rather high on average, reasonably priced meals can be found without too much trouble.

RESTAURANTS in Japan are found in tremendous variety from authentic Western cuisine to the various styles of Japanese cooking and a liberal sprinkling of Chinese restaurants. Inexpensive restaurants can usually be found near stations, in downtown areas, and on the top floors of department stores. The set lunches and dinners, which are usually served between certain hours, often include soup, coffee, and sometimes a dessert, as well as the main meal. Set lunches can usually be found for ¥600 to ¥900. Plastic models are nearly always displayed in the windows of restaurants so you can see what you are ordering. A typical Japanese meal would include miso soup, rice, fish, and pickles. Widely known traditional Japanese foods such as sashimi, sushi, tempura, shabu-shabu, and sukiyaki are considerably more expensive.

FAST-FOODS range from a variety of American-style hamburger joints and pizza restaurants to stand-up Japanese noodle shops and *bentō* take-aways. Although these places are very cheap and convenient for travellers, the hamburger joints are not always such a good deal, as you can often get a full meal in a restaurant for the same price as the packaged food at one of these places. Pizza restaurants such as Shakey's often have an "all you can eat" lunch for ¥600, which is a good deal if you are hungry. Stand-up noodle shops, where you can get a filling bowl of noodles in soup for about ¥300, are often found in or around stations. These shops often serve other dishes like rice and curry or *gyūdon* (beef on rice) for a little more. However, the most economical food is the *bentō* (box lunch) which comes in several varieties and includes rice, fish or meat, and pickles. These can be bought from the bentō chains found in most urban areas or at stations, and usually cost about ¥300 to ¥900.

COFFEE SHOPS are found everywhere in Japan and are used as places for relaxing. Coffee and tea prices at ¥300 and up are expensive, but you are really paying for the space you are occupying. During morning hours many coffee shops have a special "morning service" which includes a breakfast for the same price as the coffee. Some of these deals are about the best bargains in Japan and are well worth looking out for.

JAPANESE MEALS served at hostels, mountain huts, minshuku and ryokan are very traditional in style, and always based on rice. The breakfasts are the most difficult to stomach for unaccustomed foreigners, as they include rice with a raw egg, fish, seaweed, pickles, miso soup and green tea. Once you do become accustomed to this style of breakfast it can actually taste very good, and stand you in good stead for a day of hiking. The dinners are usually more varied and often include many kinds of seafood, fish, vegetables and soup, with rice and green tea. Seasonal fruits take the place of Western-style desserts, which Japanese are not too fond of.

CAMP AND HIKING FOOD is not available in the variety found in America and Europe, and there is a lack of special dried camp food. However, there are some alternatives such as packets of dried *ramen* noodles, which can be cooked in a few minutes, and dried soup powders. Canned foods are available, but again not in the variety found in the West. Bread is not up to the quality accustomed to in Western countries, but it is now widely available in Japan. Instead of sandwiches many Japanese hikers eat *onigiri*, which is a kind of sandwich made with rice wrapped in seaweed, with fish or seafood inside. Packed bentō meals are also convenient for taking on hiking trips, as well as the various kinds of sushi which can be bought at shops or take-aways. Energy foods such as chocolate, nuts, raisins and candies are widely available, but fairly expensive. Food prices in Japan are relatively high, especially in tourist areas, but savings can be made by shopping at large supermarkets in the main towns. Bargains can sometimes be found by shopping in the supermarkets just before closing time, when perishable foods are often sold off at half price.

Many campsites have barbecue grills, and wood is often obtainable nearby. However, in the higher mountains a cooking stove is needed if you wish to cook, as wood is not always available. Due to the generally high rainfall in Japan there is usually no problem with water supply, except on some high mountain routes. Trout can be caught in many mountain streams, but fishing is often controlled, so you should first check on the local regulations. The mountains of Japan also contain a large number of edible plants and vegetables, known as *sansai*, which are avidly collected and treated as delicacies by the Japanese.

A Note on Customs

As well as the big differences between Japanese and Western foods, there are also differences in eating etiquette. Meals are usually eaten at a low table in a tatami mat room, so it is necessary to sit either cross-legged or in a kneeling position. The first skill to acquire is that of using chopsticks (*hashi*), which are well-suited to Japanese food. Remember not to leave the hashi stuck in the rice—this is extremely bad manners because of its resemblance to a Buddhist grave. When not in use, the hashi should be rested on the special small rest.

There is no special order for eating a Japanese meal—all the main and side dishes, rice, and soup are eaten at will. The Japanese take care in the presentation and appearance of the food, and usually make a comment about how nice it looks before eating. Before starting your meal you should say *itadakimasu*—an expression of thanks for receiving the food. After finishing your meal you should say *gochisōsama deshita*—an expression of thanks for having eaten. The main dishes are placed in the center of the table and separate hashi should be used to transfer the food to your plate or dish.

Soup is eaten by lifting the bowl in both hands and raising it to your lips. The rice bowl is held in one hand while eating the rice with the hashi held in the other. If the food is hot you should never blow on it—the Japanese suck air into their mouth to cool hot food. When eating noodles or soup you should make a sucking noise—this is good manners. Quiet noodle and soup eaters are looked on in the same way as noisy eaters in the West!

Preparing Yourself

Before you set out into the mountains it is essential to be well-prepared, plan your route, have the necessary equipment and be ready for adverse changes in the weather, which can occur at any time and very rapidly in the Japanese mountains. The popularity of hiking and mountain climbing has boomed in Japan, as in many Western countries, and specialist shops have opened up, catering to the demand for equipment. However, Japanese equipment, although improving, is not yet up to the standards of Western countries. It is therefore advisable to buy equipment before coming to Japan. Imported equipment from the U.S.A., the U.K., and Italy can be obtained in Japan, but at much higher prices. There is also a problem with sizes, and larger-sized boots and clothes are often not stocked in Japanese stores as there is little demand for them.

The following is a list of essential equipment:

BOOTS - These should be strong and give ankle support. Leather boots are not essential, as there are now some good canvas and plastic boots on the market, but they should be waterproof.

BACKPACK - The size you need depends on whether you plan on one-day hikes, in which case a small day pack will do, or long expeditions of several days camping in remote mountains, in which case a full-size pack is needed. It should be waterproof, and if it has a frame, then preferably an internal one, as these give your body more freedom on difficult climbs. I don't recommend the wide canvas Boy Scout rucksacks often seen in Japan, because they are not waterproof, and the center of gravity is too far back.

WATERPROOFS - Japan is a very wet country and so waterproof clothes should be carried at all times—even when the forecast is good. Getting wet in the mountains greatly increases the danger of exposure—it is *most* important to keep dry. Goretex material is the best, as this keeps water out and also lets perspiration out—a good point on strenuous climbs. A jacket with hood and separate trousers is preferable to a large poncho, which flaps in the wind and may be inadequate in stormy conditions. It is a good idea to pack everything in your backpack separately in plastic bags, and take spare bags for wet clothes.

WARM CLOTHES - Even in midsummer, when Tokyo is basking in tropical heat, the high mountains can be very cold, even reaching sub-zero temperatures at night. Many Japanese climbers dress for the occasion, in mountain breeches, long woolen socks, thick shirt, and woolen sweater even in hot summer weather. You may not need warm clothes, but you should always be prepared. Thick trousers, woolen sweater, warm jacket, gloves, and hat are needed for high mountains and spring and autumn hiking.

FIRST AID KIT - This should include antiseptic cream, Band-Aids, bandages, cotton wool, and aspirin. Insect repellent may also be useful—especially in Hokkaido in summer.

COMPASS - This is usually not needed in Japan due to the micro-texture of mountains and valleys, but if you are caught in bad, foggy weather in remote regions, it may be essential.

MAPS - The maps in this book give a general outline of the hiking areas and trails, and will be sufficient if you keep to the main routes. However, if you wish to plan your own routes, you should use more detailed maps. The National Survey Sheets (*kokudo chiri-in*) of the 1:50,000 or 1:25,000 series cover the whole country, and are available at large book stores. Care should be taken in their use as they are often several years out of date. Plastic hiking maps, together with a small guidebook covering each of the main hiking areas of Japan, are published in a series called *Area Maps* by Shōbunsha, and are the best maps for hiking in Japan.

WATER BOTTLE OR THERMOS FLASK - to carry drinks.
FLASHLIGHT - in case you are out after dark.

Equipment for longer expeditions:

TENT - Mountain huts tend to be rather crowded and expensive in Japan. A tent allows more privacy and camping is much cheaper. Camping sites are not found on all mountains, though, and so their locations should be checked. Notably, camping is not allowed on Mt. Fuji. Dome tents have become very popular and are especially recommended in Japan, where they are easily erected on rocky ground and do not need lots of space for guy ropes.

SLEEPING BAG - This is essential if camping, but also recommended if you do not wish to use communal blankets in the huts. Some huts, especially the unmanned ones, have no bedding or blankets. A down bag with a waterproof outer layer is recommended for high mountains, spring, and autumn camping.

COOKING STOVE - Fires are officially only permitted at designated campsites, and in the high alpine mountains there is usually insufficient fuel. However, camping stoves are much more convenient for cooking in the mountains. All kinds of fuel and gas cartridge refills are available in Japan, but should be bought in a large city.

Winter climbing in snow and ice conditions is out of the scope of this guidebook, but some mountains in Japan have permanent snowfields—notably Hakuba and Tateyama in the North Alps—where crampons and an ice axe would be useful even in mid-summer.

There are many hiking and climbing equipment stores in Tokyo and other large cities in Japan, but one I especially recommend is Ishii Sports, Towa Bldg., 210 Okubo, Shinjuku-ku, Tokyo 160 (Tel: 03-3200-7219). It is conveniently located two minutes' walk from Shin

Okubo Station on the Yamanote Line. They stock a wide array of imported equipment at reasonable prices. The staff are helpful, speak some English, are knowledgeable and can advise on hiking and climbing areas.

Insurance for mountain climbing and hiking injuries in Japan is very expensive, and so if you wish to have cover it is best to take out insurance in another country before coming to Japan and *make sure it covers Japan*. Rescue fees and medical expenses in Japan are astronomical. For example, if you break your leg in the mountains, helicopter rescue is likely to cost ¥1 million or more, and hospitalization ¥2 million or ¥3 million.

If you intend to go hiking or climbing for the first time it is strongly recommended to go with others who have had experience hiking in Japan. There are many Japanese hiking clubs which accept foreign members, and a growing number of clubs especially catering to foreigners in Japan. These clubs organize meetings and regular hiking trips which you can join.

THE INTERNATIONAL ADVENTURE CLUB is a group of foreigners and Japanese who organize hiking, rock climbing, and skiing trips out of Tokyo. They have monthly meetings in Tokyo and issue a newsletter. The annual membership fee is ¥6,000. They can be contacted through Dave Parry (Tel: 03-3327-2905) or Yuko Nakano (Tel: 03-3944-6074)

FRIENDS OF THE EARTH, the worldwide organization concerned with environmental protection, has a Tokyo office which organizes one-day hikes in the Kanto District and advertises them in the *Japan Times*. They charge a small fee to join a hike, and usually get a very good response. Their office is located at: 4-8-15 Nakameguro, Meguro-ku, Tokyo 153. (Tel: 03-3760-3644)

THE JAPANESE ALPINE CLUB (*Nihon Sangaku Kai*) is the oldest and largest mountaineering club in Japan. Founded in 1905, one of its founding members was Walter Weston—the originator of alpinism in Japan. There are 21 branches from Hokkaido to Kyushu with several thousand members, some of whom are foreigners. Their main office in Tokyo has a comprehensive library of mountaineering books and maps which can be used by members. They organize regular hikes and meetings, and the membership fee is ¥25,000 (¥15,000 entrance fee and ¥10,000 annual fee). Their main Tokyo office is five minutes' walk from Ichigaya Station: Sun View Haitsu 1F, Yonbancho 5-4, Chiyoda-ku, Tokyo 102. (Tel: 03-3261-4433)

THE JAPAN ALPINE GUIDE ASSOCIATION (*Nihon Alpine Gaido Kyōkai*) provides guides for easy hiking or difficult rock climbing in any mountain area of Japan. It is a Japanese association but foreigners are welcome, and the guide fee is approximately ¥15,000 to ¥20,000 per day. They can be contacted at: 401 Sezaru Yoyogi Koen Bldg., 2-26-1 Hatsudai, Shibuya-ku, Tokyo 151. (Tel: 03-3379-9683)

THE JAPAN ENVIRONMENT EXCHANGE in Kyoto organizes hiking trips in the Kansai District. They are located at: Tomitaya Bldg. 4F, Oike-agaru, Teramachi-dori, Nakagyo-ku, Kyoto 604. (Tel: 075-252-0737)

THE KANSAI RAMBLERS are a group of foreigners who organize regular hikes in the Kansai District, and advertise their activities in the *Kansai Time Out* magazine. They can be contacted in Kobe (Tel: 078-232-4517).

Dealing with the Language

Some understanding of the Japanese language is essential if you plan to make trips out into the country alone, as few Japanese have any practical ability in English or other languages. However, it is not too difficult to acquire a basic working knowledge of spoken Japanese for use in everyday situations. The main difficulty in Japanese is the writing system, which takes several years of study because it uses Chinese characters as well as two alphabets. It is worthwhile memorizing the alphabets and sound system of Japanese before learning vocabulary and phrases, as this will be useful in getting the correct pronunciation as well as reading menus and station names.

Kana, the Japanese alphabet system, was derived from simplified Chinese characters, as Japan had no written language before the introduction of Chinese culture about 1,300 years ago. The two systems of *hiragana* and *katakana* are used for Japanese words and foreign words respectively. The pronunciation is the same for both systems, but it would seem that the Japanese like to distinguish between native words and foreign imports. There are a considerable number of foreign words used in modern Japanese, mostly from English, but they are pronounced according to the Japanese sound system, and so are often unrecognizable without an understanding of *kana* and plenty of practice. For example, the word "English" in Japanese *kana* pronunciation comes out as *Igirisu* and "hotel" comes out as *hoteru*. Most Japanese kana are equivalent to syllables in the Roman alphabet, and except for the "n" sound, Japanese does not use consonants without their being followed by a vowel sound. Pronunciation of Japanese words is very regular, and so presents few problems. The Roman alphabet, known as *rōmaji*, is also widely understood and used in Japan.

Kanji are the Chinese characters which are used in a simplified form in Japanese. There are 1,850 kanji for regular use (*tōyō kanji*), with more being used in names. The difficulty of Japanese kanji is that one kanji may have several readings. For example, the simple kanji for mountain (山) may be read as *yama, san, zan,* or sometimes *sen* or *zen.* Memorization is the only way to learn the correct reading, and so even the Japanese themselves will not know the name of a place written in kanji unless they are already familiar with it. This can prove frustrating to travellers in remote regions of Japan where only the locals know the correct pronunciation of names of villages, rivers, lakes, mountains, etc.

When learning kanji, it's best to start with the simple ones, which are then used as radicals to build up the more complex kanji. It is easier to learn kanji recognition than the correct writing of them, and when travelling around Japan you will soon build up a considerable number which you can recognize.

HIKING VOCABULARY

What's the weather forecast? - *Tenki yohō wa dono yō desu ka.*

Tomorrow will be cloudy. - *Ashita wa kumori desu.*

Today will be rainy. - *Kyō wa ame desu.*

fine - *hare desu*

snowy - *yuki desu*

windy - *kaze desu*

cold - *samui desu*

hot - *atsui desu*

Where's the start of the trail? - *Tozan guchi wa doko desu ka.*

Is this the trail to Mount Takao? - *Kore wa Takao-san made no yamamichi desu ka.*

How long does it take to the mountain cottage? - *Sansō made dono gurai kakarimasu ka.*

How far is the summit? - *Chōjō made dono gurai desu ka.*

It's far. - *Tōi desu.*

near - *chikai*

steep - *kyū*

difficult - *taihen/muzukashii*

dangerous - *abunai*

Please help me! - *Tasukete kudasai.*

MAP VOCABULARY

map - (地図) *chizu*

mountain - (山) *yama, san, zan, sen, zen*

peak - (岳) *dake, take*

ridge - (峰) *mine*

summit - (山頂) *sanchō* (頂上) *chō-jō*

pass - (峠) *tōge*

plateau - (高原) *kōgen* (平) *taira, daira*

plain - (原) *hara, bara, baru*

valley - (谷) *tani, dani*

marsh - (沼) *numa*

pond - (池) *ike*

lake - (湖) *mizuumi, ko*

stream/valley - (沢) *sawa, zawa*

river - (川) *kawa, gawa*

waterfall - (滝) *taki, daki*

trail - (山道) *yamamichi*

mountain hut - (山小屋) *yamagoya*

mountain cottage - (山荘) *sansō*

shrine - (神社) *jinja,* (神宮) *jingū*

temple - (寺) *tera, dera, ji*

A Note on Pronunciation.

The final "e" of a Japanese word is pronounced like the "ay" in "say". The "a" of Japanese is pronounced "ah", and the "u" like the "ue" in "blue".

Each syllable is pronounced separately: *Abunai* (danger)—Ah-bue-nah-ee

The Hiking Environment

The Arena

At the beginnings of history in the Middle East, the people called the East "Asu," meaning sunrise, and the West "Eleb," meaning sunset. In English these terms became Asia and Europe.

So goes one theory concerning the origin of the names. Fact or happy myth, there is certainly a confluence of European and Japanese worldviews in the word *Nippon* (or *Nihon*), which means "origin of the sun" in Japanese. The term "land of the rising sun" is synonymous with Japan, and is depicted on the national flag. Marco Polo was the first Westerner to learn of this land from the Chinese and he used the southern Chinese name of Jihpan or Jihpangu to introduce this remote island nation to Europe.

Originally, the Japanese islands were inhabited by a different race of people, who were probably related to other groups living in the remote regions of Siberia. Remains from the Jōmon period (8,000–300 B.C.) show these people to have been cave dwellers, hunters and gatherers who produced a distinctive kind of pottery. During the later Yayoi period, the present Japanese people gradually spread from Kyushu in the south, northward to northern Honshu. They were plain dwellers who brought their knowledge of rice cultivation with them. There is a debate as to the exact origin of the Japanese people. Physical similarities relate them to the Mongols of Central Asia, while language and architectural styles relate them to the peoples of the South Pacific region. As the Japanese settled in the islands and moved northward, the indigenous population was pushed to the north, much as the Celts in Europe and Britain were also pushed northward at about the same time by the advancing Angles, Saxons and other races. The Japanese finally drove the Ainu north across the Tsugaru Straits into the northern island of Hokkaido, their last refuge, in the twelfth century. Hokkaido was not actively settled by the Japanese until the late nineteenth century, when the government began programs for its development. At present there remains a small population of approximately 15,000 Ainu in Hokkaido, but they are being rapidly assimilated into the Japanese population by intermarriage, and their culture remains as little more than a tourist attraction for the hordes of Japanese tourists from the south.

GEOGRAPHY

The four major islands of Japan—Hokkaido, Honshu, Shikoku and Kyushu—form ninety-seven percent of its total area of 377,483 square kilometers, which is divided into eight districts and forty-seven prefectures. Apart from the four main islands, there are more than 3,300 smaller islands around the coast of Japan and extending in chains south toward Taiwan and into the Pacific Ocean. The main Japanese archipelago extends 3,000 kilometers from northeast to southwest, and its coastline totals 28,600 kilometers in length. The coast is comprised of sandy beaches, as for example along much of the Japan Sea coast of Tohoku, and of ria-type coasts, as along the Pacific coast of Tohoku and the Nagasaki region of Kyushu. Hilly or mountainous terrain covers seventy-five percent of the area of Japan, and most of the mountain ranges follow the axis of the archipelago, except for the higher ranges of central Honshu, which generally run north-south. The mountainous regions are mostly forested, and natural or planted forest covers more than sixty percent of the area of Japan.

The Japanese islands are formed by the tops of submarine mountain ranges rising 6,000 meters to 10,000 meters from the ocean floor, and are located in the tectonic boundary zone between the Eurasian continent and the Pacific Ocean. They form part of the "Ring of Fire," the world's most unstable zone, which circles the Pacific Ocean and is characterized by volcanic activity and earthquakes. Tokyo shares with San Francisco and Los Angeles the unenviable position of sitting on top of a geological time bomb.

The tectonically active nature of the Japanese islands gives rise to a wide variety of volcanic landforms and frequent earthquakes, and this, together with a wet climate due to its location at the meeting point of continental and oceanic air masses, results in intense erosional processes. Valleys and rivers are generally short and densely developed, forming a complicated texture of micro-relief. The slopes are steep and rugged with a shallow soil, and swift streams carry sediment to alluvial fans and deltas which form the plains around the coasts.

Due to the rugged nature of the terrain, less than sixteen percent of the area of Japan is cultivated, and there is a tremendous population pressure on the land suitable for agriculture and housing. As the flat land is mostly on the alluvial fans around the coasts, this is where most of the population lives, and one of the largest densely populated regions of the world is to be found along the Pacific coast of Japan, extending from the Tokyo Bay area southwestward through Nagoya, Osaka, Hiroshima, and on to Kita Kyushu. However, the transition from the densely populated plains to sparsely populated mountains can be very abrupt. Areas for recreation and hiking may therefore be very near to the main population and industrial centers, and because of the well-developed transportation network they can be very easy to get to.

OCEANOGRAPHY

As well as being located in a tectonically active zone between continental and oceanic plates, and at the meeting point of oceanic and continental air masses, oceanic currents from north and south also meet along the shores of Japan. From the south, the warm Kuroshio, or Japan current, warms the southern and western regions of Japan, especially Kyushu and the islands and peninsulas jutting out into the Pacific Ocean. The influence of this current reaches up to the Bōsō Peninsula in Chiba Prefecture, and these coastal regions have little snow in winter. However, the warm Kuroshio brings generally wet weather, and steers typhoons toward the Japanese islands during the summer and early autumn. A branch of the Kuroshio flows through the Tsushima Straits into the Japan Sea, but the Japan Sea is colder and more influenced by the Liman Current, which flows from the north along the shores of Eastern Siberia. The cold Oyashio or Chishima Current flows from the North Pacific and affects the northern islands of Hokkaido and the east coast of Tohoku. Fog is more frequent along these shores due to the cooling effect of the ocean, and in winter parts of the northeastern coast of Hokkaido become ice-bound, as at the port of Abashiri.

NATURAL DISASTERS

The location of the Japanese islands at the meeting place of tectonic plates, air masses, and ocean currents results in a high frequency of natural disasters. Earthquakes occur fairly frequently and occasionally cause damage in built-up areas. About fifteen percent of the world's earthquake energy is discharged in the vicinity of Japan. Large earthquakes offshore sometimes result in tsunami waves, which can cause damage to coastal regions. Volcanic activity is also widespread and, as well as providing the Japanese with their beloved hot springs (*onsen*), showers them with volcanic ash and destroys their settlements with lava flows. At Kagoshima in Kyushu the active volcano of Mt. Sakurajima is constantly belching forth ash, smoke, and steam over the surrounding population, and occasionally volcanic explosions and lava flows destroy settlements, as happened a few years ago on the slopes of Mt. Asama in central Honshu, and on Miyake Island.

A summer monsoon circulation brings high rainfall, especially to the southern and western parts of Japan, and these regions are prone to frequent flooding and landslides. Typhoons during the summer and early autumn usually affect the same regions, and may cause severe damage with intense rainfall and high winds. During the winter a monsoon circulation blows cold air from Siberia, which picks up moisture as it passes over the Japan Sea and dumps heavy snowfall over the northern and western parts of Japan facing the Japan Sea. The deep snow causes communication problems and flooding in spring.

The nature and frequency of these natural disasters have influenced the Japanese people in the development of their culture, and the leaning of their native religion, Shinto, toward nature worship. Their efforts in confronting natural disasters have also produced a hardworking people.

NATURE CONSERVATION

The Japanese have traditionally been observers and lovers of nature and the changing seasons, but this tradition has recently been under pressure from a rapidly growing and industrializing population. Hence there has been a great need for nature conservation. In 1931 the National Parks Law was passed after the U.S. model, and sites were selected from 1934 onwards. The parks are under government control and administered by the Nature Conservation Bureau of the Environment Agency, but due to the crowded nature of Japan some private lands are included within the parks. Most of the national parks have volcanic features, and many of them have active volcanoes and hot springs.

There is a classification of parks, the most important being the National Parks (*Kokuritsu Kōen*), of which there are 28. Next come the Quasi-National Parks (*Kokutei Kōen*), whose scenic value is not quite up to the standard needed to become a full national park. Of these there are 54. The Prefectural Natural Parks (*Todōfuken Shizen Kōen*) are usually smaller and chosen by the prefecture concerned. There are 298 of these parks. Smaller areas of particular interest are designated as Scenic Places (*Meisho*), as for example Mt. Fuji, and Kamikōchi in the North Alps.

The natural environment of Japan has much of interest and beauty to offer the visitor, and the high density of scenic elements and features is best appreciated on foot. Many Japanese people escape the overcrowded cities during their short weekends and vacations, and enjoy the open spaces and fresh air on mountain trails. However, their numbers have caused severe erosion along some of the more popular trails, and bad cases of pollution due to carelessness and forgetting of old traditions. The network of trails in the parks and mountains is very comprehensive, and there are many areas little frequented and untouched which are accessible to the backpacker, and where wildlife in its natural state may be seen.

Forces Below

Japan is situated in one of the most active tectonic regions of the world and forms a part of the circum-Pacific "Ring of Fire". Sub-oceanic crustal plates meet the thicker and lighter continental plates and are subducted beneath them. Stress builds up between the plates and is released periodically, causing earthquakes. Earthquakes of various magnitudes are frequent throughout Japan. Frictional heating between plates also causes high temperatures at the plate boundaries, which results in the melting of rocks, igneous intrusions into the overlying sedimentary rocks, and volcanic activity at the surface. Japan has a large proportion of the world's active volcanoes.

TECTONICS

The Japanese islands are formed by a series of island arcs which are paralleled to the east by deep oceanic trenches. These trenches are the result of the subduction of oceanic plates, which descend beneath the lighter continental plates. Due to the great forces at the plate boundaries, upwarped zones form island arcs which rise several kilometers above the ocean floor. In the Japan region the difference in height between the ocean floor and the highest mountains is as much as ten kilometers, although the highest mountain, Mt. Fuji at 3,776 meters, is less than half of this figure. Island arcs are the result of orogeny or mountain building caused by high pressures at plate boundaries where rocks are folded and faulted, and igneous intrusions and volcanic activity combine to form mountain chains parallel to the plate boundaries.

The Japanese islands can be divided into at least four island arc systems. To the north the Kuril or Chishima Arc runs through the Kuril Islands from Kamchatka to Central Hokkaido. Another less active island arc runs from Sakhalin Island (Karafuto in Japanese) to Central Hokkaido. The Japan Arc runs down the center of the main island of Honshu, but this is divided in two by a major fault known as the Fossa Magna or the Itoigawa-Shizuoka Tectonic Line, which runs north-south across the center of Honshu. This divides the Japan Arc into the Northeast Japan Arc and the Southwest Japan Arc. The Fossa Magna is a major geological feature, and is associated with the Izu-Mariana or Ogasawara Arc, which runs southward through the chain of islands extending into the Pacific Ocean from the Izu Peninsula. The Ryukyu Arc extends from Northern Kyushu through the Ryukyu chain of islands to Okinawa and Taiwan.

Where two or more island arcs meet, the width and height of the mountains become substantial, as can be seen in central Hokkaido, central Honshu, and Kyushu. Generally, the mountain ranges run parallel with the island arc systems, but this is modified in the case of the Japan Alps, where the ranges are orientated NNE-SSW as a result of tectonic activity associated with the Fossa Magna Tectonic Line.

VOLCANISM

Japan is one of the best countries in the world for volcanic scenery. There are about 200 Quaternary volcanoes in Japan, of which about 60 have erupted since the seventh century. A majority of Japan's National Parks are centered on volcanoes which are either active or dormant. Volcanoes can be classified according to shape, and in Japan by far the most common form is the cone-shaped stratovolcano, as exemplified by Mt. Fuji, which is a symbol of Japan and Japan's highest mountain. Caldera-type volcanoes are also well represented, and Mt. Aso in Kyushu is one of the largest and best examples of a caldera in the world. Tholoide volcanoes or lava domes are also found, as for example, Mt. Koma-ga-take in Hakone National Park. Flat, shield-shaped aspite volcanoes, which pour forth basaltic lava gently, are not so common in Japan, but examples, such as Mt. Kiri-ga-mine in Nagano Prefecture, may be found.

Japan's most active volcanoes are the cone-shaped stratovolcanoes which are formed by repeated eruptions, and the build-up of lava and ash layers results in a cone shape with a crater at the apex. Conical volcanoes are usually composed of andesitic rock, which is an intermediate type of igneous rock—that is, a mixture of basaltic rock from oceanic plates and siliceous rock from continental plates. Mt. Fuji has a high basaltic content, but the silicon content of its lava is high enough to assure that violent eruptions did occur. It is situated on the Fossa Magna Tectonic Line, and the last eruption was in 1707, so that it is now dormant. Mt. Mihara on Ōshima Island is similar to Fuji in having a high basaltic content, and is also cone-shaped and is presently active. Another conical volcano situated on the Fossa Magna is Mt. Asama, which has erupted in the last few years. Other geologically recent volcanoes situated on the Fossa Magna include Mts. Yatsu-ga-take and Kurohime. One of the most active volcanoes in Japan is Mt. Sakurajima, which dominates the town of Kagoshima in Kyushu, and is also a cone-shaped stratovolcano.

Caldera-type volcanoes result from the collapse of the central part of the volcano, giving rise to a large crater, which often contains a lake. The caldera of Mt. Aso in Kyushu does not contain a lake, but has a central core of volcanic peaks which are still active. The Kussharo caldera in Hokkaido has an active core as well as a large lake, and it has a parasitic caldera which contains Lake Mashū-ko, reputedly the clearest lake in the world. Other large calderas containing lakes are Tōya and Shikotsu calderas in Hokkaido, and Towada caldera in Tohoku.

Tholoide or dome-shaped volcanoes are composed of high viscosity, andesitic lava, which rises gradually and congeals at the surface in a dome shape. These volcanoes are not violent, but pour out their lava slowly. Examples of lava domes are found in Fuji-Izu-Hakone National

Park, where Mts. Koma-ga-take and Futago-yama rise from the shores of Lake Ashi-no-ko in the Hakone caldera. Other examples are Mt. Yake-dake in the North Alps, Mt. Sambe-yama in southwest Honshu, and Mt. Tarumae-san in southwest Hokkaido, where a lava dome was born in 1909 in the middle of the crater.

The present zone of active volcanoes, which is known as the Green Tuff Zone, has been active since the Miocene, and is the youngest tectonic zone. It is found on the continental side or the inner belt of the island arc systems, where subsidence and deposition of sediments in basins has occurred. During the Miocene, large-scale submarine volcanism occurred in these subsided basins, with lavas composed of andesite, basalt, rhyolite, and pyroclastic sediments. These lavas, extruded in an aqueous environment, were altered and changed to a green color—hence the name Green Tuff. Most volcanic activity is at present found in the Honshu Arc from southwest Hokkaido to the southern end of the North Alps, where two volcanoes, Mts. Norikura-dake and Ontake are located; along the Fossa Magna, where Mts. Fuji and Asama are located, and also along the Ryukyu Arc, where Kirishima and Sakurajima are located.

STRATIGRAPHY

Due to the extensive volcanic activity, mountain building, faulting, folding, and intrusions of igneous rocks into the sedimentary strata, the geology of Japan is rather complex. Orogenic movements have been severe and almost continuous since the mid-Paleozoic era. The Japanese islands are the result of at least three major orogenic cycles during geological history. These are the Paleozoic, Mesozoic, and Cenozoic orogenic cycles. The latter cycle is still active in mountain building, and active volcanoes are located in this youngest Cenozoic orogenic belt. Metamorphic rocks are formed at the core of mountain belts—for example, the geologically young Hidaka Range in Hokkaido is composed of schists, migmatites, gneisses, and granites. Older mountain belts such as the North Alps are intruded with plutonic rocks and Cretaceous granites.

In general, exposed sedimentary strata follow the axis of the Japanese Islands and of the mountain belts, but the Fossa Magna, a major geological feature, divides Japan into two geological provinces. The northeast is widely covered with Cenozoic rocks with isolated pre-Tertiary outcrops, whereas the southwest has more Paleozoic and Mesozoic outcrops and limited Cenozoic rocks. Tertiary and Quaternary sedimentary and igneous rocks of the youngest Cenozoic era cover about two-thirds of the area of Japan, and sedimentary strata older than the Tertiary are exposed over less than one-quarter of Japan's area.

The oldest confirmed rocks are from the Silurian System, mainly exposed in Shikoku and Kyushu, and the Carboniferous System, exposed in small outcrops from Hokkaido to Kyushu. Although not absolutely confirmed, there is probably a Precambrian basement beneath Japan. The Permian System is the most widespread of the Paleozoic Systems in Japan. As these Paleozoic strata are all marine sediments, they show that Japan was beneath the sea until Permian times, and is therefore a geologically young country. The Paleozoic sedimentary strata have been metamorphosed mainly into gneiss and schists by subsequent orogeny and igneous activity.

During the Triassic period the Paleozoic strata were upwarped in a major orogeny and these strata and the subsequent orogeny formed the foundation of Japan. The Triassic is a very restricted system in Japan due to mountain building during that time, and so there is very little sedimentary strata. The Jurassic System is complex, localized, and ill-defined. The Cretaceous System is widespread from Hokkaido to Kyushu with sedimentary strata, granitic intrusions, and acidic to intermediate volcanics. The Cretaceous saw another orogenic climax.

The Cenozoic is composed of sedimentary rocks and includes the sandstones, shales, and coal seams formed in the submerged lowlands and hills during the Tertiary period. The Tertiary System is thick with widespread deposits, as, for example, in the Chichibu Basin west of Tokyo. Tertiary volcanics are mainly andesitic and basaltic, and lava from these eruptions covers more than a quarter of the area of Japan. The recent Quaternary System is also well represented, with widespread deposits accumulated over low-lying areas in basins and along the coasts. The Kanto Plain, the largest flat lowland plain in Japan, is composed of fluvial, aeolian, and marine deposits, with a system of river terraces. Sea level changes and crustal movements during the Quaternary are indicated by well-developed coastal terraces along the east coasts of Hokkaido and Tohoku. Fossil evidence also shows that the Japanese islands were connected to Asia by land bridges in the geologically recent past.

GLACIATION

Above 2,000 meters in the North, Central, and South Alps of Central Honshu, and above 1,400 meters in the Hidaka Range of Hokkaido, there is evidence of past glaciation in the form of glacial cirques, troughs, and moraines. These features are all small in scale but indicate the presence of glaciers during the Pleistocene period. Although snow patches sometimes lie year-round in sheltered hollows in the high mountains, all mountains in Japan are presently below the snow line, and so active glaciers do not exist in Japan at present. The best relict glacial landforms in Japan are to be found in the Yari-ga-take and Tateyama regions of the North Alps.

Forces Above

The Japanese, like the British, use comments about the weather in their greetings and daily conversation, and there is a large vocabulary of weather and special seasonal words, (*kigo*) in Japanese, which reflects the variable weather and changing seasons. Japan's weather is characterized by being variable and wet with distinct seasonal changes, so to plan outdoor activities and hiking expeditions to the maximum advantage it's important to get a good general picture of the geographical and seasonal changes in the weather. Accurate weather information and forecasts are an essential part of any hiking trip into the Japanese mountains, where adverse weather conditions can quickly lead to disaster, and do, in fact, claim many lives every year. Weather forecasts may easily be obtained from Japanese newspapers, radio, television, and telephone, and these sources should be used before setting out to the mountains.

SEASONAL CYCLE

Six seasons can be clearly distinguished in Japan, despite the surprise that this comment usually brings to the Japanese. This situation is generally caused by Japan's location between Asia, the world's largest landmass, and the Pacific, the world's largest ocean, which both exert their influence over the islands. During the winter the Siberian high pressure system extends its influence over Japan, bringing the cold, snowy, northwesterly monsoon. This situation is reversed in summer when the North Pacific subtropical high pressure system builds up and brings a hot, humid airflow over Japan in the southeasterly monsoon. Between these two more or less stable monsoonal circulation systems there are four intermediate natural seasons in Japan. These seasonal variations are due to the movement of the mid-latitudinal westerly circulation, and the position of the polar frontal zone. Japan's location in the temperate zone of the mid-latitudes brings it under the influence of the westerly circulation with its associated jet stream, polar frontal depressions, and mobile anticyclones. However, during winter the westerly circulation is pushed to the south of Japan by the northwesterly monsoon blowing from the strong Siberian high, and during the summer the North Pacific high pushes the westerly circulation to the north of Hokkaido.

In spring the northward movement of the westerlies brings unsettled weather with mobile depressions and anticyclones. This is followed by the *baiu* or *tsuyu* rainy season when the polar frontal zone moves slowly northwards over Japan. After the southeasterly monsoon breaks down in late summer the situation is reversed as the polar frontal zone moves southwards, bringing the wet *shūrin* or *akisame* season. This is also the season of typhoons in Japan. Following this second rainy season is the autumn, which also sees the passage of mobile depressions and anticyclones in the westerly circulation.

The timing and length of these seasons varies between the north and south of Japan. Hokkaido in the north has a much shorter summer and longer winter than Kyushu in the south, and is not much affected by the baiu rainy season. June is usually the best month in Hokkaido, when the rainy season covers much of the rest of Japan. May is usually the best month in Honshu and the south of Japan before the rainy season sets in.

The summer to winter change of seasons is faster than the winter to summer change. This is because of the strength of the Siberian high, which builds up in late autumn, and the relative weakness of the North Pacific high, which builds up slowly in late spring, resulting in a longer spring as the westerly circulation and the polar front move slowly northward. Fluctuations of several weeks may occur in the natural cycle of the seasons in Japan.

WINTER

In winter, high pressure over Siberia and low pressure over the North Pacific cause a northwesterly monsoon to blow cold continental air from Siberia over Japan. Due to the cold air mass and high pressure system extending over Asia, the upper-air westerly jet stream shifts south of the Himalayas, and generally continues south of Japan with its associated polar frontal zone so that Japan comes under the influence of a stable northwesterly monsoonal circulation. The air mass from Siberia is very cold and dry, but during its passage across the Japan Sea it picks up moisture, and becomes unstable due to the relatively warm sea temperature. On reaching the Japan Sea coast the effect of orography in lifting the air mass over the mountains causes heavy snowfall, especially in the Hokuriku region and on the mountains facing the Japan Sea. The mountains of North and Central Honshu facing the Japan Sea commonly have average maximum depths of snow greater than three meters. The absolute measured maximum depth was more than eight meters at Terano near Takada in Niigata Prefecture in 1927.

Due to the orographic effect of the mountains there is a rain shadow effect on the Pacific side of the Japanese islands during the winter northwesterly monsoon. The Siberian air mass, having released its burden of snow on the Japan Sea side of the mountains, descends on the leeward side, and becomes dry and relatively warm, creating foehn winds or *karakaze*. This can cause dry spells with a serious fire danger on the Pacific side of Japan. While the Japan Sea side of the mountains experiences very cloudy and snowy winters, the Pacific side experiences increased sunshine and low precipitation. The maximum snow depth measured in Tokyo was 46 centimeters in 1883. Most snowfall on the Pacific side occurs in late winter or early spring as migratory depressions in the westerly circulation move northwards, and the precipitation falls as snow due to the still-cold temperatures. The contrast between the amount of snowfall on the Japan Sea and Pacific sides of the mountains running down the center of Honshu can be quite abrupt and startling. This can be experienced on a train ride from Tokyo to Niigata between January and March. Tokyo usually has little or no snow lying in the city, and there may only be a light sprinkling on the Pacific facing mountains. A tunnel goes beneath the Pacific-Japan Sea watershed, and on emerging, the Japan Sea facing slopes are often covered with snow up to several meters in depth. It is also quite a strange sight in winter to see trains covered with snow pulling into a snowless and sunny Ueno Station (Tokyo).

SPRING

Towards the end of February the northwesterly monsoon begins to break down, and the westerly circulation to the south of Japan moves northwards. This is associated with the weakening of the Siberian high, and the shifting of the westerly jet stream northwards. At this time the first gale of spring occurs, known as *haru ichiban*, a sign that winter is ending. Depressions cross Japan from the East China Sea, migrating northeastwards and bringing unsettled cyclonic weather which alternates with the clearer, drier weather of migrating anticyclones. The spring season is characterized by periodic wet and dry weather, with frontal depressions bringing cloudy weather, rain, and often snow, especially to the Pacific side and southern parts of Japan. Temperatures generally become warmer as the cherry blossom front advances northwards across Japan from late March to early May.

BAIU

The *baiu* or *tsuyu* (wet) season is caused by a stagnation of the polar front for approximately 30 days, bringing cyclonic, frontal, cloudy, wet weather to most of Japan during June and early July. The rains start earlier and last longer in Kyushu and southern Japan, where they begin in early June. In Tokyo they generally begin in mid-June. The polar front moves slowly northwards and brings extended periods of cloudy, wet weather with possibly a few short breaks. The baiu generally lasts until mid-July, by which time it has moved north of Hokkaido and weakened. Rainfall generally decreases northwards. Kyushu has very heavy, intense rainfall, but Hokkaido may have very little. The Pacific side of Japan experiences rainfall maxima during this season, but the Japan Sea side, which has a precipitation maxima in winter, has less rainfall during this season.

SUMMER

A subtropical high pressure system establishes itself over the North Pacific and extends its influence over the Japanese islands during July.

The westerly circulation and polar front are pushed north of Japan, and the southeasterly monsoonal circulation establishes itself over all of Japan. Subtropical maritime air flowing from the Pacific Ocean southeast of Japan is hot and humid but fairly stable as it passes over the warm Kuroshio Current. The weather is generally fine, and dry spells can occur in July and August if the North Pacific high locates itself over Japan. However, thunderstorm activity reaches a maximum in July and August, and very heavy storms are possible. Kyushu and the Pacific side of Shikoku and Honshu are the most likely regions for thunderstorm activity.

The temperature variation over Japan in the summer is not very great, with generally widespread high temperatures. The exceptions are the high mountains and Hokkaido, which may be considerably cooler. Warm, moist air passing over the cool ocean where the Oyashio Current flows east of Hokkaido and Tohoku often causes fog along the Pacific coasts of those regions. Northern Honshu and Hokkaido may also experience cool northeasterly winds known as *yamase* in the summer. The summer begins later and is much shorter in Hokkaido than in the rest of Japan. In a bad year the North Pacific high may not be strong enough over Japan to displace the polar front northwards, and a cool, wet summer may result in Hokkaido or even further south.

SHŪRIN

At the end of August the North Pacific high begins to break down, and the polar front moves southwards over Japan during September and October, bringing the frontal rainfall which is more popularly known as the *akisame*. Northeastern Japan, and especially the Pacific coasts of Tohoku and Hokkaido, experience a rainfall maxima during this season. This is also the season of typhoons in Japan. Tropical depressions or typhoons are formed throughout the year in the tropical Pacific, but they usually only approach Japan between July and October, with their highest frequency in late August. On the average, three or four serious typhoons a year approach Japan, and these mostly affect the Pacific side of southern Japan. Very intense rainfall and high winds can cause severe damage if a typhoon hits land. Typhoons usually track northwestwards from the tropical Pacific Ocean, and thrive on the warm waters of the ocean from which they derive their energy. If they pass over land or cross to the Japan Sea they usually weaken and turn northeastwards, then soon dissipate.

AUTUMN

The autumn season is similar to the spring season in being cyclonic and unsettled with depressions and frontal systems crossing Japan in a northeasterly direction from the East China Sea. Weather is periodic with cloudy, wet weather alternating with fine weather as depressions and anticyclones migrate northeastwards in the westerly circulation. The season begins earlier in Hokkaido, at the beginning of October, and covers most of Japan by mid-October. The Siberian high builds up during November, extending its influence towards Japan as temperatures decrease and snow falls in the mountains. December sees the northwesterly winter monsoon set in as the Siberian high prevails against the westerlies.

CONTINENTAL, OCEANIC, AND OROGRAPHIC EFFECTS

The large temperature difference between summer and winter shows the effect of a continental climate due to Japan's proximity to Asia. There is generally a decrease in temperature as you move northwards from the southern islands to Hokkaido. However, this temperature gradient is twice as great in winter than in summer, and is also much greater in winter between the cold Japan Sea coast and the Pacific coast. This shows that the influence of the very cold Siberian air mass during the northwesterly monsoon is greater in the northern and western parts of Japan facing the Japan Sea. In summer, Japan is uniformly under the influence of the warm southeasterly monsoon, and regional temperature differences are not so great.

Japan is surrounded by sea and ocean, and the maritime effect can be seen in the high precipitation on the islands. Southwest Japan and the Pacific coast are particularly affected by high rainfall, and these regions experience intense rainfall during the baiu and *shūrin* rainy seasons when rainfall figures over 10- to 24-hour time periods are among the highest in the world. Sudden flooding and landslides are common occurrences, especially in Kyushu. During the winter monsoon the Japan Sea coast experiences high precipitation in the form of snow, with the highest snowfalls centered on Niigata Prefecture. Southwest Japan, the Pacific coast, and the Japan Sea coast may experience precipitation levels of more than 300 centimeters per year, but this decreases northwards, and eastern Hokkaido usually has only 80 to 100 centimeters. Frontal activity and summer thunderstorms result in no distinct dry season in Japan.

Altitudinal and orographic effects should not be forgotten, especially on hiking trips into the mountains, as the high mountains in Japan often create their own weather and large temperature differences. For example the temperature difference between Tokyo, at just above sea level, and the summit of Fuji-san at 3,776 meters, 100 kilometers WSW of Tokyo and Japan's highest mountain, is more than 20°C in both summer and winter. Rainfall and summer thunderstorms are also often much heavier in the mountains than over low-lying areas.

Flora and Fauna

Due to the latitudinal extension of the Japanese islands, four climatic or natural vegetation zones may be distinguished. In the north the cold subarctic zone covers most of Hokkaido. Tohoku and Central Honshu mostly fall in the cool temperature zone. Southwestern Honshu, Shikoku, and Kyushu fall in the warm temperate zone, and the subtropical zone covers most of the southern islands. This simple distribution is modified by the altitudinal effect of the mountains so that high peaks in the temperate zones have an alpine vegetation.

Farming in the lowlands and forestry in the mountains has modified much of Japan's natural environment, especially in southern Japan, but large areas of natural, undisturbed environments still exist and are protected by the National Parks. Sixty percent of Japan is forested, this figure only being surpassed by Finland, and a wide variety of trees, shrubs, and flowers are to be found. The islands are also rich in bird life, and a variety of wildlife still exists in its natural state. There are a remarkable number of animal and plant species which are only to be found in Japan, and some of these species are restricted to very localized areas.

SUBARCTIC FOREST
This zone covers all but the southeastern part of Hokkaido and is mainly a coniferous forest with some deciduous trees in mixed forests. It is dominated by spruce (*Ezomatsu*), and white fir (*todomatsu*), with some Japanese cypress (*hinoki*), Japanese red pine (*akamatsu*), and Japanese black pine (*kuromatsu*). Deciduous trees found in the mixed forests include birch (*kaba*), Japanese yew (*ichii*), and aspens (*doronoki*). In the mountains of Honshu the Hondo Spruce (*toranoomomi*), Maries fir (*Aomori todomatsu*), and veitch fir (*shirabiso*) are found. Bamboo grass (*sasa, také, chiku*) is usually abundant in the undergrowth of this forest. There is also the Japanese rowan (*nanakamado*).

ALPINE FLORA
Above the subarctic forest in the high mountains of Hokkaido and Honshu is an alpine zone of creeping pine (*haimatsu*) and alpine plants. In Hokkaido this zone may be as low as 1,000 meters, but in Central Honshu it is above 2,500 meters. Here a profusion of colorful alpine flowers may be seen in the summer, with many plants being found only in very localized areas. Daisetsu-zan in Hokkaido and the North Alps in Central Honshu are two of the best mountain areas for seeing alpine flowers in abundance.

COOL TEMPERATE FOREST
This zone extends from the southwestern part of Hokkaido to Central Honshu and covers most of Tohoku. It is mainly a deciduous broadleaf forest dominated by Japanese beech (*buna*). On ridges and dry slopes Japanese oak (*nara*) is often found. Other deciduous trees include elm (*ohyō, harunire*), ash (*shioji*), chestnut (*kuri*), maple (*kaede, momiji*),

cherry (*sakura*), katsura (*katsura*), zelkova (*keyaki*), and in the north and high mountains birch (*kaba*). Coniferous trees to be found in this zone include the Japanese cypress (*hinoki*), Hondo spruce (*toranoomomi*), fir (*momi*), Japanese larch (*karamatsu*), Northern Japanese hemlock (*kometsuga*), and in the south Japanese cedar (*sugi*). Bamboo grass is found in the undergrowth together with a variety of shrubs, plants, and mushrooms, a large number of which are edible.

WARM TEMPERATE FOREST

Covering southwestern Honshu, Shikoku, and Kyushu this zone extends further northwards along the Pacific and Japan Sea coasts due to the warming influence of the Kuroshio Current, and so the peninsulas of Noto, Izu, and Boso are included in this zone. It is an evergreen broadleaf forest dominated by oak (*kashi*). In the northern cooler parts deciduous broadleaves such as Japanese chestnut (*kuri*), elm (*ohyō, harunire*), ash (*yachidamo*) and zelkova (*keyaki*) are mixed in. In the southern, warmer parts pasania (*shii*) and camphor (*kusunoki*) are major species. Conifers such as pine (*matsu*), southern Japanese hemlock (*tsuga*), Japanese fir (*momi*), and Japanese cedar (*sugi*) are also widespread. A variety of shrubs is found, including the laurel (*aoki*), camellia (*tsubaki*), rhododendron (*shakunage*), and azalea (*tsutsuji*). Bamboo (*také*) and bamboo grass (*sasa*) thrive in this zone. Ferns (*shida*) are especially widespread in the shady undergrowth of forests and the young shoots of two species are prized as a delicacy. One is a bracken (*warabi*) and the other is a flowering fern or osmund (*zemmai*). In Kyushu the evergreen broadleaf forest passes into deciduous broadleaf forest at about 1,000 meters altitude.

SUBTROPICAL FOREST

This zone is found in the southern Ryukyu Islands south of Yakushima and includes the Amami, Okinawa, and Iriomote islands. Many warm temperate species are found in this zone together with such exotic species as the cycad or Japanese sago palm (*sotetsu*) and the ginkgo (*ichō*), a large deciduous tree which is one of the oldest surviving species in the world. The dominant species are the palania, various oak species (*kashi*), and the tabu tree of the laurel family (*tabunoki*). Mangroves are also found in this zone. However, on these subtropical islands much of the natural forest has been cleared to be replaced with grassland, scrub, and farmland.

FORESTRY

The large area of mountainous land in Japan is unsuitable for agriculture, but the Japanese have utilized the steep slopes for forestry to supply the large domestic market. Reforested areas are mainly planted with conifers in the following proportion: cedar (*sugi*) 33%, cypress (*hinoki*) 22.5%, larch (*karamatsu*) 18%, and white fir (*todoma-*

tsu) 12.5%. As a result the area of coniferous forest is increasing, but natural broadleaf forest still covers the largest area.

AVIFAUNA

There is a rich and varied bird life in Japan, giving excellent opportunities to spot interesting and rare species on hikes in the countryside, mountains and along the coasts. A large number of sea and shore birds and 17 endemic species are to be found in the Japanese Islands.

Situated between the large land mass of Siberia, which becomes cold and frozen in winter, and the warm islands of Southeast Asia, Japan is on the migration route or is the destination of many migratory birds. Winter migrants come from Siberia, where they breed in the summer, and include such birds as swans, ducks, cranes, and geese. Summer migrants come from Southeast Asia and breed in Japan. Examples are swifts, swallows, flycatchers, and some warblers. Transients pass through Japan, breeding during the summer in Siberia and the Arctic, and wintering in Southeast Asia or Australasia. These include many sandpipers, curlews, and plovers. Resident birds which may be seen year-round in Japan include tits, thrushes, some warblers, woodpeckers, kingfishers, owls, eagles, hawks, and pheasants.

An interesting bird found only in the alpine zone of the high mountains in central Honshu is the ptarmigan (*raichō*), which changes its plumage from white in the winter to brown in the summer. In the forests at lower altitudes, the copper pheasant (*yamadori*) may be seen. This is endemic to Honshu, Shikoku, and Kyushu, but is not found in Hokkaido. The common pheasant (*kiji*) is found in more open, low-lying areas, and a subspecies, the *kōrai kiji*, or ring-necked pheasant, is common in Hokkaido and Tsushima Island.

Bird-spotting is an interesting and enjoyable exercise on any hike into the countryside and mountains of Japan, and guidebooks are available in English for bird identification. There are also a number of bird sanctuaries specifically for the protection of wild birds. Examples are Arasaki in Kyushu and Akan in Hokkaido, both of which are famous for their cranes.

FAUNA

There are 130 species of mammal in Japan, of which thirty percent are endemic. On the main island of Honshu there are 46 species, of which 16 are endemic. The large number of endemic species is a result of the Japanese islands being cut off from mainland Asia.

The Japanese serow (*kamoshika*) is an endemic species found only in the high mountains of Honshu, Shikoku, and Kyushu. It is a goat-like antelope and may be seen in the forests, and sometimes the alpine zone, running nimbly over steep, rocky slopes. A common animal found all over Japan, and especially in the mountain forests, is the Japanese deer (*shika*). In Hokkaido the *Ezo shika* is larger than the deer further south. This phenomenon of the northern, colder climate species being larger than the species to the south is also seen in the northern fox (*kita kitsune*), and the brown bear (*higuma*), which are both found in Hokkaido and are larger than the species found to the south. In the mountains of Northern and Central Honshu the smaller black bear (*tsukinowaguma*) may be found.

The Japanese macaque (*Nihonzaru*) is the northernmost monkey in the world with its range extending to Northern Tohoku. However, its numbers are greater to the south, where it may be seen from coastal areas to mountain forests. On Yakushima, south of Kyushu, is a monkey endemic to that island only (*Yakushima zaru*). On the southern island of Iriomote the rare Iriomote wild cat (*Iriomote yamaneko*) may be seen. In Shikoku there is the rare otter (*kawauso*), which was once thought extinct, and the loggerhead turtle (*akaumigame*) may be found at a few beaches. There is also a wild boar (*inoshishi*) which inhabits the forests of Honshu. The Japanese wolf (*ōkami*) was hunted to extinction in about 1905.

Smaller mammals are commonly seen in the mountain forests of Japan. The Japanese squirrel (*Nihon risu*) is a red color and found in Honshu, Shikoku, and Kyushu. In Hokkaido the *Ezo risu* is a chocolate-brown color. The Asiatic chipmunk (*Ezo shima risu*) is common in Hokkaido, and may be seen up to the alpine zone of high mountains. It is brown with dark and light side stripes, and often makes its home amongst the creeping pine of the alpine zone. The flying squirrel (*Honshu momonga*) is found in Kyushu and Honshu with a variant, the *Ezo momonga*, being found in Hokkaido. There is also a giant flying squirrel (*musasabi*) found in Kyushu, Shikoku, and Honshu. Several species of rabbit may also be found throughout Japan, with a rare endemic species known as the crying hare or pika (*Ezo naki usagi*) Kishida found only in North, West, and Central Hokkaido. The snow hare (*yuki usagi*) may also be seen in Hokkaido. In Honshu, Shikoku, and Kyushu the field hare (*nousagi*) is widespread, and endemic to the Amami Islands is the blackish brown Amami rabbit (*Amami no kurousagi*).

Nocturnal animals living in the forests and usually only active at night include the raccoon (*tanuki*), which is similar to the North American raccoon but has no ring pattern on its tail, the yellow marten (*ten*), and the mountain weasel (*itachi*), which is found in Northern and Central Honshu. The stoat (*okojo*) is also found in high mountains. Several species of small mammals such as mice (*nezumi*), shrews (*himizu*), and moles (*mogura*) are found throughout Japan, as well as many species of bat (*kōmori*).

Lizards and snakes are also common, but the only really poisonous snake is the Okinawa *habu* found on the subtropical islands south of Kyushu. The Halys viper (*mamushi*) is the only widely distributed poisonous snake and is commonly seen in paddy fields and damp areas. It is nocturnal, slow and seldom harms humans. There is also a white snake (*shirohebi*), which is a rare white species of the blue-green snakes. In southwestern Japan the giant salamander (*ōsan-shōuo*) is a protected species.

Japan also has a large number of endemic butterflies, and alpine butterflies of the Siberian group may be seen in the mountains.

The Cultural Environment

The Japanese greatly appreciate the natural beauty of their islands and the seasonal changes in the landscape. Perhaps more than any other people they celebrate the beauties of nature en masse as, for example, in their annual cherry-blossom-viewing celebrations (*hanami*) in the spring, when crowds of people picnic and dance beneath the clouds of pink and white blossoms in the cherry groves of parks and mountainsides. The earlier blossoming of plum trees brings a similar, but milder, response. In the autumn the changing of the leaves (*kōyō*), and especially the flaming red maples, brings the Japanese out to mountain parks to take in this colorful annual show. In the winter the viewing of snow and ice is a traditional pastime which has been embodied in recent times in the annual snow and ice festival in Sapporo's Ōdōri Park.

Seasonal changes are also viewed with keen interest on the face of Mt. Fuji as the snow line descends its slopes to give a completely white Fuji in winter, and as it rises to leave a snow-free Fuji in summer.

Although the Japanese suffer from earthquakes, typhoons, and other natural disasters, they have traditionally considered themselves as a part of nature, and closely united with her. Mt. Fuji and the other sacred mountains in Japan were not climbed in the past by priests and pilgrims for the purpose of conquering nature, but for the purpose of becoming one with her, and to worship the grandeur of the mountains and the rising sun seen from the summits.

One old custom practiced by the Japanese and other Asian peoples was the abandoning of old people in the mountains to die. This practice was called *obasuteyama*. Still, in Nagano Prefecture, where the custom was most widely practiced, there is a mountain called Obasute-yama.

THE WAY OF THE GODS

Harmony with nature is the essence of Shinto, Japan's native religion. Natural sights such as mountains, forests, waterfalls, and caves inspire a sense of divinity; the Japanese idea of *kami* is related to this appreciation of nature and the environment as something sacred and living. Extraordinary events and outstanding objects that throw the attention into special activity and give a conviction of reality are designated *kami*, as opposed to events and objects of common experience. Each kami has a specific nature and may be a nor-living as well as a living thing. Men, animals, trees, mountains, sea, thunder, and echoes are some examples.

Throughout Japan, except for the northern island of Hokkaido, there are numerous Shinto shrines and *torii* gateways dedicated to the worship of *kami*, and which indicate sites of special sacred character. Mountains especially are endowed with many Shinto shrines on their slopes and summits. Examples of well-known mountains with shrines on their summits are Mt. Fuji, Mt. Mitake in Okutama, and Mt. Takachiho in Kyushu. Mt. Takachiho, an active volcano with twin craters, has a special place in the ancient legends of Japan as the mountain where Ninigi no Mikoto, grandson of Amaterasu the Sun Goddess, descended from heaven to found Japan.

Among ancient civilized peoples around the world, as well as in Japanese Shintoism, mountain worship was significant. Mountains were seen as the residence of gods, a link between heaven and earth, and a place for sacrifices and revelations. The religion of the Ainu people is also similar to Shintoism in its animistic nature worship.

SHAMANISM

Since ancient times the practice of magic and fortune-telling by shamans and especially shamanesses, known as *miko*, has been going on in Japan. Similar to the oracles of ancient Greece, the miko of Japan fall into trances, communicate with the dead, and pass messages from the spirit world to this one.

The region of Tohoku, where there are still a few practitioners, seems to have been favored by the miko. On the festival of Obon on the 24th day of the old sixth month—the feast day of Boddhisattva Jizō—in the summer, when the Japanese pay respect to their ancestors, there is a gathering of miko on Mt. Osore, located in the north of Tohoku on the Shimokita Peninsula. It is a dormant volcano with a crater lake and was believed to be a sacred mountain. A temple was built on the edge of the lake, and a terrestrial paradise was believed to exist on the summit. Along the mountain paths are stupas and statues of Jizō, a popular bodhisattva in Japan, who is believed to be the savior of the spirits of the dead and the guardian of children. This mixture of shamanism and later Buddhism is an example of the blending of religions in Japan.

BUDDHISM

It was not until the sixth century that Buddhism was introduced to Japan via China and Korea. As in China, Buddhist monasteries were built in the mountains, and mountain climbing was often practiced for religious purposes. Buddhist priests and pilgrims climbed mountains wearing white clothes and straw sandals, carrying a wooden staff and chanting a sutra for purification from the six roots of evil.

The three most important mountains in Japan for Buddhist pilgrimage, all in Central Honshu, are Mts. Fuji, Tateyama, and Hakusan. Others of lesser importance are Kōya-san, on the Kii Peninsula, Nantai-san in Nikko National Park, Daisen in Chūgoku, and Chōkai-san in Tohoku. Hokkaido has no old Buddhist monasteries or temples as it was not actively settled by the Japanese until the end of the last century. Until the Meiji Restoration in 1867–8 it was not considered safe for ordinary people to venture into the mountains unless they had first been consecrated by a priest. Buddhist saints such as Kūkai and Saichō consecrated mountains so that they were safe for pilgrimage. Mt. Yari-ga-take in the North Alps was not consecrated until 1826 when the Buddhist monk Banryū placed three Buddhist images on its spear-like summit. He repeated his feat in 1828, but he was wrong in his belief that Yari-ga-take was the highest peak in the North Alps. The nearby peaks of Hotaka are higher.

MOUNTAIN FAITH

Sangaku Shinkō, or mountain faith, as practiced by the *yamabushi*, or mountain priests of Japan, is an expression of communion with nature in arduous acts of spiritual and physical training in the mountains. Founded in the mid-seventh century as a sect of Buddhism, Shugendō, as the mountain faith sect is called, was a development of Buddhist asceticism which also incorporated many of the significant characteristics of Japanese religion. The teachings of the Buddhist Mantrayana school were mixed with naturalistic Shinto and the magical practices of shamanism to produce this sect of Japanese mountain ascetics. Belief in the Dainichi Buddha and worship of fire are part of the faith, and their objective is to attain power against evil spirits and communion with nature. Their faith sometimes led them to extreme acts such as throwing themselves into the craters of active volcanoes.

Most of the Shinto shrines in Northern Japan used to have Shugendō priests i.e., *yamabushi*, who usually travelled from mountain to mountain and shrine to shrine. They exerted a strong influence on the common people due to their supposedly magical powers. Famous mountains with temples of the Shugendō sect are Ōmine-san in the Kii Peninsula and Dewa Sanzan in Tohoku, where priests and monks of this sect can still be seen practicing their faith.

ZEN

The teaching of Zen was developed in China as the result of a mixture of Buddhist and Taoist ideas and introduced to Japan soon after Buddhism. It incorporates much of the naturalistic philosophy of Taoism and teaches its followers an intuitive understanding of life and nature through direct experience. There is no dualism in Zen, and so its attitude to nature is not one of identity, which follows from the dualist concept, or of tranquility, which is like death, but one of dynamic harmony with nature that is always in motion and one with us. Zen wants us to pay nature the fullest respect it deserves as our friend.

In Japan the three Zen sects of Sōtō, Ōbaku, and Rinzai became important influences in Japanese culture. Zen, and its appreciation of nature, found its expression in such Japanese art forms as the tea ceremony (*cha-no-yu*), landscape painting (*sumi-e*), flower arrangement (*ikebana*), and landscape gardening (*teienjutsu*).

WESTERNIZATION

A dramatic change occurred in the cultural development of Japan when it finally opened its doors to the West at the time of the Meiji Restoration in 1867–8. The import of modern technology and Western ideas had far-reaching repercussions on the landscape of Japan and the lifestyle of the Japanese. Rapid urbanization in large crowded cities such as Tokyo has taken two generations of Japanese from their previous intimate contact with nature, while rapid industrialization has caused severe pollution problems. However, as Japan is a mountainous country, mostly unsuitable for urban and industrial development, large regions of mountains have been left relatively untouched by these twentieth-century realities.

The most scenic areas are now protected as National Parks and can be enjoyed by the largely urban Japanese population during their short holidays. Modern urban Japanese, however, do not retain the traditional Japanese attitude towards nature, and bad cases of pollution and environmental damage can be found even in the National Parks.

Until the Meiji Restoration, mountaineering in Japan was a religious affair, and women were banned from climbing Japan's sacred peaks. Mountaineering as a sport was started by an English missionary, Walter Weston, who explored and climbed the Japan Alps at the end of the last century. The Japan Alps in Central Honshu were also named by a British missionary, William Gowland, in his 1888 *Japan Guide*, because of their similarity to the Alps of Europe.

Many peaks were climbed for the first time by Britons. For example, Mt. Yake-dake, an active volcano in the North Alps, was first climbed by an Englishman named Marshall in 1875. Walter Weston climbed Mt. Yari-ga-take in 1892, 66 years after Banryū, the Buddhist monk, placed his Buddhist images on its summit. Large numbers of Japanese followed Weston's lead, and now they revere him as the founder of alpinism in Japan. There is an annual festival at Kamikōchi in his honor, and a memorial plaque set in the rock face and dedicated to him can be seen in the valley below the peaks which he conquered for the first time.

Nowadays many Japanese, young and old, go hiking and climbing in their rich inheritance of mountains, but occasionally you still meet a group of white-clad, staff-wielding pilgrims climbing to a shrine on the summit of a sacred peak.

Kyushu and the Southern Islands

Wilson Sugi (Yakushima)

Kyushu is the third largest island in the Japanese archipelago, and to the south the Ryukyu chain of islands stretches to the island of Taiwan. Across the central part of Kyushu runs the Kyushu mountain range, which continues eastward on the island of Shikoku. From northern Kyushu, running south along the chain of southern islands, is the Ryukyu volcanic zone. This is an active Green Tuff region with many holocene volcanoes including Kujū-san, Aso-san, Kirishima-yama, Sakurajima, and several volcanic islands to the south. Tertiary and Quaternary volcanics intrude Paleozoic, Mesozoic, and Tertiary sedimentary strata. Yakushima Island has an exceptionally high peak formed by a granite intrusion into Mesozoic strata. Miyanoura-dake (1,935 m.), which rises precipitously in the center of Yakushima Island, is the highest peak in this southern region of Japan.

Winters are usually mild in the region, with the only snow in the northern part of Kyushu and the northwesterly facing mountains. The high peaks of Yakushima have quite a lot of snow—this being the southernmost occurrence of snow in Japan. Kyushu is notorious for its heavy rainfall, especially during the baiu season in June. Typhoons are also more frequent in this part of Japan, where they can occur from June to October. Heavy rainfall and steep volcanic ash slopes result in frequent landslides. One such susceptible area is the Shirasu Uplands of southern Kyushu.

The region is covered in warm temperate forest with subtropical forest and vegetation on the southern islands. There are also coral reefs, mangroves, and some rare animals such as the Iriomote yamaneko and the Yakuzaru. Japan's most poisonous snake, the habu, is found on the southern islands too.

The best areas for hiking are included within two national parks—Aso National Park and Kirishima-Yaku National Park. Kujū-san is included within Aso National Park and is an area of volcanic scenery. Kirishima is also an area of outstanding volcanic scenery, but Yakushima to the south is not volcanic. All of these mountain areas have popular hot spring resorts.

Apart from the parks centered on mountains, there are three centered on coastal areas and islands. Saikai National Park is a coastal and island park in western Kyushu composed of numerous islands and a submerged ria-type coast. Unzen-Amakusa National Park is found on the Shimabara Peninsula and the Amakusa Islands to the south. Unzen (Cloud Mountain) is a hot spring resort of volcanic geysers and vents with Fugendake (1,359 m.) the highest peak of a composite volcano, which erupted into violent activity in 1991. The Amakusa Islands were an outpost of the hidden Christians during the Tokugawa Bakufu regime. Iriomote National Park at the southern end of the Ryukyu chain is situated on the island of Iriomote. It is famous for its coral coast, sandy beaches, mangroves, and the endemic Iriomote wildcat. The wildcat is rarely seen as it is nocturnal and there are very few remaining. There is an easy hike on the island up the Urauchigawa River to the Mariyudo and Kampira falls, but beware the poisonous habu snake found here.

ACCESS

By Air: Domestic flights link most of the main cities in Kyushu with other parts of Japan. Fukuoka and Kumamoto also have international flights to Seoul (South Korea). The flight time from Tokyo to Kagoshima is 1 hour 55 minutes.

By Rail: The Shinkansen (Bullet Train) operates to Hakata (Fukuoka), from where it is necessary to take express trains to other cities. Travel time from Tokyo to Nishi Kagoshima by Shinkansen and Limited Express is about 11 hours, with a fare of about ¥26,220.

By Sea: Marine Express Co. (Tel: 03-3563-3911 and 0982-52-8111 in Hyūga) operates a daily ferry service between Kawasaki Port near Tokyo and Hyūga Port on the southeast coast of Kyushu, taking about 20 hours. Kawasaki-bound ferries operate on even, and Hyūga-bound on odd days of the month. Kansai Steamship Co. (Tel: Tokyo 03-3274-4271, Osaka 06-572-5181) operates a ferry on the Inland Sea route from Osaka Port to Beppu in northeastern Kyushu, taking 17 hours. Ferry services operate from Kagoshima Port to the southern islands.

ACCOMMODATION

Youth hostels are found in most of the main cities of Kyushu, with four in Nagasaki, two in Kumamoto, one in Kagoshima, one in Miyazaki, and one in Beppu. The southern islands have several hostels, and there are youth hostels at Aso and below the Kujū Mountains.

There are a few mountain huts in the mountain park areas, and many campsites in the national park areas.

The following are lower-priced accommodations in the main cities: Kumamoto Daiichi Hotel (Tel: 096-325-5151) five minutes' walk from Kumamoto Station. Senju-sō (Tel: 0958-23-1954) eight minutes' walk from Nagasaki Station. Business Hotel Kudō (Tel: 0975-32-3884) five minutes' walk from Ōita Station. Nakazono Ryokan (Tel: 0992-26-5125) six minutes' walk from Kagoshima Station. Kagoshima Gasthof (Tel: 0992-52-1401) four minutes' walk from Nishi Kagoshima Station.

1. A Volcanic Wonderland—Kirishima 霧島

True to its name the fog was hanging over the volcanic heights of Kirishima as I arrived one afternoon in early spring on the plateau of Ebino Kōgen. Making my way down the track to the campsite I was warily watched through the drifting mist and fog by a small group of wild deer grazing on an open, grassy area nearby. The campsite, amidst a forest of Japanese oak, giant red pine, cedar, and fir on a hillside about half a kilometer from the road junction, was almost empty. On a previous visit one August, the place had been crowded and noisy, but this time the small wooden cabins and campground were largely unoccupied. Most visitors during this early spring season were staying at the large mountain huts, minshuku, or hotel located around the road junction on Ebino Kōgen.

Ebino is an ideal center for exploring the Kirishima part of the Kirishima-Yaku National Park with its 23 volcanoes, 15 craters, and 10 crater lakes—a remarkable collection of volcanic features in a relatively small area. Karakuni-dake, the highest peak in Kirishima, dominates the plateau, and at the bottom of its northwestern slopes on the eastern side of the plateau, hot steam hisses forth from a scar in the mountainside. Trails are laid out through the clouds of sulphurous fumes in this area of active volcanic vents, and just 500 meters down the road you can enjoy a *rotenburo* outdoor hot spring bath near a small minshuku. This is one of the highest hot spring resorts in Kyushu. Numerous possibilities exist for short hikes around the plateau and the three crater lakes to the north. In spring and early summer the plateau and surrounding mountain slopes are adorned with a magenta-colored Kirishima azalea, known as *Miyama Kirishima* in Japanese, which is a native species of Kyushu. Takachiho-no-mine, the second highest peak in Kirishima, is the legendary mountain on which the grandson of the sun goddess descended to found Japan. This seemed a logical place to begin my hiking descriptions.

ACCESS

Bus services provide easy access to Ebino Kōgen from Nishi Kagoshima and Miyazaki train stations. The former service runs via Kirishima Shrine and Kirishima Onsen on the southwestern slopes, whereas the latter service runs via Kobayashi Station at the eastern foot of the Kirishima Mountains.

ACCOMMODATION

Campsites are found at Yunono Onsen, Takachiho-gawara, and on the lake shore of Mi-ike, as well as the one at Ebino. Minshuku and ryokan accommodation can be found near Kirishima Shrine (Jingū), at Kirishima Onsen, and Ebino Kōgen.

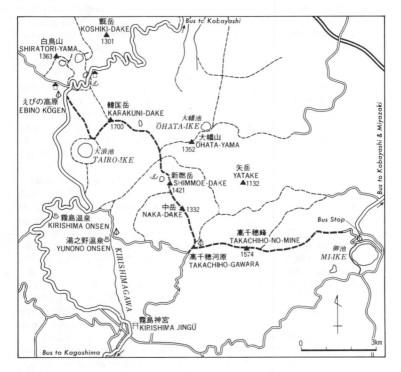

TRAILS

****

+ + +

Ebino Kōgen（えびの高原）→ 4 kms. 2 hrs. 30 mins. → Karakuni-dake （韓国岳）→ 4.5 kms. 2 hrs. → Shimmoe-dake（新燃岳）→ 4.3 kms. 2 hrs. → Takachiho-gawara （高千穂河原）→ 2.3 kms. 2 hrs. → Takachiho-no-mine（高千穂峰）→ 6.2 kms. 3 hrs. → Mi-ike（御池）

Hiking trails are fairly well signposted and easy to follow over the volcanic heights of Kirishima, but strong footwear should be worn as there are some steep volcanic rock sections. There are no streams or water on the higher slopes, so a plentiful supply should be carried on hikes from the main centers. Although there are some small shops and restaurants at Ebino, Takachiho-gawara, and Kirishima Shrine, it is best to carry food supplies from Kagoshima, Miyazaki or Kobayashi.

The best hiking route in Kirishima starts from Ebino Kōgen, climbs the peak of Karakuni-dake, and follows the line of volcanoes running southeastwards, skirting the crater of Shimmoe-dake, and passing over Naka-dake (中岳 1,332 m.) before descending to Takachiho-gawara. From here the trail climbs to the peak of Takachiho-mine, the legendary peak, and then descends to the crater lake of Mi-ike. Two days are usually required to complete this hike over the highest peaks of Kirishima, and through some of the best volcanic scenery in Japan. It may be done in reverse, but this would involve 900 meters more climbing, as Ebino is the highest plateau in the park at 1,200 meters.

Leaving the campsite at Ebino Kōgen early in the morning as the mist was still hanging thickly over the plateau and peaks, I decided to take the trail starting from near the Ebino Kōgen Hotel. This is a gentle undulating climb through pine forest up to the pass between Karakuni-dake and the large crater lake to the southwest. From the pass the trail climbs directly up the main slope of Karakuni-dake through dense bamboo grass undergrowth and forest cover, becoming steep and very badly eroded. A combination of steep volcanic slopes, numerous hiking groups churning up the trail, and high rainfall has created some enormous erosion gullies on this route where streams have been channelled down the trail. Trudging through the mud up these gullies I wished I had taken the alternative route from the hot springs to the north. Climbing out of the forest there are some steep, rocky sections, with ropes laid out to aid hikers, before you come to the peak of Karakuni-dake situated on the rim of a large crater. The early-morning mist was clearing to reveal the deep, flat-bottomed crater below, the large crater lake to the southwest, and the smoking Shimmoe-dake to the southeast with the pointed peak of Takachiho rising beyond.

The trail follows the crater rim before descending steeply, then climbing a small peak on the way to the rim of Shimmoe-dake's crater. Here you will be presented with a volcanic vista of active, steaming vents in the inner walls of the crater, and a bright green lake on the crater floor. The last eruption in 1959 showered ash over the surrounding area, and the volcano has been simmering ever since. Skirting this spectacular sight around the eastern rim, the trail then goes down to the two extinct, grassy craters of Naka-dake. As I passed, a large party of schoolchildren were having their lunch in the bottom of one of these craters, which looked like a natural baseball stadium. From here there is a good view of Takachiho-no-mine and the elliptical crater below its prominent peak.

Descending from Naka-dake to Takachiho-gawara you will pass through an area of azalea bushes covering gentle slopes before coming to the car park and Visitors' Center. Here there are displays of the local geology, flora, and fauna, similar to the one at Ebino Kōgen—both of which are well worth a visit. Takachiho-gawara was the mid-point of my hike over Kirishima with a campsite nearby and another one five kilometers down the road at Yunono Onsen. It is a convenient stopping-off or starting point for a hike in Kirishima with the surrounding slopes covered in azalea, the shortest route to the top of Takachiho-no-mine starting from here, and Kirishima Shrine and Onsen within easy access.

Kirishima Shrine, six kilometers down the road, is set amidst groves of cedar on the southern slopes of Kirishima. This splendid shrine is of central significance to the Japanese Imperial family. According to the legend, Ninigi-no-Mikoto, grandson of the sun goddess Amaterasu, descended from heaven to the peak of Takachiho to found the nation of Japan and the Japanese Imperial line.

At Takachiho-gawara there is a large torii gate with a wide, stony track leading from it up to a stone platform used for worshipping the mountain, which rises immediately beyond. The trail goes right of the platform and up through red pine forest to a ridge of loose volcanic rock and ash on the rim of the slightly active crater below the peak of Takachiho. It is a steep scramble to the summit of this sacred mountain, marked by the ruins of a stone shrine. Nearby there is a mountain hut run by an old man who sells food and drinks to exhausted and thirsty climbers.

Following the ridge eastwards from the peak the trail passes between two prominent rocks and descends through mixed forest toward the two lakes seen below—Mi-ike, the larger one and Ko-ike, the smaller one. The trail eventually comes out at Kirishima Higashi Jinja (Eastern Shrine) before reaching a road which descends to Mi-ike. This beautiful, large crater lake, surrounded by forest, has a campsite on its northwestern shore and is an excellent area for short hikes and birdspotting, with trails circling the lake and wandering through the forest to the nearby lake of Ko-ike. Buses run from the village north of the lake to Kobayashi Station, making this a convenient access or departure point for Kirishima. As well as the Kirishima Mountains to the north and Yakushima Island to the south, the Kirishima-Yaku National Park includes other smaller areas around Kinkō Bay where there are many places of interest. These include Shiroyama, scene of the 1877 Kagoshima Rebellion, the active volcano Sakurajima, and Kaimon-dake, the Fuji of Satsuma.

2. Ancient Cedars and Snowy Peaks—Yakushima
屋久島

Slipping out of Kinkō Bay between the impressive, Fuji-like Kaimon-dake at the southern tip of the Satsuma Peninsula and Cape Sata, the southernmost point of Kyushu, the four-hour trip from Kagoshima on the Yakushima ferry is an enjoyable and interesting journey in itself. As the ferry pulls into the main port at Miyanoura, the largest settlement on the island, mist and cloud enshroud the high peaks and forested mountain slopes, which loom above the small town. You are fortunate indeed if you can catch a glimpse of Miyanoura-dake (1,935 m.), the highest peak in the Kyushu region of Japan, from the sea or coast.

Usually bypassed by travellers to Southern Japan, Yakushima, a quiet, undeveloped island of about 500 square kilometers, lies some sixty kilometers south of Kyushu. Besides the soaring, granite peaks, which entice rock climbers and hikers, the island has many other attractions including thousand-year-old cedar trees called Yakusugi, an endemic species of macaque monkey known as the Yakuzaru, *rotenburo* (open-air hot spring baths) on the southeast coast, and a few sandy beaches for bathing. Much of the island forms the Yaku part of the Kirishima-Yaku National Park, a status well deserved because of its great natural beauty.

Although Yakushima lies on the edge of the subtropical zone with an average annual temperature of 19.3°C around the coast, its unusually high peaks give rise to special climatic and weather conditions. The high mountains are snow-covered during winter and spring, forming the southernmost occurrence of snow cover in Japan. One negative factor for hikers on the island is the high rainfall—Yakushima has the highest precipitation statistics in Japan with up to 400 centimeters around the coast and 1,000 centimeters in the mountains. August is generally the best month, but with a little luck you may get a few breaks of clear weather at other times. I was fortunate on my visit during the last week of March to get two and a half days of dry weather with some clear, blue skies. Two days or more are required to complete this spectacular hike over the island, with an overnight stay at one of the huts or campsites along the way.

ACCESS

A regular ferry service operates between Kagoshima Port and Miyanoura Port on the northern coast of Yakushima. Bus services run most of the way around the periphery of the island except for the section between Nagata and Kurio on the west coast, where the road is still under construction. Forestry tracks go part of the way into the central mountains, and it is possible to take a taxi to the start of the trails, of which there are six main ones to the central high peaks.

ACCOMMODATION

As yet there are no modern hotels on the island, but there are several small minshuku in the villages around the coast. Near the port of Miyanoura is the large Yakushima-sō guest house (Tel: 09974-2-0175), offering convenient accommodation. In the central mountains there are a number of simple mountain huts offering basic accommodation, and camping is possible at a few locations in the mountains and around the coast.

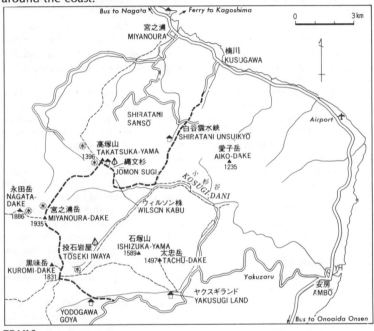

TRAILS

****
+++

Miyanoura (宮之浦) ⟶ 10 kms. 4 hrs. ⟶ Shiratani Sansō (白谷山荘) ⟶ 10 kms. 4 hrs. ⟶ Takatsuka Goya (高塚小屋) ⟶ 5.5 kms. 5 hrs. ⟶ Miyanoura-dake (宮之浦岳) ⟶ 7.5 kms. 3 hrs. 45 mins. ⟶ Yodogawa Goya (淀川小屋) ⟶ 22.5 kms. 7 hrs. 30 mins. ⟶ Ambō (安房)

This is one place where waterproofs and strong, waterproof boots must not be forgotten. Food supplies can be obtained in the main villages around the coast, and everything you need should be carried with you into the mountains. There is a plentiful supply of fresh water available from mountain springs and streams along the route.

After arriving at the port of Miyanoura it is a short, ten-minute walk into the small, main settlement on the island. From here you can take a bus or walk the three kilometers east to the start of the Kusugawa Trail (楠川登山道). Alternatively you can take a taxi up the forestry track to Shiratani Unsuikyō Gorge (白谷雲水峡), which will save you the climb up through the lower forest. However, if you have the time, the lower forest contains some interesting subtropical species including tree ferns. Shiratani Unsuikyō Gorge is set amidst a mixed forest, including cedar, and has a number of small waterfalls.

A little further up the forestry track the trail for Shiratani Sansō goes off to the right. This small mountain hut can easily be reached on the same day you arrive by ferry, and is a convenient place to spend the first night. It has a tatami mat floor large enough to sleep twenty or so people, and has only basic facilities.

The trail over the pass into Kosugi-dani is quite an easy one, and on descending you will come to the narrow-gauge railway tracks used for logging operations in the valley. Following the tracks up the valley there are occasional views through the forest to the rushing river below, and in clear weather good views of the peaks, including Miyanoura-dake, towering above the valley head.

Eventually the trail leaves the tracks and climbs steeply up to the Wilson Kabu (ウィルソン株), an enormous stump of a Yakusugi which was cut by seven men in 1586, and later rediscovered by an American botanist, Ernest Wilson, in 1914. The area of the stump is equivalent to ten tatami mats, and inside the hollow trunk has been placed a small shrine. A freshwater spring issues from the ground beneath the trunk, and flows out past a wooden torii gate standing outside the hollow trunk. The shrine and torii show the Japanese respect for the *kami* of this awe-inspiring cedar, possibly 3,000 years old, of which only the stump now remains.

Climbing through the mixed forest, which includes oak as well as Yakusugi, it takes about two hours before the trail brings you to the mighty Jōmon sugi (縄文杉), named after the era in which it started to grow, about 2,200 years ago. This ancient, massive cedar with a gnarled trunk six meters in diameter was standing in snow when I encountered it by the trail in late March. From the Jōmon sugi it is a short walk to Takatsuka Goya, a small mountain hut situated on top of the forested ridge. With two wooden floor levels big enough to sleep sixteen people at a squeeze I spent one warm night here when it was filled to capacity. A group of young Boy Scouts who arrived late had to put their large tent up in melting spring snow on a nearby area of flat ground.

The peak of Miyanoura-dake (宮之浦岳 1,935 m.) is a five-hour climb up the ridge from Takatsuka Goya. At 1,600 meters the cedar forest gives way to the open, subalpine vegetation of rhododendron bushes and bamboo grass which cloaks these high peaks. Hiking is a lot easier as you approach the pass between Nagata-dake (永田岳 1,886 m.) and Miyanoura-dake. From the pass it is a twenty-minute climb to the rocky summit, the highest point in Southern Japan. If you arrive on one of the rare, clear days, you will be blessed with a panoramic view of the nearby lower peaks, the forested valley below, and the surrounding sea possibly as far as Tane-ga-shima.

Continuing over the peak the narrow trail is fairly easy going as it passes large, granite domes on the roof of Yakushima. Most of the island is composed of granite rock, which is unusual in Japan, but good for hikers and climbers due to its rough-grained texture and weathering properties. The trail passes a natural rock shelter known as Tōseki Iwaya (投石岩屋) beneath a massive granite boulder, before coming to the eastern-facing, granite dome cliffs of Kuromi-dake (黒味岳 1,831 m.). Passing beneath the cliffs, the trail leads to Hananoego (花之江河), a flat, marshy area laid out with wooden planks, where marsh plants can be seen flowering from May through summer.

Descending through mixed forest in Yodogawa Valley, the trail crosses a bridge over the river to Yodogawa Goya, a large, wooden hut constructed in the spring of '86 with the help of a New Zealander, whom I met on my way down the mountain.

A thirty-minute hike from the hut brings you to the forestry track which leads down to Yakusugi Land. This is a major tourist attraction with well-laid-out trails and bridges in the valley offering magnificent forest scenery, including Yakusugi, and the sound of fast-flowing mountain streams.

Possibly the best place on the island for a chance of sighting the Yakuzaru is the track down from Yakusugi Land to Ambō. This track is used by tourists, who feed the monkeys on their way to and from Yakusugi Land, and so the groups of wild macaques often wait by the track for free hand-outs from passing cars and backpackers. A university team on the other side of the island at Nagata is engaged in studying this endemic species in an area less frequented by tourists.

If you feel like taking a bath after the hike, you should make your way south around the coastal road to Onoaida Onsen (尾之間温泉), where there is a hot spring bath at the entrance to another mountain trail. For more adventurous souls there is a rotenburo on the shore one kilometer away at Yakushima Onsen.

3. A Popular and Populated Caldera: Aso-san 阿蘇山

Explosions of enormous force have created some very large volcanic craters or calderas on the earth's surface, but few can be compared with that of Aso in Central Kyushu. Its central, active peaks rise from a large, flat crater floor surrounded by steep inner walls—volcanic scenery on a grand scale. Ngorongoro Crater in Northern Tanzania with lions, rhino, and buffalo roaming over its flat crater floor—one of the best places in Africa for wildlife viewing—is one contender for comparison. Another is Thira or Santorini, an arc-shaped island in the Greek Aegean Sea with a small volcanic island rising from the center of its submerged caldera, which is associated with the legend of Atlantis. Ngorongoro has a very sparse population of Masai nomads, who live on the rim and floor of the crater. Thira is populated with a sizable Greek population living in towns and villages on its island rim. Aso supports a Japanese population of about 70,000 living in towns, villages, and on farms within the caldera—a phenomenon which seems incredible, but can be explained by the force of population pressure in Japan, which has put a premium on all flat land despite the potential dangers from natural disasters. All of these calderas are big tourist attractions, and Aso-san is a must on many tour itineraries around Kyushu.

The Aso caldera measures 24 kilometers north-south, 18 kilometers east-west, 80 kilometers in circumference, and forms the main part of Aso National Park, which also includes the Kujū Mountains to the north. Its central composite volcano has five peaks known as the Aso-gogaku, of which Taka-dake (1,592 m.) is the highest. The nearby crater of Naka-dake is still very active, and many people have been killed in its eruptions—the last major one being in 1979, which destroyed the cable car on its northeastern slopes. The western rim of this steaming crater is the ultimate destination of most visitors to Aso, who stare down into its seething inferno, and buy a chunk of yellow sulphur rock as a souvenir. Rising above the crater are the barren, rocky peaks of Naka-dake and Taka-dake, which look formidable from below, but are easily climbable by a marked trail. Contrasting with the desolate scenery around the crater and high peaks, the gentle, grassy pastures and two lakes of Kusasenri, where cattle and horses may be seen grazing, lie only three kilometers to the west. Apart from these volcanic mountain scenes, Aso also attracts visitors to the several hot spring resorts found within its large caldera.

ACCESS

Roads and railways run through the crater basin, making access very easy. From Kumamoto direct bus services operate up to the cable car station on Naka-dake, or a train may be taken on the Hōhi Line to Aso Station, from where local buses operate up the mountain. If coming from the north, buses run along the Yamanami Highway from Beppu via the Kujū Mountains to Aso, and then on to Kumamoto.

ACCOMMODATION

There is plentiful ryokan and minshuku accommodation in the numerous towns and villages within the Aso caldera. From Aso Station the bus service up the mountain passes Aso Youth Hostel (Tel: 0967-

34-0804), which is otherwise a 20-minute walk, and there is a campsite a little further up the road. This is a very good location and base for visiting the area. There is another youth hostel at Kumamoto YMCA Aso Camp (Tel: 0967-35-0124), which is a 30-minute walk from Akamizu Station.

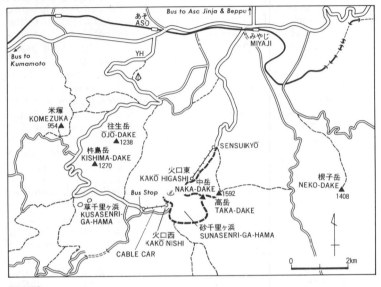

TRAILS

***

+++

Kusasenri-ga-hama （草千里ヶ浜）⟶ 3 kms. 1 hr. ⟶ Kakō Nishi (Western Rim) (火口西) ⟶ 3.5 kms. 1 hr. 50 mins. ⟶ Naka-dake (中岳) ⟶ 1 km. 25 mins. ⟶ Taka-dake （高岳）⟶ 2.5 kms. 1 hr. 15 mins. ⟶ Kakō Higashi (Eastern Rim) （火口東）⟶ 2 kms. 1 hr. ⟶ Sensuikyō (仙酔峡)

Although there are trails which climb Aso-san from the lower slopes, nowadays hardly anyone uses these, and most visitors drive or take the bus up the toll road to the western rim of Naka-dake's crater. Few venture beyond the road and main tourist sights, but a spectacular hike may be made over the highest peaks to the eastern side of the crater, easily done in one day. Strong boots are recommended for the climb, and as there is no water at all on the high peaks, plenty should be carried.

The toll road up Aso-san passes by a small, grassy side cone about 50 meters high, which looks like an inverted rice bowl and is known as

Komezuka (米塚). A legend says that the gods of Aso-san handed out the rice to the poor people living below the volcano. Trails lead from the road to the top of this hill. About ten minutes further up the road by car or bus brings you to the wide, open, grassy plains and the two lakes of Kusasenri (草千里). This is a good place to leave the bus and start a hike over Aso-san. Next to the road is the Volcano Museum, restaurant, and souvenir shops. Horses may be hired to ride over the green plains with a view eastwards to the smoking crater of Naka-dake. A popular hiking trail leads to the top of Kishima-dake (杵島岳 1,270 m.) to the north—one of the five peaks of Aso-san.

From Kusasenri a trail keeps to the left of the road towards Naka-dake, passing artificial ski slopes on the way. These ski slopes see the real thing for only one or two months in mid-winter, making it one of the southernmost ski resorts in Japan. The trail and road cross a flat area to the bottom of the cable car which climbs to the crater rim, but it is not really worth waiting for as it only takes about 20 minutes to walk up by the road. On the western rim of the crater you will meet a desolate scene of barren volcanic rocks, and the 100-meter deep active crater. My first visit in the summer of '81 was a relatively quiet time when I could see right into the bottom of the crater, but in the spring of '86 it was more active and full of steam billowing forth into the clear blue sky. Around the rim are several circular concrete bunkers—just in case anything more substantial than steam issues forth from the depths below. The last eruption in 1979 closed the trail around the northern rim.

For most people the western rim of Naka-dake is as far as they wish to go, and they return back down to the road or cable car, satisfied with one or two glimpses into the inferno. For others this is only the start of a spectacular hike over a stark volcanic moonscape to the peaks overlooking the crater. The trail starts about 300 meters down the road from the crater rim, where a signpost and wooden posts mark the way across the flat volcanic sands of Sunasenri-ga-hama (砂千里ヶ浜). You walk over this Sea of Sand until the trail eventually brings you to the base of the rocky crater wall. Here the way up is marked by white paint on the rocks, and the air is heavy with sulphur fumes. It is not a difficult climb to the top of the crater rim, from where it is a level walk along the brink of the cliff to the peak of Naka-dake, with fantastic views of the crater below.

Taka-dake (1,592 m.), the highest peak of the Aso-gogaku, is an easy climb up a rocky ridge from Naka-dake. Just below the peak on a flat area is a mountain hut providing accommodation for climbers. To the east can be seen the rocky spires of Neko-dake, and looking back to the west the grassy plains of Kusasenri can be seen beyond the smoking crater. There is a steep, craggy trail descending directly down the northern slopes to Sensuikyō, but after being warned by a group of

Japanese climbers about its steepness I decided to make my way over to the disused cable car station on the eastern side of Naka-dake's crater. So I returned to Naka-dake and then made my way over the precarious trail of crumbling volcanic rock and ash to the desolate scene of the destroyed top station of the eastern cable car, which ceased operations after the 1979 eruption.

It is a fairly steep descent from here down a rocky trail next to the cable car pylons to the lower station. Here there is a car park and road down to Miyaji Station with an infrequent bus service. If you miss the bus it takes about one and a half hours to walk, but it's all downhill.

Aso Shrine (Jinja), a 20-minute walk from Miyaji Station, is well worth a visit. This elegant shrine was built of zelkova wood at the end of the Edo Period, and is dedicated to the twelve gods of Aso-san and to Takei Watatsuno Mikoto—the grandson of Emperor Jimmu, Japan's first emperor. Amongst the festivals celebrated at this shrine there is one in March called the Hifuri Shinji.

4. The Roof of Kyushu: Kujū-san 久住山

Overlooking the Aso caldera to the south, but overshadowed by it in popularity, the Kujū Mountains rise from the high Senomoto Plateau to form the highest peaks on the island of Kyushu. These mountains are included in the Aso National Park, and although there are no special outstanding features this is a really excellent area for hiking, with plentiful hot spring resorts in and around the mountains, and easy access via the Yamanami Highway. Most travellers bypass Kujū-san on their way between Aso-san and Beppu, but if they realized what wonderful scenery and ideal hiking lay just off the highway they would be persuaded to stop off and take to the hills, if not for a few days, at least for a few hours.

Formed of lava and pumice the grassy upland plateau of Senomoto Kōgen (瀬の本高原) at a height of 600 to 1,100 meters is an area of wide, open pastures used for cattle grazing. The lower slopes of the Kujū Mountains rising from this plateau are forested, with cypress giving way to alpine flora in the higher mountains. Here the Kirishima azalea cloaking the mountainsides burst into pink and magenta flowers during May and June. Although these mountains are called the Kujū Mountains, the peak of Kujū-san (1,786.9 m.) is not the highest. This title goes to Taisen-zan (大船山 1,787.1 m.), about four kilometers to the east, which squeaks through by a few centimeters. Kujū-san is an extinct volcanic peak, but there is an active area of steaming fumaroles on the slopes of the mountain to the north. Taisen-zan peak is situated on the rim of a crater which is also extinct. There are many lower peaks in the area, some of which were formed by tholeitic lava domes.

ACCESS

Access to the Kujū Mountains is made very easy by the new Yamanami Highway, which runs between Beppu in the north and Aso in the south, making it a major route across Kyushu. The highway passes to the west of the highest peaks, and reaches its highest point at Makinoto-tōge Pass at over 1,300 meters. This is a good place to start a hike over the mountains. Another popular starting point is Chōjabaru to the north of the pass at just over 1,000 meters. Buses stop at both places on the route between Beppu and Kumamoto, which takes about one hour from Aso and two hours from Beppu.

ACCOMMODATION

In the midst of these peaks is a wide, flat valley known as Bōgatsuru which is completely enclosed by the mountains, and is an excellent base from which to explore the surrounding peaks. With two camp-sites on the valley floor, and accommodation at the remote hot spring resort of Hokkein Onsen (法華院温泉), this valley can only be reached by trails over the mountains and a rough, but drivable, track coming up the valley to the north. There is a convenient campsite at Chōjabaru (長者原) situated on the Yamanami Highway, which is a major gateway to the Kujū Mountains. Here you can also find lodges, and one and a half kilometers up the road is the hot spring resort of Makinoto. On the southern side of Makinoto-tōge there is Senomoto Kōgen Youth Hostel (Tel: 0967-44-0157), one kilometer off the Yamanami Highway. Campsites can also be found on the southern side of the mountains at Akagawa (赤川) and Sōzu (沢水).

TRAILS

***
+++
Makinoto-tōge (牧ノ戸峠) ⟶ 5 kms. 2 hrs. 30 mins ⟶ Kujū-san (久住山) ⟶ 4 kms. 2 hrs. ⟶ Bōgatsuru (坊ガツル) ⟶ 3 kms. 2 hrs. ⟶ Taisen-zan (大船山) ⟶ 3 kms. 1 hr. 15 mins. ⟶ Bōgatsuru (坊ガツル) ⟶ 5 kms. 2 hrs. 30 mins. ⟶ Chōjabaru (長者原)

Arriving at Makinoto-tōge one clear day in early April there were only a few patches of rapidly melting snow remaining in the high moun-tains, which usually see snow cover from December to March. Small groups of hikers were standing around the shops on the pass and some could be seen making their way up the relatively low mountain of Kuroiwa-san (黒岩山 1,503 m.) to the north, which can easily be climbed in one hour from the pass. Following the advice I had been given by a Japanese hiker who had climbed these mountains just a cou-ple of weeks earlier, I set off up the concrete trail to the southeast, behind the shops. My plan was to climb over the peak of Kujū-san and then down to the campsite at Bōgatsuru.

It is a steep climb up from the pass through a bushy vegetation of

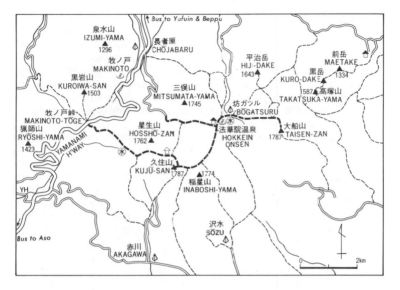

azalea and bamboo grass to the top of the ridge from where Kujū-san can be seen poking its sharp peak above the ridge to the east. Following the top of the ridge it is a very pleasant walk to a trail junction where you go left and cross a flat area with the rocky peak of Kujū-san directly ahead. The trail goes over a col and descends to a small stone hut situated below the peak. This is the highest hut in the mountains, but it is not in good enough condition for anything but a short stop in bad weather. Steep cliffs rise to the summit of Kujū-san from the flat area around the hut, and the trail makes its way up the ridge to the east of the peak. From the summit, steaming hot springs can be seen rising from the mountain to the north, and beyond the many small peaks to the east can be seen the slightly higher Taisen-zan. On a fine day there are good views southwards across the Senomoto Plateau to the caldera and peaks of Aso-san.

This hike to the top of Kujū-san and back to Makinoto-tōge can easily be done in about four hours, but amongst the placards on the exposed rocky summit I was surprised to find a wooden post commemorating the ascent of this mountain by a ninety-year-old hiker. The pronunciation of the name Kujū in Japanese sounds the same as the pronunciation of "ninety," and so to celebrate her ninetieth birthday she had climbed this peak.

The trail down to Bōgatsuru goes east down a slope to a flat area and comes to the top of a narrow valley. Descending this valley through bushy vegetation, the large, flat valley and campsite at Bōgatsuru can be seen below. Eventually the track comes out at a small campsite and wooden huts next to the large wooden building at Hokkein Onsen, where hot spring baths and accommodation are provided for hikers to this remote resort. The track across the valley floor leads to the Bōgatsuru campsite next to a clear mountain stream. This mountain stream, flowing down from the western slopes of Taisen-zan, provides a plentiful supply of water to the camp, and on one of my trips down to the stream I watched a marten creep along the bank and disappear into his burrow. These small mammals are usually only seen at night.

A well-used trail leads from the camp up through forest towards the peak of Taisen-zan. The higher slopes of the mountain are covered with a bushy vegetation, including Kirishima azalea, as the trail comes up to the crater rim of this extinct volcano. Near the trail junction there is a small stone hut in very bad repair and from here it is a steady climb up the crater rim to the summit. This trail was covered in melting snow and ice as I made my way up one day in early April. On the other side of the peak there is a small lake and flat area good for a picnic in fine weather, with good views of all the peaks of the Kujū Mountains, and Aso-san to the south. There is an alternative trail back down to the valley, but it is best to return the same way.

From Bōgatsuru Valley there are two routes over the mountains to Chōjabaru, but the most interesting climbs up the gully behind Hokkein Onsen and over Sugamori Pass, where there is a small wooden hut, then descends to the head of a barren, rocky valley of steaming vents. The sulphur fumes are almost overpowering as you cross this valley and follow the track down to Chōjabaru. This track becomes concrete as you descend the sparsely vegetated slopes with a view of the Yamanami Highway and Makinoto Onsen in the valley over to the west.

Chōjabaru has a campsite across the river, a Visitors' Center with a small display explaining the local natural history, and a nature trail around the valley. There are also shops and a restaurant near the bus stop. Buses run from here over Makinoto Pass to Senomoto Plateau and Aso-san or north to Beppu. If you are heading towards Beppu there is an interesting area for hiking around Yufuin, and a hiking trail from the highway leads to the top of Tsurumi-dake (鶴見岳 1,375 m.), which overlooks the hot spring resort of Beppu. Thirty minutes before arriving at Beppu Station the bus stops at Shidaka, where there is a pleasant lake and campsite.

Takasaki-yama, the warm, temperate, broadleaved forest habitat of wild monkeys, is situated a few minutes by bus from Beppu Station on the coast between Beppu and Ōita. If you want a close look at the Japanese macaque, this is the place to come, but be warned—it has become very commercialized with a regular flow of large tour groups and walking in the forest is not allowed.

Southwest Japan
—Kinki, Chugoku,
and Shikoku

Yamabushi at Sanjō-ga-take shrine
(Ōmine-san)

This part of Japan has relatively low mountains and few volcanoes, but there are some interesting and spectacular hiking areas. The mountains generally run east-west, and are composed mainly of Paleozoic and Mesozoic sedimentary rocks. There are some prominent volcanic peaks in the Chugoku Mountains. Through these mountains runs the Hakusan Volcanic Zone, of which Daisen is the highest peak, composed of Quaternary volcanics. Sambe-san is another volcanic peak west-southwest of Daisen. Small basins are found in the Chugoku Mountains, with karst landforms in the western areas. Akiyoshidai Cave in Yamaguchi Prefecture is cut into Permo-Carboniferous limestone and is one of the largest and most famous caves of Japan.

The Shikoku Mountains are an extension of the Kyushu Range, separated from Honshu and Kyushu by the shallow Inland Sea (Seto Naikai) depression. Ishizuchi-san (1,982 m.) is the highest peak in Western Japan and composed of crystalline schists overlain with volcanic rocks and granite intrusions. The Kii Mountains are a continuation of the Kyushu and Shikoku ranges and are composed mostly of Mesozoic strata with granite intrusions.

The Japan Sea coast, known as the San-in Kaigan, is affected by the northwesterly monsoon in winter, and the mountains facing the sea get a lot of snow, but less than in the Hokuriku region to the northeast. Shikoku and the Kii Peninsula have a mild climate, but wet summers with heavy rainfall in the tsuyu season and a high chance of typhoons from mid-summer to early autumn. The Inland Sea and Central Lowlands, where Osaka, Nara, and Kyoto are situated, are relatively dry and sunny throughout the year.

Daisen (1,729 m.), the highest peak in the Chugoku district, falls within the Daisen-Oki National Park. Hakken-zan (1,915 m.) is the highest peak on the Kii Peninsula and falls within the Yoshino-Kumano National Park, together with the nearby Ōmine-san. Ishizuchi-san on Shikoku forms the main part of Ishizuchi Quasi-National Park. These three mountain areas are the most outstanding for hiking in this part of Japan.

There are also four national parks in the region centered on coasts. The San-in Kaigan National Park has beautiful sandy bays and includes the famous Tottori sand dunes and Amanohashidate (Heavenly Bridge), a pine-covered sand spit three kilometers long cutting off a lagoon from the sea and one of the three classic sights of Japan. Seto Naikai National Park, with its submerged coasts and islands, has many beaches and campgrounds and includes another of the three classic sights—Miyajima with its torii gate standing in the shallow sea. Shikoku's only national park, Ashizuri-Uwakai National Park, has a ria coast and is famous for turtles, otters, and the shells washed up on its beaches. Ise Shima National Park on the Kii Peninsula is famous for its pearl farms centered on Toba, where there are sheltered bays, and also for Ise Shrine, where Amaterasu Ōmikami (the sun goddess) is enshrined.

Shikoku is well known for the long religious pilgrimage to its 88 Buddhist holy places, starting from Tokushima and going clockwise around the island, taking 40 to 60 days on foot. This is in memory of Kūkai (Kōbō Daishi), who was born in Shikoku and was the Buddhist priest who introduced the esoteric Shingon Sect from China to Japan.

ACCESS

By Air: The largest cities are connected by domestic flights with the rest of Japan, and Osaka has many international connections.

By Rail: The Shinkansen (Bullet Train) runs through the region with the following times from Tokyo: Kyoto—2 hours 40 minutes (¥12,970), Osaka—3 hours (¥13,480), Hiroshima—about 5 hours 30 minutes (¥17,700). Local lines provide access to all other parts of the region. A direct rail service and road connection is provided by the Seto Ōhashi Bridge between Kojima in Honshu and Sakaide in Shikoku, opened in spring 1988.

By Sea: A regular ferry operates between Hiroshima and Matsuyama on Shikoku. The Kansai Steamship Co. operates a daily ferry between Osaka and Beppu which stops at Takamatsu and Matsuyama on Shikoku. A ferry runs every other day from Tokyo via Nachi-Katsuura to Kōchi on Shikoku, taking about 21 hours. It is operated by Blue Highway Line Co. (Tel: Tokyo 03-3578-1127, Kōchi 0888-31-0520). A ferry also operates between Shimonoseki at the western tip of Honshu and Pusan in South Korea.

ACCOMMODATION

Youth hostels are found in or near most of the main cities of the region, but there were none in Osaka at the time of writing. The mountain parks have mountain huts and campsites as well as plentiful minshuku and ryokan accommodation in the villages.

The following is a list of lower-priced accommodation in the main cities of the region: Ryokan Ohto (Tel: 075-541-7803) 15 minutes' walk from Kyoto Station. Ryokan Kyōka (Tel: 075-371-2709) eight minutes' walk from Kyoto Station. Ebisu-sō Ryokan (Tel: 06-643-4861) five minutes' walk from Ebisucho subway station in Osaka. Mikawa Ryokan (Tel: 082-261-2719) seven minutes' walk from Hiroshima Station. Takamatsu Terminal Hotel (Tel: 0878-22-3731) three minutes' walk from Takamatsu Station. Hotel Ruri (Tel: 0899-41-6606) three minutes' walk from Matsuyama Station. Bizenya Ryokan (Tel: 0832-22-6228) seven minutes by bus from Shimonoseki Station.

5. Shikoku's Sacred Peak: Ishizuchi-san 石鎚山

My first attempt to climb Ishizuchi-san was made at the beginning of April, when I was surprised to find the higher peaks still covered in deep snow. There were a few people trying to make the ascent, but about halfway along the trail from the ropeway to the summit only a few footprints could be seen in the snow, and the going became difficult. I gave up and returned to the upper ropeway station, where the last skiers of the season were practicing on the last remaining snow of the ski slopes.

April is the month when the first climbers and yamabushi reach the summit, and the mountain is a popular destination from then until August. From July 1 to 10 there is a mountain-opening festival, when thousands of climbers and pilgrims visit the mountain, and yamabushi wearing their traditional white clothes and blowing conch shells climb the mountain to the summit shrine. Women are not allowed on the mountain for the first day of this festival on July 1—a remnant of older, stricter practices. My second attempt to climb Ishizuchi-san was made at the end of July, when the climbing season was well under way. This time I was successful in scaling the rocky peak soaring above the lower, forested slopes.

Ishizuchi-san (1,982 m.) is the highest mountain on the island of Shikoku and the highest in all of western Japan. It has been a sacred mountain since ancient times, and is one of the seven most sacred mountains of Japan. Until recently the mountain was only climbed by yamabushi and pilgrims, and women were strictly forbidden to climb its sacred peak. The first climber, a mountain ascetic or yamabushi named En no Ozunu, climbed to the summit 1,305 years ago. Kūkai, whose birthplace was Shikoku, climbed Ishizuchi-san 1,190 years ago. The pilgrimage around the 88 holy places of Shikoku includes Ishizuchi's Ōhōji Temple (横峰寺), the 60th place on the itinerary, which is located in the valley below the mountain.

The mountains of Shikoku are part of the range which runs from Northern Kyushu to the Kii Peninsula, and are composed mainly of sedimentary strata, lacking the volcanic features so common elsewhere in Japan. With a relatively warm climate, the forests reach the tops of the peaks, and the heavy rainfall on the Pacific side of Japan has gouged out deep, precipitous valleys. The general characteristics of the mountains of Shikoku and those of the Kii Peninsula are similar.

Ishizuchi-san and the surrounding area falls within the Ishizuchi Quasi-National Park, and is covered with a natural mixed forest of cedar, pine, fir, beech, cherry, and maple. A local variety of bamboo grass grows in the undergrowth. Tsurugi-san (剣山 1,955 m.), the second highest peak on Shikoku, is situated on the eastern side of the island in Tsurugi-san Quasi-National Park, and is another interesting hiking area on the island. This mountain, composed mainly of limestone, has also been sacred since ancient times.

Climbing Ishizuchi-san has been made easy by the construction of a ropeway on its northeastern slopes, which climbs from 450 to 1,300 meters. The ropeway operates for most of the year, taking skiers up to the ski slopes when the ski season starts in December, and hikers and

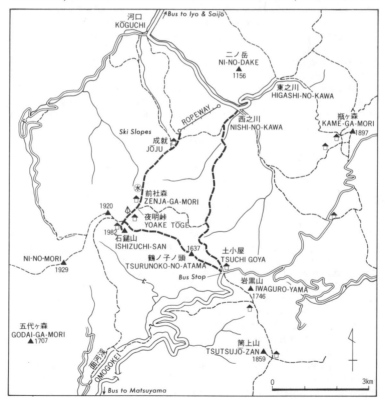

pilgrims from April to November. In November the changing leaves (*kōyō*), especially the maples, transform the mountains into blazing reds, and a *momiji* (Japanese maple) festival is held in the valley.

ACCESS

Access to Ishizuchi-san can be made by bus from Iyo Saijō Station, which is on the JR Line between Takamatsu and Matsuyama. The bus leaves from stand no. 2 and takes about one hour to the lower ropeway station just before the village of Nishi-no-kawa. It takes only six minutes on the ropeway to the top station. An alternative approach is by a long bus ride from Matsuyama Station to Omogokei or Tsuchi Goya, from where trails also climb the mountain, taking about four hours and two hours respectively. The route from Saijō via the ropeway is the fastest, and allows a climb up and down the mountain in one day from Saijō Station.

ACCOMMODATION

There are several ryokan and minshuku near the station at Saijō, and a few near the lower ropeway station. On the mountain there are several mountain huts providing accommodation and meals, and there is a large lodge at Tsuchi Goya. Camping is allowed near the hut below the steep climb to the peak, and there is another campsite in the mountains to the east at Kame-ga-mori Hut. Kammon Youth Hostel (Tel: 089258-2311) is situated in Omogo Village southwest of Ishizuchi-san, and can be reached by bus from Matsuyama in two hours and thirty minutes.

TRAILS

***
++++
Ishizuchi Ropeway (石鎚ロープウェイ) ⟶ 1 km. 20 mins. ⟶ Jōju (成就) ⟶ 4 kms. 2 hrs. 50 mins. ⟶ Ishizuchi-san (石鎚山) ⟶ 4.6 kms. 2 hrs. 30 mins. ⟶ Tsuchi Goya (土小屋) ⟶ 7 kms. 3 hrs. ⟶ Nishi-no-kawa (西之川)

The route described here is a circular one over the mountain, taking the ropeway up, descending the other popular trail to Tsuchi Goya, and then taking a little-used trail back down to Nishi-no-kawa Village, which is just up the road from the lower ropeway station. This route can be done in one day from Saijō if the weather is fine and you leave on an early bus. There are no streams or water on the climb so it is a good idea to carry water or drinks with you, as prices at the mountain huts tend to be expensive.

It was a clear, bright morning as the bus made its way up the narrow road next to the river in Kōguchi-dani—a beautiful forested valley leading up to the ropeway and Nishi-no-kawa Village. From the bus stop it is a short walk up the hill, passing a shrine and souvenir shop on the way to the ropeway station. There were a few tourists and hikers waiting for the next car up the ropeway. As the car glided over the green forests the view of steep valleys and peaks was spectacular. Coming out of the building at the top station the wide trail climbs steadily to the shrine and village at Jōju, passing disused ski lifts on the nearby slopes.

Several mountain huts, lodges, souvenir shops, and restaurants are found in the village of Jōju, where the large Ishizuchi Shrine is situated on the flat-topped hill. Framed in the window at the back of the small shrine on the south side of the courtyard, the peak of Ishizuchi-san can be seen to the south on fine days. From Jōju the trail passes through a large, old, wooden gateway, and descends through mixed forest. After fifteen minutes the trail passes a torii gate, and soon starts to climb the ridge.

Higher on the ridge at Zenja-ga-mori (前社森) there is a small hut where food and drinks are sold. Climbing from here the trail reaches Yoake-tōge (夜明峠) where the forest thins out and there is a marvelous view of the rocky cliffs and peak rising from across the pass. It is a wide, easy trail to the huts and campsites below the cliffs and the steep climb to the summit.

This is where the real fun starts on Ishizuchi-san as the pilgrims' route to the top scales the vertical rock walls via thick chains known as *kusari*. There are three of these vertical rock faces to climb before reaching the summit, with heights of 33, 65, and 68 meters of sheer rock. On weekends and holidays it may be a very slow climb as young children and old pilgrims alike scale these formidable cliffs. Clinging to the vertical rock walls the line of climbers, including the white-clad pilgrims, making slow progress to the rocky summit is an impressive sight from the pass below. For those who prefer to keep their feet on the ground, there is an easier trail around to the right (west) which is also used as the descending route from the summit.

As I pulled myself up the last kusari I was greeted by the sight and sound of a group of pilgrims chanting in front of the small shrine perched on the solid rock of the summit. To the left, two yamabushi were selling souvenirs in a small hut—even mountain ascetics in Japan are reduced to the function of servicing and profiting from tourists and climbers. The yamabushi told me they spend the whole of July and August on the mountain. Just behind the rocky peak, food and drinks were being sold at a mountain hut.

This peak with the shrine and hut on it is not actually the highest. The slightly higher peak called Tengu-dake is reached via a rocky knife-edge ridge taking about ten minutes from the shrine. Views down into the valleys are terrific, and the road and lodge at Tsuchi Goya can be seen far below to the southwest. Very spectacular and exposed, the peak of Ishizuchi-san would not be a nice place to hang around in bad weather. Luckily I was there on a beautifully clear day and the green peaks of Shikoku stretched out to the horizon.

From the hut at the summit the descent is much easier than the kusari route up. On reaching the huts and campsite at the bottom of the cliffs, a sign marks the trail to Tsuchi Goya. This is a very pleasant, easy trail through forest, first passing below the cliffs, and then descending a ridge to the road and lodge. Buses operate to the end of the road here from Matsuyama, and the forestry track continuing northeastwards eventually leads to Kame-ga-mori (瓶ヶ森), where there are huts and a campsite. This area promises some enjoyable hiking.

The trail down to Nishi-no-kawa starts from the large car park below the lodge at Tsuchi Goya, and is little used. It is a fairly long descent through the forest and thick undergrowth before coming to a stream, cedar stands, forestry workers' huts, and then the picturesque mountain village of Nishi-no-kawa. Stone pathways lead through this very simple, but neat, village of wooden houses with corrugated iron roofs, which nestles in the valley with small fields growing vegetables and corn. Life in the village couldn't be easy, but to the eyes of a transient hiker in midsummer it is peaceful and serene.

6. Big Mountain: Daisen 大山

Standing majestically above the San-in coastal plain, Daisen's profile has inspired inhabitants and travellers below since ancient times with its similarity to Fuji-san. Depending on the direction from which it is viewed, it is called "Hōki Fuji" or "Izumo Fuji" after the names of the former provinces to the east and west respectively. It is an extinct conical strata-volcano situated in the volcanic zone of the Southwest Honshu Arc, and the highest mountain in the Chugoku District. Compared with other mountains in Japan, Daisen (1,729 m.) is relatively low, in fact the district of Chugoku has the lowest peaks of any district on the main islands of Japan, but as it rises almost directly from sea level it is as impressive as many taller peaks. Its low height should not deceive prospective climbers into thinking that its peak is a walkover—the summit ridge is one of the most difficult traverses in Japan.

Daisen is a Sinitic and, by implication, Buddhist reading of the characters for Ōyama—meaning big mountain. Daisen-ji Temple on its northern slopes was founded by the Tendai Sect of Buddhism in 718, and the temple became a major landowner, involved in later political intrigues. The mountain was also popular with the Shugendō sect of mountain ascetics in days gone by, but they seem to have deserted this mountain for others. Just up the mountainside from the temple the large, rustic, wooden Ōgami-yama Jinja (Shrine) is one of the largest shrines in Chugoku. Ōgami-yama, one of the old names for the mountain, means "mountain of the great god." A mountain-opening festival is held at the village and shrine on the first Sunday in June.

Forming the main parts of the Daisen-Oki National Park, the view from Daisen's summit takes in most of the other areas of the park down to the Shimane Coast and across the Japan Sea to the Oki Islands, with the lower volcanic peak of Sambe-san (1,126 m.) far to the west. Most of the mountain is forested, with pine up to the middle section, where beech, yew, oak, and maple grow in mixed forest. A species of dwarf creeping yew is found on the higher slopes of volcanic, rocky crags. Around the mountain at a height of about 1,000 meters are grassy plains, which are good for camping and skiing, and to the southeast are the Hiruzen Plains—another promising hiking and camping area.

In winter the mountain catches the full force of the northwesterly monsoon, bringing deep snow to its slopes and making Daisen the best ski resort in southwest Japan. At this season the mountain is also used as a practice ground for Himalayan climbers. According to a policeman in Daisen village who knew the mountain like the back of his hand, there is an average of one death per year due to climbing accidents on Daisen, and these accidents usually occur in winter.

ACCESS

The most popular and convenient base from which to climb Daisen is the village below the mountain at about 800 meters on its northern slope, where the ski resort is located. This village can be reached by bus from either Yonago (50 minutes) or Daisen-guchi (30 minutes), both on the JR San-in Line.

ACCOMMODATION

Two campsites, Daisen Youth Hostel (Tel: 0859-52-2501), mountain huts, and many lodges are located in the village. Other campsites are found on the west and south sides of the mountain, and there are a few huts on the mountain itself.

TRAILS

***
+ + + + +

Daisen Village (大山村) ━━▶ 0.9 km. 40 mins. ━━▶ Ōgami-yama Jinja (大神山神社) ━━▶ 0.8 km. 50 mins. ━━▶ Shimohōju-koshi (下宝珠越) ━━▶ 0.5 km. 25 mins. ━━▶ Nakahōju-koshi (中 宝 珠 越) ━━▶ 0.8 km. 40 mins. ━━▶ Kamihōju-koshi (上宝珠越) ━━▶ 0.5 km. 25 mins. ━━▶ Utopia Goya (ユートピア小屋) ━━▶ 1.7 kms. 1 hr. 15 mins. ━━▶ Ken-ga-mine (剣ヶ峰) ━━▶ 1.2 kms. 50 mins. ━━▶ Misen (弥山) ━━▶ 1.5 kms. 50 mins. ━━▶ 6th Stage (六合目) ━━▶ 3 kms. 1 hr. 50 mins. ━━▶ Daisen Village (大山村)

There are five routes up to the jagged ridges of peaks on top of Daisen, and two of them start from the village, which, with its temple and shrine buildings, is the most interesting base. So the routes described

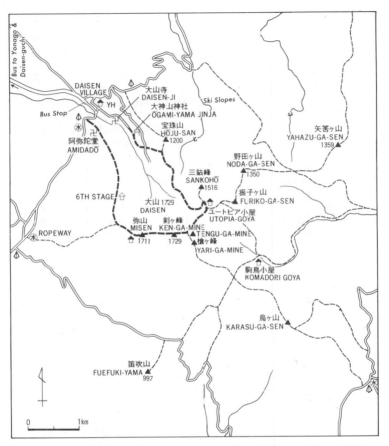

here over the peaks can be done in either direction from Daisen Village, and both take one day. The section along the summit ridge between Tengu-ga-mine and Misen peaks has several dangerous, narrow ridges to traverse, and if you should lose confidence it is best to return back down the same route. There is no water on the routes, so plenty should be carried.

Climbing up through the tourist village of lodges, restaurants, and souvenir shops, the road stops at a flight of steps leading up to Daisen-ji Temple. On the left of the torii gate is the start of the stone pathway up to Ōgami-yama Jinja, but this shrine can also be reached via the temple. Sitting on a terrace amidst the forest, the square, wooden temple building has a miniature waterfall next to it, and there are views through the trees to the ridges and peaks of Daisen soaring above. Much-trodden moss-covered stones on the path and steps up through giant cedars lead to a beautiful, large, wooden gateway, and beyond it Ōgami-yama Shrine.

Passing through the deserted grounds of the shrine, the trail climbs up to, and crosses, a dirt track which leads to a quarry in the rugged valley beneath Daisen's peaks. The trail climbs steeply from the track to the top of the ridge at Shimohōju-koshi or lower shoulder, and then follows the top of the ridge, passing the middle and upper shoulders with some precipitous crags dropping off into the valley.

Utopia Goya, situated near the trail junction on the main ridge to the summit, is a small concrete hut with two wooden-floored sleeping levels big enough to accommodate ten people. The nearby trail descending into the valley on the southeast side of the mountain leads to Komadori Hut and campsite in the bottom of the valley. The ridge trail climbs the exposed, rocky ridge to the peaks of Tengu-ga-mine and Ken-ga-mine—the peak at the summit of Daisen. Tengu-ga-mine is named after the goblin with the long nose, and Ken-ga-mine means "knife-edge ridge." These peaks are reached by traversing very narrow ridges of loose rock with sheer drops down rocky crags on both sides. The bare crags of light-gray volcanic rock have been severely eroded on the summit of Daisen to create these hair-raising ridges.

From the summit ridge the views down the crags into the rocky valleys and beyond to the coast are spectacular. Over the peak on the ridge to Misen there is one rocky section called Rakuda no Se—Camel's Back. After this stomach-churning ridge traverse the trail comes to Misen Peak and Chōjō Goya (Summit Hut), a supervised hut providing accommodation, food, and drinks. The trail down the ridge from Misen to Daisen Village is relatively easy after the more difficult route up and the dangerous summit ridge.

Descending the ridge from the hut the trail crosses exposed, rocky slopes with another trail leading directly down to the road on the west side of the mountain. Staying on the ridge trail it descends into the forest and passes the small hut at the Sixth Stage of this old staged route to the summit. It is a straightforward descent from here through the forest to the village area below.

The trail first comes out at a track junction, with the old, wooden, Buddhist temple building of Amida-dō a few hundred meters to the left in the midst of the quiet forest. Mountain lodges are located in the forest on the way down to the road. Just across the road is the campsite, and a few minutes down the road a bridge crosses the river into Daisen Village. From the bridge there is an impressive view up the valley to the light-gray, craggy peaks darkening in the dying light of dusk. Daisen—the big mountain—lives up to its name.

7. Mysterious Mountain: Ōmine-san 大峰山

Having decided to climb the highest peaks on the Kii Peninsula, I set about trying to collect information on hiking routes and conditions in these mountains. However, in Tokyo it seemed that few people knew about the area, and the only replies I got to my questions were that this was a little off the beaten track and a mysterious place. So after studying maps, I planned the route which seemed the most interesting and accessible. Then I went and hiked over these mountains of mystery. It was only after my hiking experiences, on reading Carmen Blacker's book *The Catalpa Bow: A Study of Shamanistic Practices in Japan*, that I realized the religious and symbolic significance of these forested, craggy peaks.

Derived from *ki no kuni*—province of trees—the name of the peninsula is apt, with its lush virgin forests of cypress, cedar, pine, and fir covering steep valleys and high peaks alike. Since ancient times the rugged mountains of the peninsula have been a sanctuary for mountain hermits and ascetics. In 1185 Minamoto Yoshitsune found protection here from his brother Yoritomo, the first Kamakura shogun, and in the fourteenth century the emperor Godaigo hid from another shogun amidst the mountains and valleys of Kii.

Previously under the protection of Shinto *kami*, the mountains of Ōmine-san and Yoshino-yama came to be invested with much Buddhist symbolism after the introduction of Buddhism to Japan in the sixth century. En no Ozunu, the greatest of Japan's mountain ascetics, was the first climber of Ōmine-san about 1,300 years ago. He was the founder of Shugendō, and Ōmine-san became the center of the Shugendō sect, which developed towards the end of the twelfth century. Ōmine-san became associated with paradise in the early Heian period, possibly because the Kii Peninsula, on which it is situated, points toward India, the origin of Buddhism. The other main center of Shugendō is Haguro-san in Tohoku.

The ascent of Ōmine-san became one of the principal power-giving practices of Shugendō, and a long pilgrimage route over the mountains from Yoshino to Kumano became popular in the tenth and eleventh centuries. In those days, the yamabushi pilgrimages began with a procession from Shōgoin Temple in Kyoto and proceeded on foot to Yoshino for the start of the austere mountain pilgrimage over Ōmine-san and south to Kumano. Every member of the sect was expected to go on a pilgrimage once a year. A remnant of this long pilgrimage is carried out on August 1, when the Ōmine Okugake *shugyō* (pilgrimage) is held by the Shōgoin branch of Shugendō. The pilgrimage is now much shorter, with fewer of the austerities which, in the old days, were strictly enforced.

Purification and correct preparation before the climb were essential, otherwise there was the risk of being thrown down the precipices and dashed to pieces. On the climb the only food allowed was the roots and herbs found in the mountains. The rules were enforced by the inhabitants of the mountain villages, particularly those of Dorogawa—an isolated village in the valley below Ōmine-san. The people of this village claimed descent from Goki, one of the demonic attendants on En no Ozunu. If they caught any of the pilgrims breaking the rules, they tied him upside down to a tree overhanging a precipice, and left him to his fate. Those who became sick on the way were either left to help themselves or thrown into the valleys below.

As far as I know, this is the only mountain in Japan where women are still strictly banned from climbing to the summit. (Ishizuchi-san in Shikoku bans women on July 1 only.) Carmen Blacker was not allowed to go to the top of this mountain, but she mentions that from 1969 women were allowed to approach 12 miles closer, as far as Gobanseki on the trail from Yoshino to the north. To the east, women must stop at the trail junction at Amida-ga-mori, and to the west they can climb Inamuraga-dake (1,726 m.), which is actually higher than Sanjō-ga-take, the peak of Ōmine-san (1,719 m.). The area around the peak of Ōmine-san where women should not venture is about three kilometers in radius. I would advise women climbers to stay away as there are some strict Shugendō practitioners who may resort to ancient methods of punishment.

ACCESS

Access to Yoshino is made by the private Kintetsu Railway, which takes one and a quarter hours from Osaka. This line can also be taken from the JR Yoshino-guchi Station on the Wakayama Line. From Yoshino Station at the end of the line a cable car runs up the hill to Yoshino-yama and the mountain village of temples, shrines, ryokan, minshuku, and souvenir shops.

ACCOMMODATION

Yoshino-yama is the most famous place in Japan for cherry blossoms. In April the whole mountain bursts into delicate shades of pink. At this time it may be difficult to find accommodation in the village, but there is a campsite at the lake of Tsufuro-ko several kilometers to the east. On the summit of Ōmine-san there are large mountain huts for pilgrims, and there are other mountain huts and campsites in the surrounding mountains and valleys. The Yoshino-yama Kizōin Youth Hostel (Tel: 07463-2-3014) is situated in Yoshino Village.

TRAILS

***
+++

Yoshino-yama (吉野山) ⟶ 5 kms. 1 hr. 50 mins. ⟶ Kimpu Jinja (金峰神

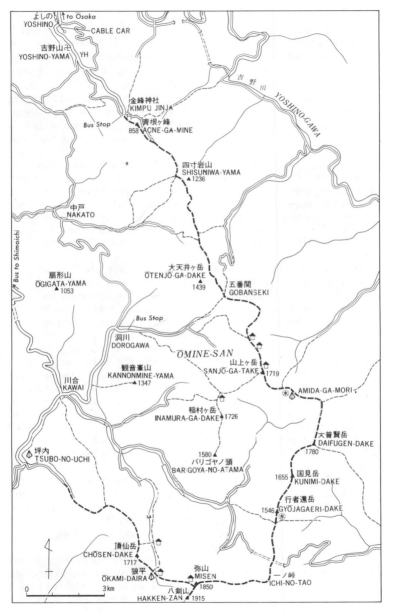

よしの ↑to Osaka
YOSHINO
CABLE CAR
吉野山卍
YOSHINO-YAMA   YH

金峰神社
KIMPU JINJA
Bus Stop   青根ヶ峰
858 AONE-GA-MINE

吉野川
YOSHINO-GAWA

四寸岩山
SHISUNIWA-YAMA
▲1236

中戸
NAKATO

扇形山
ŌGIGATA-YAMA
▲1053

大天井ヶ岳
ŌTENJŌ-GA-DAKE
▲1439

五番関
GOBANSEKI

Bus Stop

洞川
DOROGAWA

ŌMINE-SAN

観音峯山
KANNONMINE-YAMA
▲1347

山上ヶ岳
SANJŌ-GA-TAKE   1719

川合
KAWAI

稲村ヶ岳
INAMURA-GA-DAKE   1726

AMIDA-GA-MORI

大普賢岳
DAIFUGEN-DAKE
1780

坪内
TSUBO-NO-UCHI

1580
バリゴヤノ頭
BARIGOYA-NO-ATAMA

1655   国見岳
KUNIMI-DAKE

行者還岳
1546   GYŌJAGAERI-DAKE

頂仙岳
CHŌSEN-DAKE
1717

狼平
ŌKAMI-DAIRA

弥山
MISEN
1850

一ノ峠
ICHI-NO-TAO

八剣山
HAKKEN-ZAN   ▲1915

0   3 km

↑Bus to Shimoichi

社) ⟶ 14 kms. 6 hrs. ⟶ Gobanseki (五番関) ⟶ 6 kms. 3 hrs. 45 mins. ⟶ Ōmine-san (大峰山) ⟶ 16 kms. 6 hrs. 30 mins. ⟶ Gyōjagaeri-dake (行者還岳) ⟶ 7 kms. 5 hrs. ⟶ Misen (弥山) ⟶ 2.5 kms. 1 hr. ⟶ Ōkami-daira (狼平) ⟶ 10 kms. 5 hrs. ⟶ Tsubo-no-uchi (坪内)

Although the route from Yoshino is the traditional Shugendō route up the mountain, nowadays most climbers take the much shorter route up from the village of Dorogawa. Dorogawa can be reached by a long one and a half hour bus ride from Shimoichi Station on the Kintetsu Yoshino Line. The climb up and down from Dorogawa, where there is a campsite, ryokan, and minshuku accommodation, can easily be done in one day.

Ōmine-san is the name for the whole range of mountains down the center of the Kii Peninsula as well as the sacred peak, which is also known as Sanjō-ga-take. The Shugendō route going south from Ōmine-san goes over the highest peak of Hakken-zan (1,915 m.) before continuing southwards along the range to Kumano. Trails to the peak of Hakken-zan and the nearby Misen start from the villages of Kawai and Tsubo-no-uchi, which can be reached by bus from Shimoichi.

The hike described here starting from Yoshino, climbing Ōmine-san, continuing over the ridges of peaks to Misen and Hakken-zan, and descending to Tsubo-no-uchi, requires about three days and takes in the main points of interest in the area. The ancient yamabushi route continuing south from Hakken-zan along the mountains to Kumano would need a week or more to complete. These mountains fall within the Yoshino-Kumano National Park, which also includes Torokyō Gorge and Nachi-no-taki Waterfall (130 m.)—the highest in Japan.

From the upper cable car station at Yoshino-yama the narrow road winds its way up through the cherry trees and a village, and passes the large bronze torii of Hosshimmon (Gate of Awakening), which marks the boundary between this world and paradise. On the way up through the village there are many shrines and temples with special resthouses for pilgrims. There is an infrequent bus service from the village up to the small wooden Kimpu Shrine at the start of the trail, but otherwise it is a pleasant walk.

An interesting ritual for pilgrims performed at Kimpu Jinja Shrine is described by Carmen Blacker in her book. The pilgrims are ushered into a small hut near the shrine. The door is shut and, for several minutes and in total darkness, the pilgrims chant:

The Kakuredō, in the depths of the Yoshino mountains,
Here has always lain the abode of Emptiness.

This chant is interrupted by the deafening sound of a bell clanging, and the door is opened, letting in the sun. The ritual is designed to simulate the shock of birth. Nearby there is a small tea house, and as I took a rest here before starting the hike, an old priest was explaining to a group of young schoolchildren about the shrine and mountain. Just up the hill behind the shrine a statue marks the place where women had to turn back until 1969. Now they can proceed further.

The trail generally follows close to the ridge through pine and cedar forest with bamboo grass undergrowth, and is a very pleasant but long hike up to the trail junction at Gobanseki. Here women must turn back or take the trail down to Dorogawa Village. Continuing up the ridge the trail is a little steeper to a large corrugated iron hut at the junction with another trail from Dorogawa. Here I met my first group of pilgrims and yamabushi wearing white clothes, baggy pants, deerskins, colorful beads and pendants, small black caps on their heads, and carrying staffs. Bells tinkled as they walked.

There is another hut about half a kilometer further on, just before the steep climb up to the summit. Chains are secured to the rock face, making the climb easier. A nearby precipice called Nishi-no-nozoki is the place from which pilgrims are dangled head-first while they confess their sins. Before coming to the large huts and shrine on the summit, the trail passes through a narrow cleft in the rocks, which symbolizes passage through the womb.

Groups of pilgrims were being conducted between the huts and shrines on the summit by the colorful yamabushi, whose main occupation seemed to be that of guides. I was surprised by the fairly large number of yamabushi and pilgrims I saw around the summit, and they looked very surprised to see a foreigner who had wandered so far off the main tourist routes. However, I met three friendly old yamabushi outside the wooden summit shrine and they pointed out for me the trail continuing over the peak.

It was a short, easy hike to a campsite by the stream at Kosasa-no-juku (小笹宿), where there was a small shrine, a statue, and a tiny hut. There are several bronze statues of yamabushi along this route, each with the characteristic clothes and ringed staff. The trail on the south side of Ōmine-san is much less used, as it is a long, one-day hike over several peaks before the steep climb up Misen. The trail junction at Amida-ga-mori (阿弥陀ヶ森) has a sign in Japanese and bad English saying that women are not allowed to climb beyond this point towards Ōmine-san.

From the peak of Daifugen-dake (大普賢岳 1,780 m.) there are good views of the precipitous forested peaks and deep valleys, north to Ōmine-san and south to Hakken-zan. Far to the east is Ōdai-ga-hara (大台ヶ原)—another interesting mountain hiking area. Passing over Gyō-jagaeri-dake (1,546 m.), there is a large corrugated-iron hut with a nearby freshwater spring on the south side of the peak. After the trail junction at Ichi-no-tao (一ノ峠), the trail swings to the west, keeping to the forested ridge. At the bottom of the steep climb up Misen there is another statue of a yamabushi—probably to give strength and encouragement to those about to make the climb. Amidst the pine forest covering Misen's summit there is a manned wooden hut and campsite and a small wooden shrine. The higher peak of Hakken-zan (also known as Bukkyō-ga-take and Hakkyō-ga-take), covered in pine forest, can be seen to the south. It is a 30-minute hike to its summit—the highest point on the Kii Peninsula—marked by a wooden sign and a yamabushi's ringed staff. Precipitous crags, peaks and deep valleys present an awe-inspiring sight.

The traditional Shugendō route continues south along the ridge of mountains, but for the descent to the valley it is necessary to return to Misen. At Ōkami-daira on the trail down, there is a small, unmanned hut and campsite next to a stream in a picturesque valley. The trail from here to Tsubo-no-uchi crosses the bridge over the stream. Another trail descends via Misen River and its deep gorge, but I was warned that it was hazardous, with many ladders and chains to scale, although the views are supposed to be good.

Descending through lush forest on the trail to Tsubo-no-uchi there is a good chance of spotting monkeys or serow. Two trails descend to the village, but the newer one, which is reached first, is the fastest and best. This passes through cedar stands before coming out onto a track in the valley. The track follows the stream down to the village.

The village of Tsubo-no-uchi is famous for its ancient Tenkawa (Milky Way) Shrine, a beautiful, wooden structure situated on a small hill of cedar. This shrine was one of the earliest places where Noh drama and dance were performed, and it was the home of Kūkai (774–835) for three years before he went to Kōya-san, not so far away, to establish the famous temple there.

A campsite is located next to the river at Tsubo-no-uchi. Bus services operate to the nearby villages of Kawai and Dorogawa, and over the mountains to Shimoichi Station.

▲▲
Chubu:
The Roof of
Japan

Yari-ga-take (Kamikōchi)

In the central, widest part of the main island of Honshu are to be found Japan's highest mountain ranges—the Hida, Kiso, and Akaishi ranges—which are referred to more popularly as the North, Central, and South Alps. These three ranges have an echelon (step-like) arrangement, with the Fossa Magna Tectonic Line forming their northern boundary.

The Japan Alps are mostly formed by Paleozoic and Mesozoic sedimentary strata, which have been intruded by igneous rocks, including Cretaceous granites, and metamorphosed. Cretaceous and Tertiary volcanics are found in the active belt of the Honshu Arc, which runs through the region.

The Yatsu-ga-take Range lies north of the Fossa Magna and is a dormant volcanic area. To the west of the Alps lies Hakusan, an extinct volcanic mountain. Two high volcanoes—Ontake-san (3,063 m.) and Norikura-dake (3,026 m.)—are situated to the south of the North Alps. The former erupted in 1979. Yake-dake (2,455 m.) at the southern end of the North Alps, is still active.

The clearest signs of former glacial activity in Japan are to be found in the Japan Alps, with many cirques in the high mountains, especially in the North Alps. There are no glaciers in these mountains now, but there are many snowy valleys and ravines with perpetual snow. The best examples are found in the Tateyama and Shirouma mountains—the northern part of the North Alps.

The region has very cold winters and the Hokuriku District on the Japan Sea side of the mountains is one of the snowiest regions of the world, where three to four meters of snow may accumulate. Some of Japan's best ski slopes are located here. The Pacific Coast side of the mountains has clear, mild winters with the relatively little snow mostly falling in late winter or early spring. Summers are hot, and intense thunderstorms may occur. Typhoons may cross the region from late summer to early autumn.

The mountains are forested up to about 2,500 meters, above which is the alpine zone of creeping pine and alpine flora. The alpine peaks of this region are the only ones in Japan where the ptarmigan may be seen. This is also probably the best region to see the serow (*kamoshika*).

It was during the late nineteenth century that the Alps of Japan acquired their name from some British travellers who compared them with the Alps of Europe. The North Alps were also the area where Walter Weston, the British missionary, introduced alpinism to Japan. This new sport was taken up enthusiastically by the Japanese, who had previously only climbed mountains for religious reasons. Weston was the first man to conquer Hotaka-dake, the highest peak in the North Alps, and the third highest in Japan. To commemorate Walter Weston's introduction of alpinism to Japan there is a monument to his memory set into the rock face at Kamikōchi, below the mountains he loved to climb. There is also a festival in his honor held every year in Kamikōchi on the first Sunday in June.

Kamikōchi, meaning "Highland," is a very beautiful valley in the midst of the North Alps, through which the sparkling-clear Azusagawa River flows. This is a very popular base for climbing the 3,000-meter peaks of the North Alps which I think are the most magnificent of all Japan's mountains. There are more than 100 mountain huts and campgrounds in the North Alps, reflecting the popularity of this area for hikers and climbers.

The North Alps fall within the Chubu Sangaku National Park. The South Alps are in the Minami Alps National Park. Hakusan is also a national park. Yatsu-ga-take is in the Yatsu-ga-take Chūshin Kōgen Quasi-National Park.

Shinshū was the old name for Nagano Prefecture, which includes most of the Alps ranges and Yatsu-ga-take. Matsumoto City is a gateway to the North Alps and the Alps Mountain Museum is to be found here. The city of Ōmachi to the north is another gateway into the North Alps and has a mountaineering museum.

ACCESS

From Tokyo's Shinjuku Station the Chuo Line runs directly to Matsumoto, taking three hours by express (about ¥6,580). The South Alps can be reached by taking a bus from Kōfu Station and Yatsu-ga-take can be reached by taking a bus from Chino Station. Ōmachi and Hakuba are north of Matsumoto on the Oito Line. The Central Alps are reached on the Iida Line south of Matsumoto. There is also a direct bus service from Shinjuku Station Nishi (West) Exit to Komagane—the base for climbing the Central Alps. Hakusan is best reached from Kanazawa which is seven hours by express from Ueno Station in Tokyo via Nagano, or a one-hour flight from Haneda, Tokyo.

ACCOMMODATION

The mountains of the Chubu District have a plentiful supply of mountain huts and lodges. Campsites are also numerous and camping is usually allowed next to the mountain huts. The towns and cities of the region have a large choice of hotels, ryokan, and minshuku, with youth hostels in most of the main centers including Kōfu, Matsumoto, Komagane, Kanazawa, and Toyama.

Following is a list of lower-priced accommodation in Matsumoto and Kanazawa: Shinshū Kaikan (Tel: 0263-33-0165), seven minutes' walk from Matsumoto Station, rooms are communal. Matsumoto Tourist Hotel (Tel: 0263-33-9000), six minutes' walk from Matsumoto Station. Murataya Ryokan (Tel: 0762-63-0455), 12 minutes by bus from Kanazawa Station. Shibaya Minshuku (Tel: 0762-22-3270), three minutes' walk from Kanazawa Station, with several more reasonably priced minshuku in the area.

8. White Mountain: Hakusan 白山

Travelling along the Hokurikudō—North Land Road—in days gone by, travellers looked inland to the large, white mountain, snow-covered much of the year, and the dwelling place of the gods who protected travellers. Standing on its own, west of the North Alps, this high mountain is exposed to the cold Siberian winds of the winter monsoon, and so catches very heavy snowfalls with snow patches lying around its peaks all year—hence its name. Old names for the mountain also describe its white appearance—"Shirayama" and "Koshi-no-Shirane."

Hakusan is one of the three great spiritual mountains of Japan, together with Tateyama and Fuji-san. Overlooking the old castle town of Kanazawa, which used to be a Buddhist stronghold and the home of the powerful Kaga clan, Hakusan sits on the Ishikawa-Gifu prefectural border. As with other mountains in Japan, its previous Buddhist significance has been superceded by Shinto worship and there is a Shinto shrine on its summit—Gozenhō—Peak of the August Presence.

Situated in the Hakusan Volcanic Zone, which runs through Southwest Honshu to Northern Kyushu, Hakusan is an extinct strato-volcano composed of hornblende andesite. The volcanic domes forming its three central peaks are Gozenhō (2,702 m.), Ōnanji-mine (2,684 m.), and Ken-ga-mine (2,660 m.). Their rocky peaks dominate the beautiful summit scenery of seven small crater lakes and mountain slopes covered in colorful alpine flowers. At the foot of the mountain there are many hot springs which tap the thermal waters beneath the mountain.

The lower slopes of the mountain are covered with virgin forests of white fir, beech, and oak, with pine on the higher slopes and creeping pine in the alpine zone above about 2,200 meters. Twenty-three species of mammals are found on Hakusan, including the serow and monkey. The ptarmigan may be seen in the alpine zone, and the rare Japanese eagle—the *inuwashi*—may be found here.

In winter the thick snow falling on the mountain is perfect for skiing, and five ski resorts are located on the lower slopes. The climbing season is fairly short, with the official "opening" of the mountain at a big festival on July 17 and 18 in Shiramine village, in the valley on the west side of the mountain. This *kaizan matsuri* is followed by many people climbing up to the shrine on the summit. In days gone by, Hakusan was climbed and worshipped by Buddhists and yamabushi of the Shugendō sect. The official climbing season is over at the end of August, but climbing is still possible if you go well prepared. However, July and August are best for weather and viewing the alpine flowers.

ACCESS

Access to Hakusan is easiest via the historic town of Kanazawa, from where buses run directly up the mountain to Bettōdeai—the start of the trail to the summit. The private Hokuriku Railway can also be taken from Nomachi to Hakusan-shita, where the lower shrine is situated, and a bus from there up the valley to Shiramine, Ichi-no-se, and Bettōdeai. Bettōdeai is the start of the shortest and most popular hiking route to the summit.

ACCOMMODATION

There is plenty of ryokan and minshuku accommodation in the villages below the mountain, but this will often be full during July and August. At Ichi-no-se, just below the start of the trail, there is a mountain hut and campsite. There is a mountain hut on the trail to the summit and two large huts at Murodō and Nanryū Sansō below the summit peaks, with a campsite near the latter hut. Several more huts and campsites are found on the mountain.

TRAILS

*****
+++
Bettōdeai (別当出合) ⟶ 6 kms. 5 hrs. ⟶ Murodō (室堂) ⟶ 1 km. 50 mins. ⟶ Gozenhō (御前峰) ⟶ 2 kms. 1 hr. 15 mins. ⟶ Ōnanji-mine (大汝峰) ⟶ 2 kms. 1 hr. ⟶ Murodō (室堂) ⟶ 2 kms. 1 hr. 30 mins. ⟶ Nanryū Sansō (南竜山荘) ⟶ 4.5 kms. 3 hrs. ⟶ Bessan (別山) ⟶ 2.5 kms. 2 hrs. ⟶ San-no-mine (三ノ峰) ⟶ 6 kms. 4 hrs. 15 mins. ⟶ Kamiko-ike (上小池) ⟶ 6 kms. 2 hrs. 30 mins. ⟶ Hato-ga-yu Onsen (鳩ヶ湯温泉)

Many alternative routes can be taken over Hakusan, but I chose a route which passes the main points of interest as well as having ease of access. So taking the short route to the summit from Bettōdeai the route goes over the peaks, passes the lakes, and then goes south on the

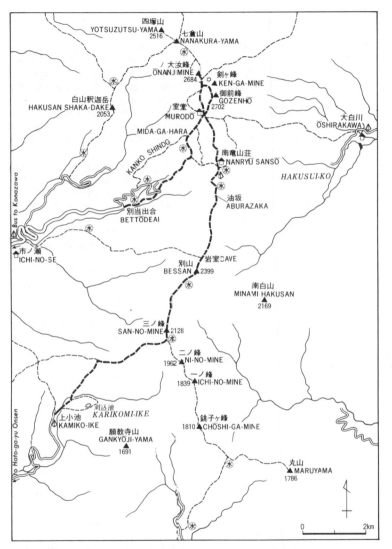

ridge to Bessan—a secondary peak which also has a small shrine on its summit. Down the ridge and into the valley at Kamiko-ike, where there is a campsite, the route continues down the road to Hato-ga-yu Onsen, from where buses run to the famous pottery and temple town of Echizen Ōno. This route is a full two days of hiking through wonderful scenery.

After spending a day wandering around the old samurai and geisha districts of Kanazawa City, I took the early-morning bus from the station up to Bettōdeai. The journey took about two hours, the bus becoming crammed with hikers at Ichi-no-se Hut and campsite for the last climbing section up to the end of the road.

Two trails climb from the shelter, but both meet high on the mountain at Mida-ga-hara (弥陀ヶ原), an alpine plateau at about 2,400 meters. The trail to the right, which I took, called Sabō Shindō (砂防新道), is faster and more popular than the Kankō Shindō (観光新道).

It is a long, steep climb, crossing a track and passing a disused hut, before coming to a wooden hut higher on the route, where many hikers stopped for drinks and snacks. From here it is a further climb up through bushy forest to a trail junction where you go left for the alpine plateau of Mida-ga-hara, passing the top of the other route on the way. It is a gentle climb up the open, flower-covered slopes with snow filling the gullies to Murodō—a very large wooden hut and mountain center built on a flat area below Gozenhō peak.

A small shrine and torii gateway marks the start of the rocky trail to the summit. Here another small wooden shrine nestles amidst the rocks just below the highest peak of Hakusan. The view from the peak is terrific, with the lower peaks of Ken-ga-mine and Ōnanji to the north, small crater lakes sitting in the rocky hollows between the peaks, and best of all the panoramic profile of the North Alps stretched along the horizon to the east. Along this North Alps profile the peaks of Tateyama, Yari-ga-take, and Hotaka can be clearly distinguished.

Descending on the north side of Gozenhō peak, the trail passes the crater lakes, which are still partly snow- and ice-covered in mid-August. On the rocky slopes around the lakes, colorful alpine plants grow in profusion, with many local varieties named after the mountain. The largest lake of Midori-ga-ike sits on a terrace with a magnificent view across its glittering, ice-cold water to the North Alps—this has to be one of the best sights on Hakusan.

Ōnanji can be reached via a steep trail to its flat, rocky summit, where there is also a small wooden shrine enclosed by a stone wall. Two trails lead back to Murodō over beautiful alpine slopes of creeping pine and flowers. There are also two trails from Murodō to the hut and campsite at Nanryū Sansō. The trail directly south crosses a snowy gully and is steeper and faster.

From the campsite the trail crosses the valley to the south and climbs steeply to Aburazaka-no-kashira (油坂の頭 2,256 m.). Over this peak it is a wonderful ridge walk to the peak of Bessan (2,399 m.), with very picturesque meadows of yellow mountain lilies and other alpine flowers on the way. Just before the peak of Bessan there is a shelter in a small rock cave below the ridge. A small shrine sits in a hollow below the peak, surrounded by rock walls to protect it from the bad weather.

Continuing on the ridge, the trail passes a small pond, whose Japanese name means "hand washing pond," on its way to San-no-mine (2,128 m.). Over this peak the trail divides at a small unsupervised wooden hut with the shortest route down the mountain on the trail to the right (west) of the hut. This trail was very narrow and overgrown as I followed it down the slippery, muddy ridge. Cloud and mist were moving in during the afternoon, and the thick bamboo grass and bushy vegetation were dripping with moisture. After entering the forest, a trail goes off the ridge to the left and descends steeply into the valley. I had some difficulty here because recent dam works made the trail difficult to follow in places.

Coming out at the end of a track the campsite is a short walk down to a junction by some huts. The paved road leads down this beautiful valley cut by the Uchinami River to Hato-ga-yu Onsen—an old wooden ryokan with natural hot spring baths. For a small fee you can enjoy the hot baths without staying the night. On my way down to this remote, rustic hot spring resort I saw a large wild monkey crossing the road on his way from the river below, going up into the thick forest covering the mountainside.

Three buses a day run from the onsen to Echizen Ōno—an interesting town where old temple buildings and the famous Echizen-yaki pottery may be seen. Trains run from here to Fukui. Rising from the old towns of Echizen and Kanazawa, and the old North Land Road the white mountain has inspired people below since ancient times.

9. White Horse Mountain: Shirouma-dake 白馬岳

Year-round snow-filled valleys make this mountain an exciting and cool climb during midsummer, when you can be hiking on snow and ice within two hours of leaving the nearest railway station at Hakuba on the Oito Line. Actually Hakuba, the name of the town below the mountain, and Shirouma, the name of the mountain, are different readings of the same Chinese characters meaning "White Horse." The "white" part of the name can be accounted for by the perpetual snow lying on the mountain, but the "horse" part of the name is more difficult to explain. Although this is the only mountain in Japan with this name, there are several mountains bearing the name *Koma* (駒), which also means horse or pony. One explanation is that the shape of the snow lying on the mountainside, especially during the spring, looks like a horse. There is also an interesting parallel with the two white horses found on the northern slopes of the chalk hills of Southern England, which were sculpted in the white bedrock in pre-Roman times. Their explanation is also a mystery.

The mountains of Shirouma form the highest peaks in the north-eastern section of the Hida Range, more popularly known as the North Alps. Just north of Shirouma-dake is the junction of three prefectures—Niigata to the north, Toyama to the west, and Nagano to the east. Shirouma has three high peaks of which Shirouma-dake (2,932 m.) is the highest, with Shakushi-dake (2,812 m.) and Yari-ga-take (2,903 m.) to the south. On a fine day the higher peaks of Tateyama can be seen to the west across the deep Kurobe-gawa Gorge.

Midsummer snow, alpine peaks, alpine flowers, a chance to spot a ptarmigan, and easy access, make the Shirouma Mountains very popular with hikers from July to October, and especially during the month of August. My hike up the mountain in mid-August was done as part of a long procession of hikers. We sometimes came to a standstill on the trail up the snowy valley, and the large mountain huts were filled to capacity. The scenery here is terrific and it's worth putting up with the crowds, which, however, can be largely avoided during the less popular months of September and October.

Most climbers use the same route up and down the mountain direct-ly from the town of Hakuba, and it is possible to do this climb up and down in one day, although many climbers stay at one of the five moun-tain huts along this route. With a little extra planning, however, there are many more spectacular, and less crowded, hikes to be done in these mountains. The trail going northeast along the ridge from Shirouma-dake comes to a beautiful area of mountain lakes and mar-shes, while the trail going south goes over the other peaks of Shirouma and comes to Karamatsu-dake, from where another trail can be taken down to the ski lifts on the lower slopes and then back to Hakuba. These lower mountain slopes are some of the most popular ski resorts in Japan, as the area falls in the Hokuriku District with its heavy snowfall during the winter monsoon. The snowfalls are so deep in these mountains that even the hot, sunny summers are not enough to melt all the snow away. Described here is a hike over Shirouma-dake taking the popular route up, but then a much-less-used trail on the western side of the mountain down to Keyaki-daira in the Kurobe-gawa Gorge, which is itself an excellent base for hiking, with many hot springs in the area. This hike normally takes two days, but it is possible to do it in one very hard day's trek.

ACCESS

Access to Hakuba is fairly easy, taking the Chuo Line from Shinjuku to Matsumoto, and then the Oito Line from there. If coming from the Japan Sea coast at Toyama or Niigata, the Oito Line can be taken from Itoigawa. Hakuba is a small tourist town catering to motorists and hikers during the summer, and skiers during the winter, and is not par-ticularly interesting. Just in front of Hakuba Station is the bus stop for the bus which goes up the mountain to Sarukura-sō—a mountain cottage at about 1,200 meters, and the start of the popular trail up to the summit. The first buses leave in summer at 0540 and are crowded with hikers eager to get an early start. Winding up the small road, the last part steep and unpaved, the bus journey takes about 30 minutes.

ACCOMMODATION

Sarukura-sō is the first of the five cottages and huts on the way to the summit which offer basic accommodation, food, and drinks. Accommodation in these huts, with two meals, costs upwards of ¥5,000, and canned drinks sell for two or three times their normal price, because they are either carried up the mountain or flown in by helicopter. It is best to carry your own food and drink supplies. There is a campsite behind the Chōjō Shukusha hut, situated on the pass southwest of the summit, and camping is also allowed at Babadani Onsen on the route down to Keyaki-daira.

TRAILS

****
++++
Sarukura-sō (猿倉荘) ⟶ 2.8 kms. 1 hr. 15 mins. ⟶ Hakubajiri-sō (白馬尻荘) ⟶ 4.5 kms. 3 hrs. 45 mins. ⟶ Chōjō Shukusha (頂上宿舎) ⟶ 1 km. 40 mins. ⟶ Shirouma-dake (白馬岳) ⟶ 5 5 kms. 2 hrs. 30 mins. ⟶ Shōzu-dake (清水岳) ⟶ 3.2 kms. 1 hr. 50 mins. ⟶ Hinan Goya (避難小屋) ⟶ 10 kms. 5 hrs. ⟶ Babadani Onsen (祖母谷温泉) ⟶ 2.5 kms. 50 mins. ⟶ Keyaki-daira (欅平)

A wide, unpaved track continues up the valley from the bus terminus at Sarukura-sō, passing through natural forest, and soon there is a view up the valley to the rocky crags and peaks of Shirouma. The track ends and a wide trail leads to Hakubajiri-sō and Hakubajiri Goya—two huts situated below the snow valley at about 1,550 meters. From here there are good views of the snowy ravines on the mountain and Daisekkei—the name of the snow-filled valley on the route. Simple iron crampons are sold at the huts for fastening to your boots and giving you a grip on the snow, but in summer the snow is usually soft and crampons are not really needed, especially when following the well-trodden trail. There is a sign just after the huts saying that climbing beyond this point is not allowed after 2:00 P.M., as it is reckoned that you will not have enough time to reach the huts at the top before dark.

Climbing through the top part of the forest from Hakubajiri, a 15-minute walk will bring you directly onto the open snow slopes at the bottom of Daisekkei. The next part of the climb is completely on snow, and is steep in places, but steps are worn into the snow by the thousands of hikers who take this route. People descending this route seem to have a much more difficult time staying on their feet than those climbing. The climb up Daisekkei takes about one and a half hours, after which you will come out onto rocky alpine slopes with colorful flowers and creeping pine. There are more snow patches higher up the mountain and fresh water from snowmelt all the way up to the pass below the summit, so it is not necessary to carry much water on the hike up. Climbing up to Chōjō Shukusha hut, the alpine scenery is spectacular, with the peaks of Shakushi-dake and Yari-ga-take rising to the south, and Shirouma-dake to the north. Chōjō Shukusha is a large hut with a dining room and small store, and the campsite is just behind it on rocky ground. From here you can see Hakuba-sō, an even larger mountain hut, sitting on the rocky slopes up to the summit. This is only a 20-minute walk away up a wide trail. I was told that this hut can accommodate up to 1,500 people in intimate, communal style, and a regular helicopter service brings in supplies. A party of young people were on their way up to this hut as I was on my way to the summit, which is only another 20-minute hike up behind Hakuba-sō.

The summit of Shirouma-dake is a jagged, rocky peak with precipitous crags on its eastern side over which there is an aerial view of the snowy valley you have just climbed. To the north, south, and west is an endless vista of alpine peaks, and if the weather is really fine, the peaks of Tateyama can be seen to the southwest.

For the trail down the west side of the mountain to Keyaki-daira you must return down to the pass just above Chōjō Shukusha hut, where there is a trail junction and signboard. From here the trail goes west, passing over gentle alpine slopes covered with flowers before crossing snow on the southern side of Asahi-dake. It is a great alpine walk, generally keeping close to the ridge as the trail makes its way to Shōzu-dake (2,590 m.). There are lots of alpine flowers and creeping pine on this high ridge trail, with a good chance of seeing a ptarmigan—the symbol of the North Alps.

After passing over the gentle peak of Shōzu-dake, the trail descends from the colorful, flowery, alpine slopes into the forest, and eventually comes to the small, unmanned Hinan Goya hut. It is rather a long trek down through the forest, crossing some streams lower down and some badly eroded sections along the trail, before coming to Babadani Onsen in the valley. As you come down a ridge on the last part of the descent into Babadani valley, you will see the steam rising from the hot spring next to the river. The trail comes out onto a track which passes the hot spring across the river and then comes to a bridge. Babadani Onsen Hut is about 100 meters down the track on the right before the bridge. Here the small wooden hut provides accommodation and meals, with a small area for camping near the outdoor spring (*rotenburo*). Natural hot spring water is piped from the steaming vents just upstream to the large bathing pool next to the hut. Here you can soak away the aches and pains from tired muscles and feet after the hike over "White Horse Mountain."

Across the bridge and about 50 minutes' walk down the track, which was just being paved on my visit, is Keyaki-daira, set in a magnificent gorge of precipitous forested and craggy cliffs. This is the gorge cut by the Kurobe-gawa River, which is dammed upstream at the famous Kurobe No. 4 Dam. In the Kurobe Gorge there are several hot springs, most of which are downstream on the way to Unazuki Onsen. Keyaki-daira is the end of the private Kurobe Kyokoku Railway Line, which connects with the Toyama Dentetsu Line at Unazuki Onsen, and so access between the gorge and Toyama is very easy. Keyaki-daira is an excellent base or starting point for hiking in the Shirouma and Tateyama mountains. The hike over Shirouma-dake can be done in reverse by starting here, but this would involve a much longer climb and a tricky descent of Shirouma's snowy valley. From Keyaki-daira there is a spectacular trail up the Kurobe Gorge to the dam, and trails into the Tateyama Mountains. Both of these hikes take two days, with many mountain huts and campsites on the way.

10. Buddhist or Shinto? Tateyama 立山

After Buddhism was introduced to Japan, many mountains were consecrated by Buddhist priests, but there were three mountains which stood out as being especially holy—they were Fuji-san, Hakusan and Tateyama (the last was consecrated in 703). Hakusan and Tateyama overlooked the Hokurikudō, while Fuji-san overlooked the Tōkaidō, these being the two main routes between the Kanto and Kansai

Districts. Hence, they have always presented their awe-inspiring profiles to the many travellers along these old roads. In addition, Tateyama has a pre-Buddhist association with the other world. Travellers in the mountains in olden times heard noises, probably due to volcanic activity, from beneath the earth, so it came to symbolize the entrance to hell. But although these three mountains are well-known as Buddhist consecrated peaks, a hike up any one of them will present you with, not a mountain crowned by temples, and statues of Buddha, but a definitely Shinto-imbued peak, with torii gateways and shrines. The change is probably a post-Meiji Restoration phenomenon, a result of the late-nineteenth, early-twentieth-century encouragement of Shinto as the national religion. So, perched on Tateyama's Oyama peak is a wooden Shinto shrine and just below it, a torii gateway.

A nearby, lower peak in the Tateyama Mountains has the name Jōdo-san which means Pure Land Mountain—clearly a Buddhist name, but on its summit, too, you will find a Shinto shrine. This can be confusing for foreigners, who usually think in terms of exclusive categories, especially when it comes to different beliefs and philosophies. The Japanese, however, are able to accommodate apparent contradictions in their beliefs, because their categories are basically socially oriented, with the major categorical boundary being around their islands. Contradictions are allowed if they are for the harmony and good of society and the nation. In Japan, Buddhism is the religion for funerals, whereas Shinto is the religion for new babies, children, and marriage. Each particular situation is seen separately without the universalistic views and principles held by most Westerners. So here we have a Buddhist-consecrated mountain with a Shinto shrine on its summit.

The Tateyama Range forms the northwestern part of the North Alps, and its metamorphic and volcanic rocks are the building material for some of the grandest alpine peaks in Japan. Tsurugi-dake (2,998 m.) to the north of Tateyama's highest peaks, but only a few meters lower, is one of the severest peaks in Japan, with sharp cliffs and rocky peaks composed of diorite. It is one of the two most popular alpine peaks for rock climbers to test their skill and strength against, the other being Hotaka-dake, also in the North Alps. Below the peaks are several lava plateaus, as seen at Murodō-daira and Mida-ga-hara. Near Murodō there is a crater centered on Jigoku-dani (Hell's Valley), and to the southwest there is a large caldera.

Snow lies in the valleys and ravines of these mountains year-round, and alpine flowers bring color to the rocky and snowy slopes during the summer. These mountains are perhaps the most likely place to see a ptarmigan. I made four sightings in these mountains in three days, whereas I saw none on Shirouma-dake or in the mountains around Kamikōchi—the two other popular areas of the North Alps.

ACCESS

The best base for hiking in the Tateyama Mountains is Murodō, situated on a lava plateau at about 2,400 meters, and overlooked by the highest peaks in the range. Murodō is the highest point on the popular Tateyama-Kurobe Alpine Route—a combination of train, bus, cable car, and ropeway passing over and under the Tateyama Mountains, and across Kurobe No. 4 Dam in the deep gorge to the east of the range. Since its opening in 1971 one million tourists and climbers have used this spectacular route each year. The route can be travelled in either direction: from east of the North Alps from Shinano Ōmachi Station on the Oito Line, or from the west from Tateyama Station on the Toyama Dentetsu Line. From Shinano Omachi Station take a bus and trolley bus to Kurobe Dam; from Tateyama Station you can take a cable car and then bus to Murodō. A ticket for the complete route or tickets for each separate part of the journey can be bought.

ACCOMMODATION

There are many hotels, ryokan, and mountain huts providing accommodation along the route, and Sugita Youth Hostel (Tel: 0764-82-1754) is situated near Tateyama Station at the end of the private Toyama Dentetsu Line from Toyama. A campsite is located thirty minutes' walk from Murodō Bus Terminal in the valley below Tateyama's peaks, and there are several campsites and mountain huts for climbers in the mountains. The summer months, and especially August, may see the huts filled to capacity in the area around Murodō and in the central peaks, but there are many trails leading to less frequented parts of the Tateyama Mountains to the south and east.

TRAILS

* * * * *
+ + +

Murodō (室堂) —→ 2.5 kms. 1 hr. —→ Ichi-no-koshi (一ノ越) —→ 1 km. 1 hr. —→ Oyama (雄山) —→ 0.6 km. 20 mins. —→ Ōnanji-san (大汝山) —→ 3.5 kms. 1 hr. 50 mins. —→ Tsurugi-gozen Goya (剣御前小屋) —→ 2.8 kms. 1 hr. 40 mins. —→ Jigoku-dani (地獄谷) —→ 1 km. 40 mins. —→ Murodō (室堂)

The hiking route described here is not very long and can be done easily in one day from Murodō. It includes all of the sights around Murodō and goes over Tateyama's highest peaks, with views of all the surrounding peaks on a fine day. As Murodō is already above the forest and in the alpine zone, the whole hike goes over rocky mountain slopes with eternal snow lying in the gullies, colorful alpine flowers, and many ptarmigan resident in the area. Hiking boots are recommended on the rocky trails, but are not absolutely essential.

At the large bus terminal complex on the Murodō Plateau, an in-

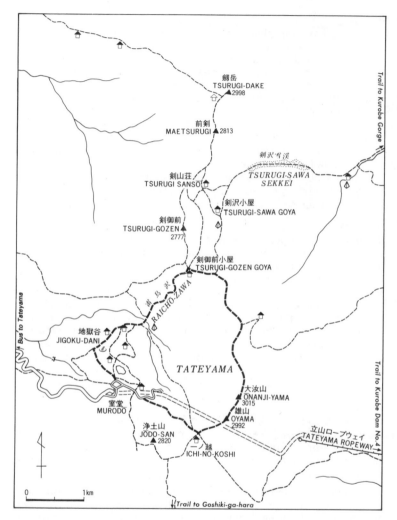

congruous sight in these alpine mountains, there is a modern hotel, restaurants, and souvenir shops. Nearby there is a nature center with displays of the mountains and wildlife to be found in the area, the main exhibit being the ptarmigan. The plateau area around Murodō, including Jigoku-dani, a crater lake, several lodges with natural hot spring baths, and a campsite, is well laid out with trails, the Tateyama peaks forming an impressive backdrop. Taking the main track from the bus terminal up the slope towards the highest peaks you will soon come to a mountain hut from where two trails go up into the mountains. The trail to the right (south) goes over Jōdo-san (浄土山), and is a longer route to the main peaks, but most people take the direct trail (southeast) straight up to Ichi-no-koshi Hut on the pass below the peaks. This is a wide, easy trail with wonderful views back down to the Murodō Plateau. Accommodation, food, and drinks are available at the hut, which is a good place to rest before the steep, rugged climb up to the peaks.

From the hut the trail climbs 300 meters almost vertically to the peak of Oyama (2,992 m.), without any let-up in its steep gradient. I was amazed to see large groups of young children being coaxed up by their teachers, and families with young children who were sometimes carried up by their parents. There is no other country where I have seen so many children climbing rocky, alpine peaks.

On the summit of Oyama stands a wooden Shinto shrine with a torii gateway on the trail leading up to it. While I was there a Shinto priest in colorful robes stood on the exposed peak next to the shrine making a truly impressive sight. However, this is not the highest peak of Tateyama. That distinction goes to Ōnanji-san (3,015 m.), just to the north, and reached in fifteen minutes along a rocky trail. (The hard rocks of these peaks are composed of granodiorite gneiss.) Clouds often build up quickly around these peaks, and so early morning is the best time for clear views when the craggy Tsurugi-dake (2,998 m.), a mecca for rock climbers, may be seen to the north.

Many people return the same way back to Murodō, but it is more interesting to continue on the trail over Ōnanji, descending a rocky ridge with a little more climbing over a lower peak and keeping left at two junctions before coming to Tsurugi-gozen Goya—a large hut situated on a pass. The valley to the northeast of the pass has perpetual snow, and a couple of skiers were getting some midsummer skiing practice in as I passed by. From the hut there are trails going north to the notorious Tsurugi-dake, and other trails leading down to a campsite at Tsurugi-sawa Goya, the large snowy valley of Tsurugi-sawa Sekkei, and eventually down into the Kurobe Gorge and Keyaki-daira, which is a full day's hike from here.

If the weather is fine, the plateau of Murodō can be seen from the pass. The trail leading down into the valley below Murodō keeps close to a gully known as Raichō-sawa (Ptarmigan Vale), and indeed I did spot a female ptarmigan with several chicks as I descended the trail. Situated on flat ground, next to the river in the valley below, the campsite can be seen with the desolate, steaming valley of Jigoku-dani just beyond it. Coming to the bottom of Raichō-sawa, a bridge crosses the river to the campsite, and a trail leads from there to Jigoku-dani, where you can walk through the active area of bubbling, steaming, sulphurous vents. Taking the trail from here up the hill, you come to Mikuri-ga-ike—the crater lake in which, on calm, clear days, can be seen the reflection of Tateyama's impressive peaks. From the lake it is only a five-minute walk to the Murodō Terminal.

For the more adventurous souls who wish to make a longer trek through the North Alps, I can recommend the route from Murodō going south along the Tateyama Range of mountains, passing Goshiki-ga-hara (五色ヶ原), where there is a hut, cottage, and campsite on a beautiful plateau, and continuing south to Yakushi-dake (薬師岳 2,926 m.), Mitsumatarenge-dake (三俣蓮華岳 2,841 m.), Yari-ga-take (槍ヶ岳 3,180 m.), Hotaka-dake (穂高岳 3,190 m.), and finally down to Kamikōchi. The latter part of this hike is described in the following section on Kamikōchi. Most of the route is above 2,500 meters, and so it is pleasantly cool in the summer, with magnificent alpine scenery, and many mountain huts and campsites along the way. From five days to one week is needed to complete this trek, which is one of the best long-distance alpine treks in Japan.

11. The Birthplace of Japanese Alpinism: Kamikōchi
上高地

By height they rank third in Japan, below Fuji-san and the South Alps, but amongst all of Japan's impressive mountainscapes of soaring alpine peaks and active volcanoes, there are none to compare with the noble splendor and magnificence of the North Alps. The name "Japan Alps" was made popular for these mountains at the end of the nineteeth century by William Gowland, whose *Japan Guide* was published in 1888, and another Englishman—Walter Weston, who scaled many of the peaks in the North Alps and introduced the sport of alpinism to Japan for the first time. Until Weston set out on his expeditions into uncharted areas of the North Alps, mountain climbing in Japan was a purely religious affair undertaken by Shinto, Buddhist and Shugendō priests and pilgrims.

The spear-like peak of Yari-ga-take (3,180 m.) was not consecrated until 1826, when the Buddhist monk Banryū placed three Buddhist images on its summit, after many years of trying to scale its rocky peak. Weston conquered this peak 66 years later in 1892, and also Hotaka-dake (3,190 m.), the highest peak towering above Kamikōchi. It was yet another Briton named Marshall who first climbed the active volcano of Yake-dake (2,455 m.) in the southwestern part of the range. Kamikōchi—the alpinists' base, set on the banks of the Azusagawa River and surrounded by the highest peaks in the North Alps—was beloved of Weston for its outstanding natural beauty. A memorial in his honor can be seen set in the rock face near the banks of the Azusagawa River, and on the first Sunday in June each year a festival is held here to open each new summer climbing season.

The original Japanese name for the North Alps is Hida, and this range runs from the Japan Sea Coast in the north, where the mountains run right into the sea, to the volcanic peaks of Norikura-dake and Ontake in the south. They are composed of Paleozoic and Mesozoic strata which have been extensively metamorphosed and intruded by igneous rocks. The Cretaceous, Tertiary, and Recent volcanics of the range form part of the active Honshu Arc. Japan's best relict glacial features are to be found in these mountains above 2,500 meters, with many rocky, ice-scoured areas in the high peaks, and several glacial cirques which are the result of past glacial activity. Permanent snow lies in the valleys and hollows of these mountains, but there are no glaciers at present.

Heavy snow falls on the range in winter, making for popular ski resorts on the lower slopes, and exciting winter climbing for specialists. Mixed forests of pine, fir, spruce, cedar, beech, and maple cover the lower mountain slopes, while above 2,300 meters are the rocky alpine slopes with their brilliant splashes of summer color. This is the domain of the ptarmigan—a friendly resident of these harsh peaks, and the emblem of the North Alps.

Within this range there are many areas of interest, but three popular centers for hiking stand out. They are: Kamikōchi, situated in the Azusa valley, dominated by the highest, most impressive peaks of the range, and described here; Tateyama to the northwest; and Shirouma to the northeast, both of which are described separately. Kamikōchi offers some fine mountaineering for all levels of ability, from easy strolls along the beautiful Azusa Valley, to strenuous rock climbing on the sheer walls of Hotaka-dake. The circular route described here includes the hike up the Azusa Valley to the peak of Yari-ga-take, then along the ridge of peaks to Hotaka-dake, which I consider *the* alpine route to do in Japan, and finally the descent back down to Kamikōchi. Three days are needed to complete this route. This area and this route are extremely popular with Japanese mountaineers, and one ridge trail just to the north, which also climbs Yari-ga-take, is known as the "Ginza Traverse" (Ginza Jūsō), after the busy shopping street in central Tokyo.

ACCESS

Access to Kamikōchi is usually made via Matsumoto, the nearest large city, which can be reached by Chuo Line from Tokyo, and from where bus services operate direct. Alternatively, a combination of train and bus can be used for the journey by taking the private Kamikōchi Line from Matsumoto to Shinshimashima at the end of the line, and then a bus from there. It takes about one and a half hours from Matsumoto to Kamikōchi.

The bus leaves the main road, which continues on to Takayama, at Nakanoyu—a hot spring resort with a rotenburo in the rocks above the river—and takes a small road about eight kilometers up the valley to Kamikōchi. Private cars are stopped from entering this road at the height of the tourist season in July and August. Halfway, the road passes Taishō-ike, a small lake formed after the 1915 eruption of Yake-dake blocked the Azusa Valley with a lava flow. The dark, volcanic rock peaks of Yake-dake, the only active volcano in the North Alps, which again erupted in 1962, rise above the far side of the lake. From the bus terminal it is a ten-minute walk up the track to Kappabashi Bridge, where the campsite and most of the lodges are to be found. Trails are well laid out next to the river, and through the forested valley, with the Weston Monument, and ryokan with natural hot spring baths, a fifteen-minute walk downstream on the north bank of the river, and a trail from there to Taishō-ike. The trail climbing up Yake-dake takes about one and a half hours to its simmering peaks.

ACCOMMODATION

Kamikōchi is a major tourist destination, and is becoming more popular each year. The building of new hotels and tourist facilities is, however, restricted, to preserve the natural beauty of the valley. There are several hotels, lodges, and ryokan in the small tourist village, but advanced booking is needed to be sure of a place to stay here. Near Kappabashi Bridge, which crosses the Azusagawa River at the center of Kamikōchi, is Konashi-daira Campsite, situated in a forest of pine and fir with thick bamboo grass undergrowth. On the trails in the surrounding valleys and mountains there are numerous huts and campsites, but although accommodation is assured, it is often overcrowded.

TRAILS

*****
+++++
Kamikōchi （上高地）—→ 7 kms. 2 hrs. —→ Tokusawaen （徳沢園）—→ 4 kms. 1 hrs. 15 mins. —→ Yokoo Sansō （横尾山荘）—→ 4 kms. 1 hr. 15 mins. —→ Ichinomata Goya （一ノ俣小屋）—→ 2.4 kms. 1 hr. 15 mins. —→ Yarisawa Lodge （槍沢ロッジ）—→ 4.4 kms. 4 hrs. 45 mins. —→ Yari-ga-take Sansō （槍ヶ岳山荘）—→ 2 kms. 1 hr. 15 mins. —→ Naka-dake （中岳）—→ 2 kms. 2 hrs. —→ Minami-dake （南岳）—→ 3.5 kms. 3 hrs. 40 mins. —→ Kita Hotaka Goya （北穂高小屋）—→ 2 kms. 2 hrs. 20 mins. —→ Karasawa-dake （涸沢岳）—→ 0.5 km. 30 mins. —→ Hotaka-dake Sansō （穂高岳山荘）—→ 1 km. 1 hr. —→ Okuhotaka-dake （奥穂高岳）—→ 5.5 kms. 3 hrs. 40 mins. —→ Dakesawa Hut （岳沢ヒュッテ）—→ 4.5 kms. 1 hr. 50 mins. —→ Kamikōchi

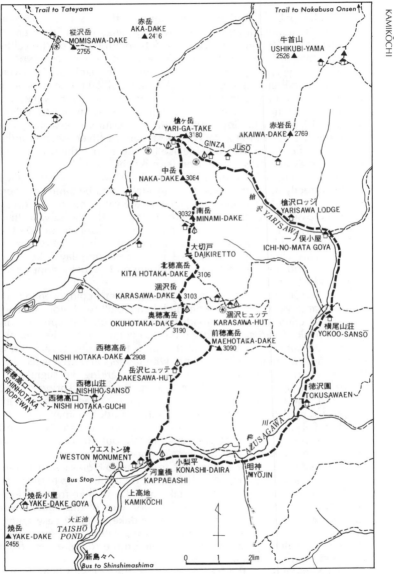

Trail to Tateyama

Trail to Nakabusa Onsen

赤岳
AKA-DAKE ▲24˙6

樅沢岳
MOMISAWA-DAKE
2755

牛首山
USHIKUBI-YAMA
2526 ▲

槍ヶ岳
YARI-GA-TAKE
3˙80

GINZA JUSŌ

赤岩岳
AKAIWA-DAKE ▲2769

中岳
NAKA-DAKE 3084

槍沢 YARISAWA

槍沢ロッジ
YARISAWA LODGE

3032 南岳
MINAMI-DAKE

一俣小屋
ICHI-NO-MATA GOYA

大切戸
DAIKIRETTO

北穂高岳
KITA HOTAKA-DAKE 3106

涸沢岳
KARASAWA-DAKE 3103

涸沢ヒュッテ
KARASAWA-HUT

横尾山荘
YOKOO-SANSŌ

奥穂高岳
OKUHOTAKA-DAKE 3190

前穂高岳
MAEHOTAKA-DAKE 3090

西穂高岳
NISHI HOTAKA-DAKE ▲2908

岳沢ヒュッテ
DAKESAWA-HUT

徳沢園
TOKUSAWAEN

新穂高ロープウェー
SHINHOTAKA
ROPEWAY

西穂山荘
NISHIHO SANSŌ

西穂高口
NISHI HOTAKA-GUCHI

梓川 AZUSAGAWA

ウエストン碑
WESTON MONUMENT

小梨平
KONASHI-DAIRA

明神
MYŌJIN

Bus Stop

河童橋
KAPPAEASHI

焼岳小屋
YAKE-DAKE GOYA

上高地
KAMIKŌCHI

焼岳
▲YAKE-DAKE
2455

大正池
TAISHŌ
POND

新島々へ
Bus to Shinshimashima

0   1   2 ㎞

101

Between Kappabashi Bridge and the campsite there is a small exhibition hall with many informative displays on the natural environment of the North Alps. Myōjin (明神) is an easy fifty-minute walk up the valley from the campsite. This small shrine is located by a picturesque pond surrounded by lush, green forest on the north bank of the river. Another fifty minutes up the valley, taking the trail on the south side of the river, will bring you to Tokusawaen Hut. Keeping to the valley going north from here is a well-worn trail, and easy hiking to Yokoo Sansō and Ichinomata Goya huts, with wonderful scenery along the sparklingly clear, rushing waters of the Azusagawa River. Accommodation, food, and drinks are available at all of these huts, but prices tend to increase as you move away from Kamikōchi.

After Ichinomata Goya the trail climbs Yarisawa, the stream valley leading directly up to the peak of Yari-ga-take, and becomes steeper. Passing Yarisawa Lodge and zigzagging up the valley out of the forest, the trail crosses permanent snow in the bottom of the Yarisawa Valley. It is a long, steep, rocky, alpine climb up to Yari-ga-take Sansō—the large hut situated below the peak of Yari-ga-take, the "Matterhorn of Japan." This climb up Yari-ga-take is a good, one-day hike from Kamikōchi and there is an area for camping on the rocky slopes near Yari-ga-take Sansō.

Dawn on top of these 3,000-meter peaks is bitterly cold, even in midsummer, and warm clothes are needed. In the chilly air before sunrise, crowds of climbers were already clambering up the spectacular, pointed peak of Yari-ga-take to see the sun come up from its summit. The twenty-minute climb up from the hut is technically easy, but it is nevertheless a strenuous rock climb, with ladders and chains fixed to the rocks. Arrows are painted on the rocks marking the slightly different routes up and down. There is a small wooden shrine on the restricted, flat area at the summit, where the rocks are covered with people's names, but no sign of Banryū's three Buddhist images. In fine weather, Fuji-san and the South Alps can be seen to the southeast, and the other peaks of the North Alps stretch out to Tateyama and Shirouma in the north, and the Hotaka Massif to the south.

It is a magnificent alpine ridge hike from Yari to Hotaka with a deep col, known as Daikiretto (大切戸), before the tricky climb up to the peak of Kita Hotaka-dake. Most people take one day to hike from Yari-ga-take Sansō to Hotaka-dake Sansō. The first part of this route, over Naka-dake to the next hut below Minami-dake, is fairly easy going, over barren, rocky slopes with little or no vegetation, and snow lying in sheltered gullies. Water is not available on the route, except from snowmelt, but it is sold at the huts.

From Minami-dake, the trail descends to the col with ladders and chains down vertical rock faces, before the climb up the formidable rocky crags of Kita Hotaka-dake. Perched near the summit, the small hut of Kita Hotaka Goya can be seen from below, and rock climbers, clinging to the sheer rock walls like flies, can be heard echoing instructions. Arrows painted on the rocks mark out the hiking trail on this difficult part of the route.

The Kita Hotaka Goya Hut has a wooden balcony with tables and benches—a heavenly place to eat lunch after the exhausting climb up. Just behind the hut is the peak of Kita Hotaka-dake (3,106 m.) with a camping site on a nearby ridge. The trail from here follows a rocky ridge up and down to the peak of Karasawa-dake (3,103 m.). Down below to the east is the Karasawa Cirque—an ice-eroded valley head which is evidence of past glaciation in these mountains—with two huts and a large campsite on the floor of its valley. It is an easy descent down the ridge from Karasawa-dake to Hotaka-dake Sansō, a popular hut situated at the trail junction on the col below Okuhotaka-dake (3,190 m.), the highest peak in the North Alps and the third highest in Japan. A trail leads down from the col to the two Karasawa huts and campsite.

Okuhotaka-dake is a steep climb from the hut at first, but gets easier going toward the summit, marked by a small stone shrine and many cairns. From the summit the trail southwest is the ridge route to Nishi Hotaka-dake and Yake-dake. The shorter route to Kamikōchi is southeast on the ridge trail to Maehotaka-dake, and then down into the Dakesawa Valley. Keeping close to the ridge at first, the main trail avoids the peak of Maehotaka before descending steeply into the valley. This is quite a long, tiring descent as you leave the higher alpine slopes and enter the forest before coming to Dakesawa Hut, where there is a campsite in the valley below a permanent snow patch. On the higher part of this route there are commanding views of Kamikōchi lying in the flat, green valley below, and the volcanic peak of Yake-dake to the southwest. After the strenuous and difficult climb over the Hotaka Massif, it is an easy, straightforward hike down the forested Dakesawa Valley to the Azusagawa River and Kamikōchi.

This three-day hike over the highest of the North Alps' peaks, and some of the best alpine scenery in Japan, is only one of the many spectacular hikes to be done in this area. A shorter, easier climb up Hotaka-dake can be made via Karasawa, taking two days, and Yari-ga-take may be climbed in two days by returning back down the Yarisawa Valley route or descending to the valley on the west side. Although the mountain scenery is some of the best in these mountains, alpine flora and ptarmigan are noticeably lacking. The best area to see alpine flowers and spot a ptarmigan is Jōnen-dake (常念岳 2,857 m.) to the east of the Yari-Hotaka mountains.

My wish is the same as that expressed by Weston 100 years ago—to see the preservation of Kamikōchi and the surrounding mountains in their natural state, and to resist any commercial tourist ventures in this area of outstanding natural beauty. I think Weston would be greatly disappointed to see the development which has already taken place. Let's hope it proceeds no further, and that the national park authorities see that it remains the domain of dedicated naturalists, hikers and climbers.

12. Alpinism with Ease: Central Alps 中央アルプス

For those who like to start hiking in high alpine scenery without any of the sweat of climbing up through the forest, this is the place to go. The Koma-ga-take Ropeway whisks you up 950 meters, from 1,662 m. to 2,612 m., in just seven and a half minutes, saving you several hours of hiking and many gallons of sweat. Although not quite as grand as the North or South Alps, the Chuo (Central) Alps offer some excellent hiking, along ridges and over peaks adorned with liberal splashes of alpine flowers. Using the ropeway up the mountain, it is an easy day's hike over the peak of Koma-ga-take (2,956 m.)—the highest in the range.

The Chuo Alps, otherwise known as the Kiso Range, run north-south in the southern part of Nagano Prefecture. In an echelon arrangement with the North Alps to the north and the South Alps to the southeast, the Chuo Alps are lower than their neighbors. The highest peaks are composed of granite with a well-defined ridge of peaks running north-south, and steep eastern and western slopes. Some glacial features are found around the peaks, notably the Senjōjiki Cirque at the top of the ropeway. However, there are no permanent snow-filled valleys, and only one or two patches of snow remain in summer.

Cedar grows on the lower slopes, where serow and other forest animals may be seen. The top part of the forest between about 2,400 and 2,600 meters includes silver birch, pine, and fir. Above this is the alpine zone of creeping pine and alpine flowers, which burst into color in July.

ACCESS

There are several points of access into the Chuo Alps, but the most popular is via Komagane on the JR Iida Line. Direct buses also run to Komagane from Shinjuku. From Komagane Station buses operate up to the ropeway at Shirabi-daira via Komagane Kōgen.

ACCOMMODATION

Many campsites and mountain huts are found in these mountains, and tend to be located either on the mountaintop ridge or in the valleys below. There are two campsites at Komagane Kōgen and another just above the lower ropeway station at Shirabi-daira. At the top of the ropeway and around the peak area of Koma-ga-take there are six huts and a campsite. Komagane City and Komagane Kōgen have plenty of minshuku and lodge accommodation, but this is a popular holiday area, so booking is essential in the summer season. Komagane Youth Hostel (Tel: 0265-83-3856) is located at Akaho, and is a fifteen-minute bus ride from Komagane Station.

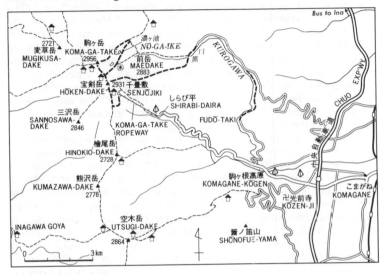

TRAILS

****
+++

Senjōjiki (千畳敷) ⟶ 1.5 kms. 1 hr. 15 mins. ⟶ Hōken-dake (宝剣岳) ⟶ 0.5 km. 30 mins. ⟶ Hōken Sansō (宝剣山荘) ⟶ 1 km. 50 mins. ⟶ Koma-ga-take (駒ヶ岳) ⟶ 2 kms. 1 hr. ⟶ Nō-ga-ike (濃ヶ池) ⟶ 1 km. 40 mins. ⟶ Komakai-no-ike (駒飼の池) ⟶ 0.6 km. 40 mins. ⟶ Hōken Sansō (宝剣山荘) ⟶ 1 km. 30 mins. ⟶ Maedake (前岳) ⟶ 2 kms. 1 hr. ⟶ Itchō-ga-ike (一丁ヶ池) ⟶ 1.5 kms. 50 mins. ⟶ Kurogawa (黒川) ⟶ 15 kms. 4 hrs. 20 mins. ⟶ Komagane Kōgen (駒ヶ根高原)

A fifteen-minute bus ride from Komagane takes you up to Komagane Kōgen—a summer holiday resort situated on the forested plateau beneath the mountain peaks, with small lakes and the rustic 1,130-year old Kōzen-ji Temple shaded beneath a grove of tall cedars. Although a little crowded in July and August, the campsites on this plateau are a good base from which to climb the mountains. The bus continues up to the ropeway at Shirabi-daira, taking about fifty minutes from the station. A few hundred meters up the trail there is a campsite, and a little further on a beautiful waterfall, which can also be seen from the ropeway above. This trail continues up through the forest to the top station of the ropeway at Senjōjiki, but these days hardly anyone uses it.

The ropeway climbs the 950 meters steeply and brings you out at the top station, situated on the floor of Senjōjiki Cirque. Sheer cliffs rise up to the peaks of Hōken-dake (2,931 m.) and Maedake (2,883 m.) at the head of this glacially eroded valley. Alpine flowers carpet the floor of the valley, which is well laid out with hiking trails. Leaving the large building, which provides food, drinks, and accommodation, there is a small shrine near where the trail divides. Most people opt for the direct and easier route to the summit of Koma-ga-take, going right. This trail can be seen as it climbs up the cliffs from the valley with a constant procession of hikers stringing along it in summer. However, the route to the left is more interesting.

Climbing this rocky trail up to Gokuraku-daira (極楽平) through alpine flower-covered slopes, you come out on the rocky ridge. The ridge trail going south from here looked very promising for a delightful three- or four-day hike down the length of the range, and several hikers were heading that way, but I had only planned a one-day hike over the peak of Koma-ga-take, and back down to Komagane. So going right on the trail to Hōken-dake I scrambled up the granite rock of the ridge which has chains fixed to the rocks to help climbers. A few hikers were crowded around the difficult area on the boulder pile at the peak. Clouds had already drifted in and so the views were restricted, but the cool temperatures were a welcome relief from the summer heat down below.

A short descent from the peak of Hōken-dake brings you to the two huts of Hōken Sansō and Tengu-sō. The latter is named after a nearby rock which is shaped like the large-nosed face of Tengu—the mythical goblin. The trail from here can be taken either over or around the small peak of Naka-dake to Chōjō Sansō—Summit Hut—with a campsite on nearby flat, rocky ground. This hut is just below the peak of Koma-ga-take.

Koma-ga-take, also known as Kiso-koma, is one of several mountains with the same name, meaning Horse or Pony peak. On a fine day the Koma-ga-take of the South Alps, known as Kai-koma, can be seen to the southeast. I was not granted this view of the South Alps' peaks, as the summit was enveloped in drifting mist and cloud. Two small shrines stand on the peak, and next to the larger one a young man was selling charms and souvenirs in a tiny corrugated iron kiosk. Hikers reaching the summit approached the shrine, clapped their hands, and offered prayers or made requests to the *kami* dwelling on this mountain peak.

Taking the ridge to the northeast from the peak it is a rocky trail through open alpine scenery. A trail descends from the ridge to the pond of Nō-ga-ike, visible down below as you approach it along the ridge. This small, muddy pond was almost dry, but the surrounding slopes were rich with colorful flowers. The track from here contours around the mountain to Komakai-no-ike—but this pond was completely dry with only a mudflat remaining. Lying on the steep slopes above was the only snow patch I saw on the mountain. It is a short climb from here up to the Summit Hut. Lazy hikers may take the trail from here back down to Senjōjiki for the ropeway down the mountain.

A long hike may be made all the way back down to Komagane Kōgen via the Kurogawa Valley by first taking the trail over Maedake—the peak to the east. The trail descends by the ridge from this peak and enters cedar forest before coming to a junction where you go left for the route down the Kurogawa Valley. A wooden bridge crosses the river and then, turning downstream, you come to the top end of a forestry track. It is a long but pleasant hike down this track to Komagane Kōgen keeping close to the river, and passing two beautiful waterfalls on the way. The first—Isedaki Falls—is left of the track near its upper end, and the second, larger, more spectacular falls—Fudō-taki—is deep in the gorge after passing a dam lower down the valley.

As I ambled down this track taking in the dark, silent cedar forest and the white chattering waters of the river, the clouds which had been building around the peaks from early morning started to make rumbling noises and I was caught in a summer thunderstorm. Thankful that I was in the valley and not on the peaks, I arrived back at the campsite on Komagane Kōgen and looked forward to the bright, warm sunshine sure to follow early next morning.

13. Alpinism for the Dedicated: South Alps 南アルプス

The mountains of the South Alps National Park are some of the most inaccessible in Japan, with few roads penetrating this large unspoilt mountainous area, no popular tourist resorts, no ropeways, and few modern developments. Some years ago the building of the South Alps Super Rindō road over the mountains to provide easier access to the central peaks gave rise to criticism from some groups of ardent alpinists and nature lovers who would like to see those mountains remain inaccessible to all but a select few. Lacking large hotels, souvenir shops, restaurants, and other tourist facilities, the mountains of the South Alps are a domain for the dedicated alpinist and hiker who likes to see the unspoilt beauty of nature and the mountains.

Lying west of Fuji-san, the South Alps, also known as the Akaishi Range, runs north-south and is the highest range in Japan. The Alps stretch for about 150 kilometers north-south, and 80 kilometers east-west, and include ten peaks over 3,000 meters and 36 peaks over 2,500 meters. Three groups of peaks can be distinguished: Koma-ga-take (駒ヶ岳 2,966 m.) to the north; Shirane-san (白根山 3,192 m.) in the central area; and Akaishi-dake (赤石岳 3,146 m.) to the south.The Shirane-san peaks include Kita-dake—North Peak—which is the second highest mountain in Japan after Fuji.

Formed tectonically, the South Alps have no volcanoes, although a few hot springs are found in the lower valleys. The Paleozoic and Mesozoic strata have been uplifted, intruded, and metamorphosed due to tectonic movements along the Fossa Magna, a major tectonic line to the east on which Mount Fuji sits. Glaciated and ice-scoured areas are found on the highest peaks, and some gullies remain snow-filled year-round—especially on Shirane-san. However, these mountains do not receive the heavy snowfalls of the North Alps because they lie on the Pacific side of Honshu and so are not subject to the full force of the winter monsoon.

July and August are the best months for hiking, and if you go prepared for colder conditions, September to November can also be good. The spring season from late February to April sees the heaviest snowfalls on these mountains. Winter and spring climbing should only be attempted by specialists with all the necessary equipment for snow and ice conditions.

Forests of beech, fir, spruce, and Japanese hemlock cover the mountain slopes, giving way to creeping pine and alpine plants above 2,600 meters. Wild animals may be seen in the forest, including the serow, deer, and, if you are lucky, the black bear, as well as smaller mammals. The ptarmigan is also found on the rocky peaks of the alpine zone.

ACCESS

The fastest and most convenient access into the South Alps is by a two-hour bus ride from Kōfu Station to Hirogawara along the Minami Alps Super Rindō. (Kōfu Station, on the Chuo Line, is easily reached within two hours from Shinjuku.) Hirogawara is situated in the Norogawa Valley below Kita-dake—the highest peak in the range—and is the most popular base for climbing the South Alps.

ACCOMMODATION

Several lodges, a mountain hut, and a campsite are located at Hirogawara. Mountain huts and campsites are found in the mountains, usually within a few hours' hike of each other.

TRAILS

****
+++++
Hirogawara (広河原) ⟶ 4 kms. 3 hrs. 45 mins. ⟶ Shirane-oike (白根御池) ⟶ 4 kms. 4 hrs. 15 mins. ⟶ Kita-dake (北岳) ⟶ 5 kms. 3 hrs. ⟶ Ai-no-take (間ノ岳) ⟶ 3.5 kms. 2 hrs. 15 mins. ⟶ Kuma-no-daira (熊ノ

平) ⟶ 5.5 kms. 3 hrs. ⟶ Kita Arakawa-dake (北荒川岳) ⟶ 3.5 kms. 2 hrs. 15 mins. ⟶ Shiomi-dake (塩見岳) ⟶ 6.5 kms. 3 hrs. 45 mins. ⟶ Sanpuku-tōge (三伏峠) ⟶ 6 kms. 3 hrs. ⟶ Shiokawa (塩川)

It is possible to make an assault on Kita-dake (3,192 m.) in only two days from Tokyo, climbing from Hirogawara and returning the same way with one night spent at a hut or campsite on the mountain. However, to enjoy these mountains at their best, several days should be planned for a hike over the peaks. One popular route goes over the peaks of Shirane Sanzan three peaks starting from Hirogawara, climbing Kita-dake and going south on the spectacular ridge to Ai-no-take and Nōtori-dake before descending to the Hayakawa Valley. Three or four days are needed to complete this route.

The route I have chosen starts from Hirogawara, climbs Kita-dake, and then traverses the range in a southwesterly direction to Shiomi-dake and down into the Shiokawa Valley on the western side of the South Alps. Buses operate from the hut in this valley to Ina Ōshima Station. This is convenient for going on to the Central or North Alps.

If arriving at Hirogawara late, it is best to stay at one of the lodges, the hut or campsite, and start the climb up Kita-dake early next morning. But if you take an early bus or taxi from Kōfu you will have time to climb up to the hut and campsite at the small pond of Shirane-oike, which is about halfway to the top. The climb up through forest is very steep, with some erosion gullies and fallen trees making the going harder. From the small pond sitting on a terrace on the mountainside it is another long, steep climb up through thinning, bushy forest to the wooden hut and campsite at Kita-dake Kata-no-koya—Shoulder Hut—situated in the alpine zone just below the peak. Kita-dake's peak can be reached in thirty minutes from here up the rocky ridge and is marked by a wooden signboard and small stone Jizō statue. The view from the summit on a fine day is breathtaking—Fuji's cone to the southeast, the white granite peak of Kai-koma to the north, the Central Alps to the west, and the North Alps beyond the peak of Senjō-ga-take to the northwest.

The other peaks of Shirane Sanzan rise from the ridge to the south. Descending the steep, rocky trail on the south side of the peak you can see the prefabricated metal hut of Kita-dake Sansō and the adjacent campsite on the flat col below. On the other side of this rock-strewn col the trail climbs Ai-no-take (3,189 m.) only three meters lower than Kita-dake. These high barren peaks have only a thin covering of alpine plants and flowers.

South of Ai-no-take is the third peak of Shirane Sanzan—Nōtori-dake (農鳥岳 3,050 m.)—with Nōtori Hut on the col between. The trail to the west descends a sharp, jagged ridge to the spectacular peak of Mibu-dake (三峰岳 2,999 m.) which is situated on the triple border of Nagano, Yamanashi, and Shizuoka Prefectures. Down to the southwest the wooden hut of Kuma-no-daira (Bear Plateau) can be seen amidst fir forest. This fairly large log hut sits above a forested valley in the remote central part of the mountains, and has an area for camping. It is a wonderful location with views of Mibudake, Ai-no-take and Nōtori-dake towering above.

Going south it is a fairly easy ridge walk through fir forest to Kita Arakawa-dake, where there is a campsite just down from the ridge in a beautiful area of alpine flowers. A freshwater spring is located a few hundred meters down a small trail. I was surprised to find only one other camper staying here at the height of the climbing season in mid-August. As I was putting up my tent a small brown and white marten popped out of the bushes and ran around my tent—startled to see another visitor to his remote mountain home.

The trail continues south on the ridge with severe erosion into deep gullies on the west side, and then climbs up the rugged slopes of creeping pine and alpine flowers to the peak of Shiomi-dake (3,047 m.). Just before the peak I spotted a ptarmigan with two young chicks scrambling over extremely steep, craggy slopes—this is the only place I have seen a ptarmigan outside the North Alps.

Shiomi's peak is very rocky and exposed, with a steep descent on the western side to the small hut and campsite located on the ridge. The peaks rising across the valley to the south are Arakawa-dake and Akaishi-dake—the southern group of the range. From Shiomi Hut the trail descends into fir forest and crosses a stream before climbing the forested Hontani-yama (本谷山 2,658 m.). Continuing south on this ridge you reach Sanpuku-tōge (2,615 m.)—the highest mountain pass in Japan. The wooden hut and campsite in the forest at the pass were swirling in mist and cloud as I arrived.

From the pass it is a steep descent through mixed forest to the Shiokawa Valley. Downstream at the end of the dirt track in the valley is the small Shiokawa Hut providing accommodation and meals. Bus tickets can also be bought here for the twice daily bus service down to Ina Ōshima Station. There were only a handful of hikers here when I arrived, and we had to walk down the dirt track for ten minutes to the waiting bus, which was prevented from reaching the hut by a massive landslide of mud, rock, and trees across the track. The bus made its bumpy way down through small, picturesque mountain villages, then on a surfaced road passing a large reservoir and dam, taking 1 hour and 20 minutes to the station.

Forestry tracks and roads are being pushed further into these remote mountains, but the *kami* often hit back with landslides and floods to destroy men's efforts. It is my wish that these mountains stay remote, and that the dedicated hikers and climbers to the peaks carry with them a healthy respect for the kami working in these mountains.

14. Eight Peaks: Yatsu-ga-take 八ヶ岳

According to the ancient legend, Yatsu-ga-take—meaning eight peaks—was once higher than Fuji, but Fuji rose and kicked its rival over, forming eight lower peaks. This legend is not so far-fetched as it may at first seem, as both Fuji and the Yatsu-ga-take peaks are situated close to the Fossa Magna tectonic line, Yatsu-ga-take being a relatively old, eroded, volcanic mountain and Fuji a relatively new volcano which has superceded it in prominence. The legend has preserved certain truths about the time sequence of geological events.

There are actually more than eight peaks along the north-south ridge which forms the border between Nagano and Yamanashi prefectures. Composed of pyroxene andesite, the strato-volcanoes of Yatsu-ga-take have long been dormant, and have been eroded to form its present jagged ridge of rocky peaks. Hot springs are found in the valleys below—the only remnants of its former volcanic activity.

Most of the ridge is above 2,500 meters with Akadake (2,899 m.) being the highest peak. The range forms the main part of Yatsu-ga-take—Chūshin Kōgen Quasi-National Park. On the western slopes below the peaks is Tateshina, and to the east, Kiyosato—both very popular summer holiday and second-home resorts.

All except the highest peaks have a forest cover of fir or mixed deciduous trees, with rhododendron and azalea growing in the undergrowth. The highest peaks above 2,600 meters have an alpine flora of creeping pine and alpine flowers. Serow and deer may be seen in the forests together with smaller mammals. I once spotted a serow on rugged alpine slopes at 2,600 meters in these mountains.

ACCESS

There are many access points into the mountains of Yatsu-ga-take. Kobuchi-zawa, on the Chuo Line, which runs south of the range, is a popular starting point for hiking into the mountains. From Kobuchi-zawa the Koumi Line runs east of the range to Kiyosato, Lake Matsubara-ko and Yachiho, which are all good starting points with bus services running further up into the mountains. However, the best access route is via Chino, taking about three hours on the Chuo Line from Tokyo, from where bus services operate up to Mugikusa-tōge Pass—at about 2,130 meters on the northern part of the Yatsu-ga-take ridge.

ACCOMMODATION

Yatsu-ga-take is covered with deep snow in winter and spring and so the best months for climbing are July and August. September to November are also good if you go prepared for cold weather. The summer resort areas and hot springs in the valleys and on the lower plateaus below the peaks have plentiful ryokan, minshuku and hotel accommodation. In the mountains there are several mountain huts and campsites within easy hiking distance of each other. Kiyosato Youth Hostel (Tel: 0551-48-2125) is a five-minute walk from Kiyosato Station, east of Yatsu-ga-take. Shirakabako Youth Hostel (Tel: 0266-68-2031) and Tateshina Shirakaba Kōgen Youth Hostel (Tel: 0267-55-6601) can be reached by bus from Chino Station, west of Yatsu-ga-take.

TRAILS

****

+ + + + +

Mugikusa-tōge (麦草峠) —→ 2 kms. 40 mins. —→ Shirakoma-ike (白駒池) —→ 3 kms. 1 hr. 30 mins. —→ Nyū (にゅう) —→ 4 kms. 2 hrs. —→ Tengu-dake (天狗岳) —→ 2.5 kms. 1 hr. —→ Komakusa-sō (こまくさ荘) —→ 1.5 kms. 1 hr. 15 mins. —→ Iwo-dake (硫黄岳) —→ 2.5 kms. 1 hr. 15 mins. —→ Yoko-dake (横岳) —→ 2 kms. 1 hr. 45 mins. —→ Akadake (赤岳) —→ 5 kms. 3 hrs. 15 mins. —→ Gongen-dake (権現岳) —→ 3 kms. 1 hr. 30 mins. —→ Amigasa-yama (編笠山) —→ 5 kms. 2 hrs. 30 mins. —→ Kannon-daira (観音平) —→ 9 kms. 2 hrs. 30 mins. —→ Kobuchi-zawa (小淵沢)

Short one- or two-day hikes may be made in these mountains, but the route I describe here is a traverse of the entire ridge of high peaks from north to south. Three days are required for this hike over Yatsu-ga-take's most spectacular scenery. Starting from Mugikusa-tōge, the route goes over several peaks culminating in the summit of Akadake,

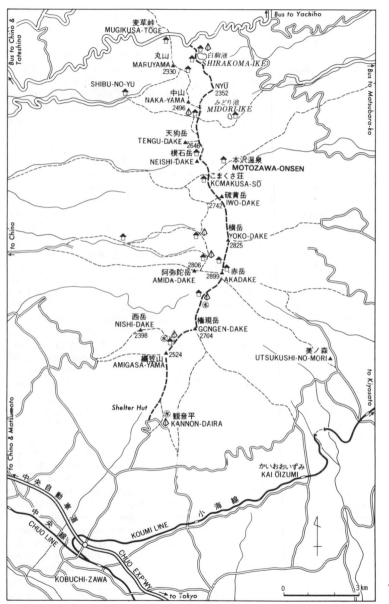

麦草峠
MUGIKUSA-TŌGE

↑ Bus to Yachiho

Bus to Chino & Tateshina

Bus to Matsubara-ko

白駒池
SHIRAKOMA-IKE

丸山
MARUYAMA
2330

SHIBU-NO-YU

NYŪ
2352

中山
NAKA-YAMA
2496

みどり池
MIDORI-IKE

天狗岳
TENGU-DAKE
2646

根石岳
NEISHI-DAKE

本沢温泉
MOTOZAWA-ONSEN

こまくさ荘
KOMAKUSA-SŌ

硫黄岳
IWO-DAKE
2742

to Chino

横岳
YOKO-DAKE
2825

阿弥陀岳
AMIDA-DAKE
2806

赤岳
AKADAKE
2899

西岳
NISHI-DAKE
2398

権現岳
GONGEN-DAKE
2704

美ノ森
UTSUKUSHI-NO-MORI

編笠山
AMIGASA-YAMA
2524

Shelter Hut

観音平
KANNON-DAIRA

to Chino & Matsumoto

かいおおいずみ
KAI ŌIZUMI

to Kiyosato

中央自動車道

中央線

小海線
KOUMI LINE

CHUO LINE

CHUO EXPWY.

KOBUCHI-ZAWA

to Tokyo

0   3 km

and then over the southern peaks of the range, before descending to Kobuchi-zawa.

Cloud and mist lay thick on the mountains as I arrived at Mugikusa-tōge one day in late August. The bus from Chino had passed through crowds of tourists as it wound its way up through the resort of Tateshina, but up on the cool, high pass, a smaller number of tourists and hikers were wandering around and finding shelter in Mugikusa Hut. The weather was not favorable for going up to the peaks, and so I decided to make my way down the road and trail on the eastern side of the pass to the nearby pond of Shirakoma-ike, where there are two more huts and a campsite.

The sun shone brightly on the lake next morning as I made my way on the trail around the forested shores. Then a climb up over tangled roots in the forest of firs brought me out at the rocky peak of Nyū—situated at the northern end of Yatsu-ga-take's high ridge. From here the trail followed the ridge through forest, descended to Nakayama-tōge, and then climbed to the eastern peak of Tengu-dake (2,646 m.)—an exposed, rocky peak and one of the eight.

After a short rest to take in the view, I made my way down the easy trail and passed a new wooden hut being constructed at Neishi-dake (根石岳). Down the trail through stunted fir forest I came to the large Komakusa-sō Hut situated in the forest on a pass. A trail from here descends to Motozawa Onsen—a remote hot spring resort in the valley on the eastern side of the ridge—taking thirty minutes to descend.

Staying on the ridge the trail climbs out of the forest onto rocky slopes of creeping pine and alpine flowers to the flat summit of Iwo-dake (2,742 m.), which is marked by several rock cairns. Low cloud and mist were hanging over this desolate peak, making ghosts out of the groups of hikers standing around on the top amongst the cairns. Taking the wide trail east from this peak, I descended the ridge to Iwo-dake Hut. The bell I had heard ringing through the mist came from the small shrine next to the hut. Nearby alpine slopes are laid out with trails for viewing the alpine flora.

Climbing up the craggy trail one has to scale lava rocks with the aid of chains fixed to the rocks over difficult sections up to the peak of Yoko-dake (2,835 m.). As I sat down for lunch overlooking the precipitous volcanic lava rock crags, a girl popped her head up from over the edge of what I thought was a sheer drop. Fixing her carabiners and ropes to the rocks on the summit, she pulled up her friend. I was mildly surprised to see them reaching the summit via such a difficult route, but some Japanese male hikers looked outraged to find girls bettering them at scaling this peak. There is still a lot of climbing to do for women in Japan.

It was a rocky descent, with more chains for support, on the ridge down to Akadake Hut. The view west from the ridge looks down red lava rock cliffs and pinnacles into the valley, where Gyōsha Hut and campsite are situated below. From the large, new, prefabricated hut it is a steep climb up loose red lava rocks to Akadake Summit Hut. This log hut perched on the summit sells drinks and food, and has a wooden terrace allowing breathtaking views into the valleys below. A tiny shrine is found at the summit on the rocks a few meters away.

The descent from Akadake to the deep col on its southwestern ridge is precipitous in places, with more chains fixed to the rock face to help climbers. Kiretto Hut and campsite are situated at the bottom of the col below the magnificent crags of Akadake. I remembered camping here several years earlier in the melting snow of early May, but there is no snow on these peaks in August and camping is a lot easier and more pleasant.

The morning was clear and bright with a classic view of Fuji above a forested mountain ridge. Gongen-dake (2,704 m.) was a steep climb with a long ladder to scale up a vertical cliff just before the top. On the south side of the peak is Gongen Hut, sheltered below the ridge. From here the trail follows the ridge then descends to Seinen Goya—a large hut on a flat area between the peaks. The round, forested peak of Amigasa-yama (2,524 m.) rises beyond the hut—this is the southern-most of Yatsu-ga-take's eight peaks.

In fine weather there is a panoramic view of the South, Central, and North Alps from the summit of Amigasa. It is a long descent through fir forest and bamboo grass undergrowth to the top of the forestry road at Kannon-daira, where there is a campsite. Unfortunately, there are no bus services from here, so it is either a long walk or a taxi ride down to Kobuchi-zawa Station.

Kanto's Mountain Borderland

Fuji-san from Koma-ga-take (Hakone)

The Kanto Plain is the largest lowland area in Japan, supporting one of the world's most concentrated populations in and around the capital city of Tokyo. Alluvial deposits of Quaternary sediments washed down from the mountains to form the flat plain, across which run the Tamagawa, Sumidagawa, and Arakawa rivers. The mountain ranges and volcanoes to the north and west are composed of Paleozoic, Mesozoic, and Tertiary sedimentary strata, with Tertiary and Quaternary volcanics. To the west the major tectonic fault of the Fossa Magna runs north-south—with the dormant Fuji-san and active Asama-yama volcanoes lying on it. To the north the Tanigawa and Nikko mountains lie on the watershed between the Japan Sea and the Pacific Ocean.

Winters are clear and sunny over the Kanto Plain region as the northwesterly monsoon dumps its moisture as snow over the Hokuriku region and dry foehn (*karakaze*) winds sweep the plain. The coastal regions of the Izu and Bōsō peninsulas have mild winters due to the influence of the offshore Kuroshio current. In June and early July, the wet season brings extended cloudy and rainy periods to the region before the hot summer sets in. In summer, thunderstorms may be expected in the mountains. A few violent typhoons usually pass over the region each year, with the maximum frequency in September. Autumn, like the spring, experiences alternating wet and dry periods as depressions and fronts pass through.

Because of the shortage of flat land in Japan, most of the Kanto Plain is urbanized, with some areas of intensive agriculture growing rice and vegetables. However, the unspoilt, natural scenery of the mountains is never far away, and these mountains can often be seen even from downtown Tokyo. The mountains are mostly forested with mixed natural forests or forestry plantations of conifers. Wildlife survives in these forests and can be seen even on one-day hikes from Tokyo. Among the animals to be seen are deer, macaque monkey, fox, squirrel, raccoon, boar, and smaller mammals, as well as a varied birdlife.

The main centers of interest for hiking are the national or quasi-national parks. Tanzawa-Ōyama Quasi-National Park to the west is the closest area of high mountains to Tokyo. Beyond it lies the Fuji-Hakone-Izu National Park, which includes Fuji-san, Japan's highest peak, the popular mountain resort of Hakone, and the peninsula and volcanic islands of Izu. Chichibu-Tama National Park west of Tokyo is a large area of high mountains excellent for hiking. To the northwest lies Jōshin-etsu Kōgen National Park, which includes Asama-yama, an active volcano, and Tanigawa-dake, an exciting mountain for rock climbing as well as hiking. Nikko National Park lies north of the Kanto Plain and is a very popular park offering many attractions.

ACCESS

Due to the high population density on the Kanto Plain, transport networks are very convenient and efficient in the urban areas, and access to the parks and mountains is quite easy and fast. Many private railway lines operate out to the surrounding mountains and parks. These lines are cheaper and often more convenient than the JR lines.

By Rail: Private railway lines include the Keisei Line which provides a connection between Narita International Airport and Ueno Station in downtown Tokyo. From Shinjuku Station there are two private lines which are convenient for reaching the mountains. The Odakyu Line passes to the south of the Tanzawa mountains on its way to Hakone Yumoto, the gateway to Fuji-Hakone-Izu National Park. The Keio Line goes as far as Takao-san Guchi, a popular mountain for hiking. From Ikebukuro Station runs the Seibu Ikebukuro Line which goes to Chichibu, the gateway to the Chichibu area of the Chichibu-Tama National Park, from where the Chichibu Line runs to Mitsumine-guchi further up the valley. The Tobu Nikko Line running from Asakusa Station in downtown Tokyo is the most convenient way of reaching the Nikko National Park.

JR lines are needed to reach the other mountain regions. The Chuo Line from Shinjuku Station operates to Takao-san and beyond, and by changing at Tachikawa to the Itsukaichi or Ome lines, access is provided to the Okutama mountains. The Takasaki Line from Ueno Station provides access to Jōshin-etsu Kōgen National Park. The Shinetsu Line from Takasaki goes to Asama-yama, and the Jōetsu Line from Takasaki provides access to Tanigawa-dake.

By Bus: Bus services operate from many stations and provide access to the start of many hiking trails. Convenient stations with bus services into the mountains are: Hadano, Shibusawa, and Hakone Yumoto on the Odakyu Line; Musashi Itsukaichi at the end of the Itsukaichi Line; Okutama at the end of the Ome Line; Mitsumine-guchi at the end of the Chichibu Line; and Nikko at the end of the Tobu Nikko Line.

Bus services also run direct from Tokyo to Fuji-san, and there is a bus service between Narita International Airport and various points in Tokyo.

By Road: Road Transport out of Tokyo is often very slow due to congested, narrow roads, and it can take twice as long as by train to reach the mountains and parks on the outskirts.

ACCOMMODATION

Tokyo is full of expensive hotels, but there are also many reasonably priced business hotels and ryokan. The tourist offices at Narita Airport and near Yurakucho Station in Tokyo are very helpful in providing information and maps. The most economical form of accommodation is the youth hostels. There are two in downtown Tokyo: Tokyo Kokusai Youth Hostel (Tel: 03-3235-1107) is on the 18th floor of the tall Central Plaza Building just outside Iidabashi Station; Tokyo Yoyogi Youth Hostel (Tel: 03-3467-9163) is northwest of Meiji Jingū shrine grounds, and is a five-minute walk from Sangubashi, the second station on the Odakyu Line from Shinjuku, or can be reached from Yoyogi or Harajuku stations on the Yamanote Line. The length of stay at these hostels is usually restricted to a few days.

For longer stays in Tokyo the most economical accommodation is found at one of the *gaijin* (foreigner) houses which are listed in the monthly *Tokyo Journal* magazine. A few such places are: Mickey House (Tel: 03-3936-8889) eight minutes' walk from Kami Itabashi Station on the Tobu-Tojo Line; Tokyo House (Tel: 03-3391-5577) near Ogikubo Station on the Chuo Line from Shinjuku; Tokyo English Center (Tel: 03-3360-4781) near Higashi Nakano Station on the Sobu Line; Tokyo English House (Tel: 03-3332-0940) has three locations, but the main English House is in Nishi Ogikubo on the Chuo and Sobu lines.

Charges at these gaijin houses are usually about ¥50,000 and up per month.

One economical Japanese inn located near Shin Okubo Station on the Yamanote Line is Okubo House (Tel: 03-3361-2348), which provides basic shared accommodation for ¥1,700 and up.

The mountains and parks around the Kanto region have plentiful hotel, ryokan, and minshuku accommodation. There are also several youth hostels, but booking is often necessary, especially during holiday seasons. There are also a surprising number of campsites in the mountains within easy access of Tokyo, and most of the national parks have several campsites.

15. Symbol of Japan: Fuji-san 富士山

Climbing Fuji-san is rather a dull, bleak undertaking, likened by one writer to walking up a giant ashtray. The beauty of Fuji-san completely vanishes when you touch it and trudge up its barren, gray, volcanic ash and lava slopes, which are devoid of green vegetation or mountain streams. It is one more example of the ephemeral beauty praised by the Japanese. Gazing on the profile of Fuji-san from afar it is seen to be asymmetrical—the Mayon volcano in the Philippines has a much more impressive symmetry—but this is also consistent with the Japanese sense of beauty, as seen for example, in the asymmetry of tea bowls used in the tea ceremony. The conical asymmetry of Fuji-san moves the Japanese by its seasonally changing appearance, and not for any one static face it may present. In winter the slopes are entirely covered by snow, and the white profile is often visible from downtown Tokyo through the crystal-clear winter air. The snow line rises up the slopes during the spring, and a snowless Fuji is presented in the warm, humid summer. From September, snow falls on its summit again, and the snow line descends its slopes during the autumn. Different aspects of Fuji can be viewed from various locations as depicted in the famous woodblock prints of Hokusai, and the Japanese sensibility can even be moved by the charm of Fuji when it is completely obscured by clouds and rain.

The ultimate goal of a Fuji climb is to see sunrise from its summit, viewing one symbol of Japan from the top of another, and the cherry blossom, yet another of Japan's symbols, is worshipped at the Sengen Shrine located on the crater rim of Fuji. Crowds of climbers gather on the summit, waiting in the icy-cold dawn air for the sun to burst over the sea of cotton clouds. This is the highlight of the climb, and as the sun brings heat, and sometimes builds clouds on the slopes of Fuji, most climbers disperse for the dusty trek or slide back down. On my last climb up Fuji I saw one young Japanese man who had carried his bicycle to the top, and there were others carrying hang gliders up.

Fuji-san is a dormant volcano with parasitic volcanoes deforming its conical shape. The oldest lava dates from 8,000 years ago, and so it is a relatively young volcano, situated in the volcanic zone which extends from Asama-yama to the north southwards through the Izu Peninsula and the chain of islands stretching out into the Pacific Ocean. It is Japan's highest mountain at 3,776 meters, but an ancient legend says that Yatsu-ga-take, a nearby mountain, was once the highest until Fuji-san kicked it over to form its eight lower peaks. From 781 to 1707 eighteen eruptions were recorded, with the last one in 1707 at the side cone of Hōei-zan on the southeast side of Fuji's slopes. The crater on top of Fuji is about 100 meters deep and 700 meters in diameter, but shows no signs of activity at present. Numerous smaller Fujis may be seen throughout Japan, all of which have a similar conical shape—for example, Akan Fuji in Hokkaido and Satsuma Fuji in Kyushu.

People have been climbing Fuji-san for over 1,000 years, but until just over 100 years ago this was an activity for Shinto or Buddhist priests and pilgrims only. Women were not allowed to climb to the summit of Fuji-san until 1872. The oldest mention of ascent to the summit was in the 870's. In 1149 the Dainichi Temple was built near the summit, and this became the inner branch of the Sengen Shrine. The main sanctuary is in Fujinomiya, below the mountain, where the world's oldest picture of mountain climbing can be seen, dating from the 1400's and depicting the ascent of Fuji-san.

Monks of the Shugendō sect first opened the climbing route on the south side of Fuji-san, and from about 1430 mountain huts were built for the monks and pilgrims climbing the mountains. Another route for pilgrims which became more popular during the 1600's was opened on the north side of Fuji-san, and this is the most popular route today. The first foreigner to climb Fuji was Sir Rutherford Alcock, the first British minister to visit Japan, who made a successful expedition in 1860. Nowadays most climbers climb Fuji-san for the fun and challenge of climbing Japan's highest peak, but a few pilgrims may be seen wearing the traditional white clothes and straw sandals, and carrying the pilgrim's wooden staff, known as a *kongōzue*. Many climbers purchase a wooden staff and have it branded at each of the numbered stages on the climb, but nearly all climbers now start from the fifth stages, which are more than halfway up the mountain and easily reached by road.

In 1932 the world's highest, constantly manned weather station was established on the summit of Fuji-san, and its building and dome can be seen perched on the highest point of the crater rim. Here the average January temperature is $-20°C$, and temperatures dip below $0°C$ even in mid-summer, so plenty of warm clothes should be taken for the climb, even if you are sweating in a T-shirt in downtown Tokyo.

The open season for climbing on Fuji-san is from July 1 to August 31, when the mountain huts along the trails are open for accommodation and sell food and drinks. There are often lines of hikers snaking their way along the trails during these two summer months, and especially at weekends, when you may be brought to a complete standstill on the trail at times. During open season, the number of climbers who head for Fuji is in the hundreds of thousands. Those who wish to sleep in one of the huts are packed in like sardines—a space on the floor or in the bunks with two meals usually costs about ¥4,500. Many plod on during the night.

The Subashiri and Gotemba Trails to the east have long ash slides and are used for a fast descent. Nowadays just about everyone starts a Fuji climb from one of the fifth stages, but there are trails starting from the base of the mountain. There is also a circuit trail which circles Fuji-san at the timber line, the level of the fifth stages, at about 2,500 meters, with the green sea of forests below and the barren lava and ash slopes above. This trail is about 19 kilometers around, and takes eight to ten hours to hike.

ACCESS

From downtown Tokyo the most convenient way of reaching Fuji-san is by taking the direct bus service from either the Hamamatsucho or Shinjuku Bus Terminal to the Fifth Stage of the Lake Kawaguchi-ko Trail. These bus services run daily from mid-July to the end of August, and on Sundays and holidays from mid-April to early November. The journey takes about two and a half hours. An alternative way of reaching the Fifth Stage of the Lake Kawaguchi-ko Trail is by taking the Chuo line from Shinjuku Station to Ōtsuki (大月), where you change to the private Fuji Kyuko line to Lake Kawaguchi-ko (河口湖) Station. From here there are daily bus services to the Fifth Stage between mid-April and early November. The Fifth Stage of the Gotemba Trail can be reached by taking the bus service from Gotemba Station, which operates during the months of July and August. The new Fifth Stage of the Fujinomiya Trail can be reached by taking the bus service from Mishima Station (三島駅), which operates from early July to the end of August.

To get to Lake Yamanaka-ko, take the Fuji Kyuko line from Ōtsuki to Asahi-ga-oka. Or, the Chuo Kosoku bus can be taken from Shinjuku Station to Yamanaka-ko (2 hrs.).

For Lake Saiko, take the Fuji Kyuko line from Ōtsuki to Fuji Yoshida, then Fuji Kyuko bus (40 mins.) to Saiko. The bus stop is in front of the youth hostel.

ACCOMMODATION

The lakes below Fuji-san also offer some good hiking, and youth hostels are located at three of these lakes: Kawaguchi-ko Youth Hostel (Tel: 0555-72-1431), Fuji Saiko Youth Hostel (Tel: 0555-82-2616), and Yamanaka-ko Marimo Youth Hostel (Tel: 0555-62-4210). Fuji Yoshida Youth Hostel (Tel: 0555-22-0533) and Gotemba Youth Hostel (Tel: 0550-82-3045) are located in those towns below Fuji's slopes.

There are about 30 huts on the Lake Kawaguchi-ko Trail to the north, and eleven on the Fujinomiya Trail to the south, which are the most popular routes up.

TRAILS

*
++++
Kawaguchi-ko 5th Stage (河口湖五合目) —→ 2 kms. 50 mins. —→ 6th Stage (六合目) —→ 1.5 kms. 1 hr. 15 mins. —→ 7th Stage (七合目) —→ 2.5 kms. 2 hrs. 30 mins. —→ 8th Stage (八合目) —→ 0.9 kms. 1 hr. —→ 9th Stage (九合目) —→ 0.6 kms. 40 mins. —→ Summit —→ 2.8 kms. 2 hrs. 30 mins. —→ 7th Stage (七合目) —→ 5 kms. 1 hrs. 15 mins. —→ Gotemba 5th Stage (御殿場五合目)

Before setting out to climb Fuji, make sure you have plenty of extra

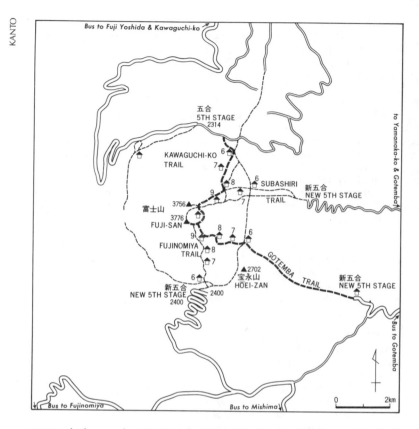

Bus to Fuji Yoshida & Kawaguchi-ko

五合
5TH STAGE
2314

KAWAGUCHI-KO
TRAIL

6
7
8
9

6 SUBASHIRI
新五合
NEW 5TH STAGE
TRAIL
7

to Yamanaka-ko & Gotemba

富士山
3756▲
FUJI-SAN
3776

8 7 6
9
FUJINOMIYA
TRAIL
8
7

▲2702
宝永山
HŌEI-ZAN

GOTEMBA TRAIL

新五合
NEW 5TH STAGE

6
新五合
NEW 5TH STAGE
2400
2400

Bus to Gotemba

Bus to Fujinomiya

Bus to Mishima

0   2km

warm clothes and waterproofs. Strong boots are also recommended, as the lava rock is hard and sharp, and the small stones and ash easily get into shoes on the scree runs. It is also wise to carry your own food and drink supplies, as prices at the huts rise with the altitude. The recent popularity of canned drinks and bad littering habits caused the formation of slopes of glittering aluminum cans until the authorities, fearing the advent of a completely aluminum-covered Fuji, installed can crushers on the mountain in 1985. You are meant to crush your cans and carry them back with you.

If you are planning to climb Fuji-san from Tokyo, the best route up is the Kawaguchi-ko Trail, which is the easiest and fastest to reach, and also the most popular. To avoid backtracking, the Gotemba Trail is recommended for the descent as this has some fast scree runs, and allows a close look at the Hoei side cone. Most climbers start from the

5th Stage late in the evening, not only to reach the summit for sunrise, but to avoid the relentless, scorching sun during fine days.

From the car park it is a five-minute walk up the road to the start of the trail. It is an easy walk up through the last trees on Fuji's slopes to the 6th Stage, where there is a Safety Guidance Center providing information and assistance for climbing Fuji-san. Z gzagging its way up the volcanic rock and ash slopes, the trail comes to the mountain huts at the 7th Stage, where there is a First Aid Station open from mid-July to late August. The long section up to the 8th Stage is marked by ropes, chains, and metal posts, with many huts along the way. After the 8th Stage the trail zigzags up a scree slope of loose volcanic rocks and ash to the crater rim. It is not unusual for this section of the trail to become jammed with climbers on a weekend night in midsummer, as everyone begins to tire after the climb, and gasp for breath in the thin air. A continuous thread of torch lights and lamps may be seen winding its way to the top of Fuji's crater. It is just as well to take this section slowly, as this is where altitude sickness may affect a few people. If you get a bad headache or start vomiting, you should not continue the climb but return back down. On reaching the crater rim you may be surprised to see what looks like a village, including shops, restaurants, and a small shrine. The summit, crowned with the observatory, can be reached by either going around the crater rim to the east, passing the Sengen Shrine on the way, or around to the west of the large crater.

It is not wise to reach the summit too long before sunrise (about 4:00 A.M.) as dawn is the coldest time to be hanging around. However, the restaurants never close during the open season, and serve hot food and drinks through the night to cold and weary climbers. On a fine day the sunrise is spectacular, preceded by a glowing horizon, along which the golden, plastic sun distends, squeezes upwards, and blazes free, showering light and warmth on the summit of Fuji while the rest of Japan lies in dark shadow. Far to the west, the peaks of the North Alps may be seen beyond those of the nearer South Alps, to the north the peaks of Yatsu-ga-take, Okutama and Nikko, and to the south the Izu Peninsula stretch out into the Pacific Ocean.

From the observatory at the summit the trail down to the Sengen Shrine passes the junction with the top of the Fujinomiya Trail, and the Gotemba Trail starts further on to the north of the shrine, which is situated on an area of flat ground on the crater rim. The Gotemba Trail zigzags down over rough volcanic rock and passes just north of the Hōei crater, where the last eruption of Fuji occurred in 1707. There are steep scree runs of loose volcanic rock and ash down this route, where you may dig your heels in and slide down at alarming speeds, making the descent much faster than the ascent. If the sun is blazing, there is no shelter on these barren slopes, and the dust and heat will drive you on to the bottom of the trail. Buses run from the car park at the 5th Stage to Gotemba Station, from where JR trains can be taken.

Around the base of Fuji-san there are some popular tourist sights including the beautiful Five Lakes of Fuji (Fuji Go-ko) spread around the northern base of the mountain. Lava caves can be visited on the western side, and the large forest of Aoki-ga-hara covers its southwestern slopes. There are a few youth hostels and many min-shuku and ryokan to be found in this area. The views of Fuji-san from the lakes is especially impressive during spring and autumn, when snow covers its higher slopes. During their long history of Fuji-viewing and Fuji-climbing, the Japanese have realized where Fuji's beauty lies—they have a saying which goes, "He who climbs Fuji-san once is a wise man, he who climbs it twice is a fool."

16. Tokyo's Vacationland under the Shadow of Fuji: Hakone 箱根

Travelling along the old Tōkaidō road which linked Edo (old Tokyo) with Kyoto, travellers and *daimyō* processions of the Edo Period had to pass over the Hakone Mountains on the section between Mishima and Odawara. As they came to the southern shore of Lake Ashi-no-ko they had to pass through the Hakone Checkpoint (*sekisho*)—one of the barriers which the Tokugawa Shogunate used to control the movement of people and ensure its continued power. This was one of the most beautiful parts of their journey as they looked out across the large, mountain-enclosed lake to the familiar profile of Fuji-san rising beyond. Just across the lake on the nearby shore stood the vermilion torii gateway, lapped by gentle waves, marking the entrance path to Hakone Shrine concealed in the lush green forest of tall cedars. Above the torii and invisible shrine, the forested slopes rose to the central peaks of Hakone towering over the lake. This beautiful landscape has been depicted by Hiroshige (1797–1858) in his famous ukiyo-e prints.

Nowadays the views are much the same, but the old road has been superceded by highways, and the route of the old Tōkaidō is now a popular trail for hikers. It is one of the oldest roads in Japan, built by the Tokugawa Shogunate in 1619, and the checkpoint was reconstructed in 1965 together with an adjoining museum of Edo period exhibits. Parts of the old road retain the *ishidatami* stone paving, which was mostly laid in 1862, but some sections are older. Enjoyable hiking awaits those who wish to follow in the footsteps of the Edo period travellers, and there are some wonderful hikes over the peaks, with the profile of Fuji never far from view.

Hakone, situated southeast of Fuji-san and north of the Izu Peninsula, forms part of the Fuji-Hakone-Izu National Park. It was previously a large conical volcano resembling the present-day Fuji, but its central part collapsed to form a caldera. Later Tertiary and Quaternary volcanic activity in the caldera built the triple volcanic cones of Kamiyama (1,438 m.), the highest peak in Hakone, the neighbouring Koma-ga-take (1,327 m.), and the nearby Futago-yama (1,091 m.). Within the caldera and west of these peaks lies the picturesque Lake Ashi-no-ko, which is 20 kilometers in circumference. There are a number of steam vents in the area, and the local ryokan inns are supplied with natural hot spring water—the onsen baths being one of the main attractions for Japanese visitors to Hakone. Ōwaku-dani on the northern slopes of Kamiyama was the last point of eruption in Hakone's long volcanic history, and visitors may wander through the active steaming vents of this area on well-laid-out trails.

The lakeshore and mountains of Hakone are forested with a natural mixed forest of cedar, cypress, spruce, beech, cherry, and azalea. There is a large and varied bird population and wildlife may be seen away from the crowded areas. Situated close to the Pacific Coast, Hakone has a warm climate with relatively mild winters—snow usually not falling until February.

Described here are two popular hikes: along the course of the old Tōkaidō road and the central highest peaks. There are many more mountain trails in the area, including a pleasant hiking trail around the western shore of Lake Ashi-no-ko.

ACCESS

Only 90 kilometers west of Tokyo, with fast and easy access on the private Odakyu Line from Shinjuku, and good transport within the park, Hakone receives about 17 million visitors annually. Most go on day trips or for short weekend stays. The express train called the "Romance Car" makes few stops between Shinjuku and Hakone Yumoto—the gateway to Hakone—taking about 85 minutes. Alternatively, buses run from Odawara Station, which can be reached by Odakyu or JR trains, to Hakone Yumoto and other destinations in the Hakone area. There is an amazing variety of transport within the park on which it is possible to make a spectacular circular tour. The Hakone Mountain Railway runs from Hakone Yumoto up to Gōra, from where a cable car climbs the mountains to Sōunzan. A ropeway starts from Sōunzan and glides you over the mountains to Ōwaku-dani and Sengendai on the northern shore of Lake Ashi-no-ko. Boats ply the lake between Sengendai and Hakone-machi on the southern shores. From Hakone-machi, bus services operate to Hakone Yumoto and Odawara. A ropeway and a cable car also run to the top of Koma-ga-take. The Hakone Free Pass, available at Odakyu stations, allows one return journey from Tokyo and free use of most of the transport services in Hakone for a four-day period, saving you a lot of money if you intend to travel all around Hakone.

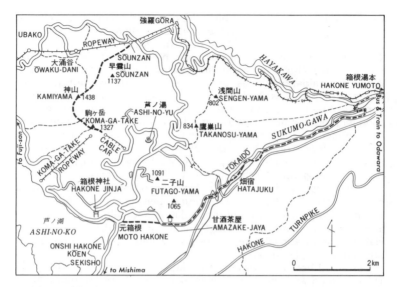

ACCOMMODATION

Accommodation in Hakone is often fully booked, especially at holiday times and weekends, and so it is best to book in advance if you want to be sure of a place to stay. There are plenty of hotels, ryokan, and minshuku, many with natural hot spring baths. A convenient minshuku for hiking in the area is the Moto Hakone Guest House (Tel: 0460-3-7880) located near Lake Ashi-no-ko and offering spectacular views of Mt. Fuji. Two campsites are located in the park at Otamaga-ike near the Tōkaidō road beneath Futago-yama, and on the northern shore of Lake Ashi-no-ko near Sengendai.

TRAILS

Hiking the Old Tōkaidō Road (*Kyūkaidō*)

*
+

Moto Hakone (元箱根) ⟶ 4.5 kms. 1 hr. 40 mins. ⟶ Hatajuku (畑宿) ⟶ 2 kms. 55 mins. ⟶ Sukumo-gawa (須雲川) ⟶ 4.5 kms. 1 hr. 35 mins. ⟶ Hakone Yumoto (箱根湯本)

The old Tōkaidō road can be hiked in either direction from Moto Hakone on Lake Ashi-no-ko or Hakone Yumoto, but most people choose to start from Moto Hakone and do the route downhill. On the southern shore of Lake Ashi-no-ko the Hakone Checkpoint (*sekisho*) can be visited, and the nearby Hakone Detached Palace Garden (Onshi Hakone Kōen) lying on a peninsula landscaped with fine trees and commanding a fine view of the lake and Fuji is worth a visit. Further around the shore is the Hakone Shrine, also know as Hakone Gongen, which was built in 757 by priest Mangan.

An avenue of 420 giant cedar trees lines the route of the old Tōkaidō road along the southeastern shore of Lake Ashi-no-ko. These cedar trees were planted in 1618 to protect travellers from snow in winter and to give shade in summer. Now forming an impressive sight, this cedar avenue is designated a "Natural Treasure." Climbing from Moto Hakone, the old road leaves the lake and passes through forest. After crossing the newer tarmac road it comes to the quaint old Amazake-jaya tea house where you can rest, drink sweet non-alcoholic *saké* and eat rice cakes, just as the travellers in the Edo period did.

From the tea house the old road continues through forest, then follows close to the newer road before descending to the village of Hatajuku. This village is the center for Hakone-zaiku marquetry (*yosegi*)—a woodcraft using inlaid and mosaic techniques developed around the ninth century to produce very attractive boxes, toys, and accessories. The old paved road comes out at the tarmac road near an old tea house where the woodcrafts can be seen in the making. Across the road, the Yosegi Kaikan Hall has an impressive exhibition of the local craft. The road through the village passes several small workshops and there is a beautiful old ryokan garden which can be visited.

The old stone-paved road leaves the tarmac road and resumes its way down through forest, across a stream, and then back up to the road again. After following the road for five minutes there is a section of stone paving dating from the Edo period as the old road runs parallel to the newer one. Crossing the road again, the trail descends to and crosses the Sukumo-gawa River, with a nearby camp of small holiday cabins in the forest. The trail is well marked as it follows the old road through cypress forest and comes out at the road near a bridge in the village of Sukumo-gawa.

From Sukumo-gawa Village to Hakone Yumoto the tarmac road follows the same course as the old road with the modern highway running parallel. A bus can be taken or you can continue to walk on the road to Shōgan-ji Temple with a nearby pine tree which was used as a marker on the old Tōkaidō road. Ten minutes after Shōgan-ji you come to the small, old Sōun-ji Temple—up a flight of steps from the road. This temple was established in 1521 as the family temple of the Hojo clan who were the lords of Odawara Castle in the late fifteenth century.

The road opposite Sōun-ji Temple leads to a trail over a forested hill which comes to Homare Bridge across the Hayakawa River. This is the center of Hakone Yumoto, the hot spring resort town and gateway to Hakone.

Hakone's Central Peaks
***
+ + +

Koma-ga-take (駒ヶ岳) ⟶ 2.8 kms. 1 hr. ⟶ Kamiyama (神山) ⟶ 1.8 kms. 1 hr. ⟶ Ōwaku-dani (大涌谷) ⟶ 2 kms. 1 hr. 30 mins. ⟶ Sōunzan (早雲山)

Hakone's central peaks can be climbed from many directions, but perhaps the easiest route is to take the Koma-ga-take cable car up to the top of the second highest peak and hike from there. Buses run to the cable car station from Hakone Yumoto via Ashi-no-yu, and from Moto Hakone. The cable car runs fairly frequently up the southeast side of Koma-ga-take and takes five minutes to reach the top. You may be surprised to find a large building housing an ice-skating rink in a hollow at the summit with the top ropeway station on the other side of it. The summit is occupied by Hakone Mototsumiya Shrine—a branch of Hakone Shrine. To the north the peak of Kamiyama can be seen and to the northwest a splendid profile of Fuji-san presents itself in fine weather.

It is an easy trail, first descending to the pass and then climbing through a forest of beech, mountain plum, and cherry to the peak of Kamiyama, from where views are obscured by the low, bushy forest. I was very surprised on one of my hikes along this highest trail in Hakone, when I almost had a head-on collision with a fox coming along the trail in the opposite direction. However, he was even more surprised and quickly darted off into the undergrowth.

A steep descent from the peak of Kamiyama passes a trail on the left for the lower peak of Kammuri-ga-take (冠ヶ岳), and then a small, red torii gateway. The hot spring vents of Ōwaku-dani soon come into view below and to the left before coming to another trail junction with the trail right leading to Sōunzan. Ōwaku-dani is about a fifteen-minute descent from this junction, where well-laid-out trails allow close inspection of the steaming, hissing vents of sulphurous vapors. Blackened eggs boiled in the steam are sold here. Nearby is the Ōwaku-dani Natural Science Museum, with displays of the local geology, flora, and fauna. The ropeway may be taken from here to Sengendai on Lake Ashi-no-ko or over the mountain to Sōunzan. For those fitter souls, the trail can be taken to Sōunzan through the forest, and passing the active, desolate, yellow volcanic rock valley of Sōun-jigoku on to the long descent to the Sōunzan cable car and ropeway station.

17. The Guardian Peaks of the Kanto Plain: Tanzawa 丹沢

Rising abruptly from the Kanto Plain, the Tanzawa Mountains are the nearest peaks over 1,000 meters to the sprawling conurbation of Tokyo and Yokohama. At the eastern end of the range, the conical peak of Ōyama (1,252 m.) commands a prominent position, overlooking the megalopolis to the east and the shimmering ocean to the south. Previously called Kunimi-yama (Guardian of the Land) it has been worshipped as a deity since ancient times by people living below it and fishermen along the coast of Kanagawa Prefecture. Earthenware vessels from the Jōmon period, circa 1,000 B.C., have been found near the top of the mountain. Another old name for the mountain is Afuriyama, a descriptive term for the high rainfall and cloud often seen hanging around its peak.

The wooden buildings of the Afuri Upper Shrine are found on the forested peak of Ōyama, with the larger main shrine, or Afuri Shimosha, set amidst cedar forest on the southeastern side of the mountain. Below the lower shrine is the Ōyama Fudōson Temple, which was also called Daisan-ji and Sekison Daigongen in olden days. This Buddhist temple was founded by the Shingon sect in A.D. 755, and was a favorite place for mountain hermits. It is especially noted for the beautiful *keyaki* wood carvings on the temple structure. The temple was visited every year by Minamoto Yoritomo, who used to offer a sword for protection against disasters. Nowadays wooden swords are sold at the market below the mountain, which is visited by many pilgrims, tourists, and hikers on their way up the mountain. Colorful spinning tops (*koma*) are another specialty of Ōyama market, and the restaurants offer bean curd (*tōfu*), mountain vegetables (*sansai*) and boar stew in winter.

Two trails lead from the market up to the lower shrine. The less steep women's slope (*onnazaka*) passes the temple before rejoining the men's slope (*otokozaka*) on the way to the shrine. A cable car also runs up the mountain from the market to the lower shrine. Two trails climb the mountain from the lower to the upper shrine on the summit, taking about one hour. From the summit another trail leads down the southwest side of the mountain to Yabitsu Pass and the higher peaks of Tanzawa to the west.

Ōyama is a very popular mountain for day-trippers from Tokyo, but the best hiking is to be found in the higher peaks. The route I describe here is a two-day hike over Tanzawa's highest peaks from south to north, but there are several options for covering the first part only and making a one-day hike over Tō-no-dake. Tanzawa, with its fine mountain scenery, is a good place for novice hikers, but some routes offer a challenge even to those more experienced.

Apart from easy accessibility, the other attraction of Tanzawa is the possibility of year-round hiking, with snow usually only covering the mountains from late February to early April. Much of the winter is snow-free, with fine weather due to the effects of the *karakaze* dry wind, which blows across the Kanto Plain during the winter north-westerly monsoon. This season is best for the magnificent views of Fuji-san, with its snow-covered cone rising to the west.

Extending from east to west across Kanagawa Prefecture, the Tanzawa Range is composed of Tertiary volcanics with some exposures of Miocene granite. The mountains are covered with forest to the highest peaks with forestry stands of cypress, cedar and fir, and natural mixed forest including pine, cherry and maple. The undergrowth is bamboo grass, laurel, and azalea. Opportunities are good for spotting resident copper pheasant and woodpeckers in the forests. An amazing variety of wildlife is present in these mountains, where wild boar and bear are still occasionally hunted.

ACCESS

Tanzawa can be reached on the Odakyu Line from Shinjuku, and with trains starting to run at about 0530 it is best to leave early on an express train, which takes just over one hour to the stations south of the range. The "Tanzawa-Ōyama Free Pass—B Ticket" can be bought at any Odakyu station and allows two days' free use of Odakyu trains up to Shibusawa Station, and buses to the mountains, and may save you a lot of money. For the trip to Ōyama, the best station to get off is Isehara, from where buses run to Ōyama market from bus stand no. 4 outside the station. Hadano is the best station to get off for hiking the ridge from Yabitsu-tōge Pass with buses running to Minoge Village and the pass (except December to February) from bus stand no. 2 outside the station. For the route described here, get off at Shibusawa Station and take the bus to Ōkura Village.

ACCOMMODATION

There are many mountain huts in Tanzawa, and especially on the route up from Ōkura Village. Wooden huts offering accommodation, food, and drinks are found on Tanzawa's highest peaks, and are open for most of the year. A long list of huts with phone numbers is found at the bus stop just outside Shibusawa Station. Campsites are also fairly plentiful in the Tanzawa Mountains, and on this route there is one at Ōkura Village and another on the ridge between Tanzawa-yama and Hiru-ga-take—the highest peaks. There is a youth hostel in Sagami-ko Town north of Tanzawa—Sagami-ko Youth Hostel (Tel: 04268-4-2338). Water is available from streams, freshwater springs and the huts, but on ridge routes it is best to carry a good supply. Food supplies should be brought with you because the villages and huts have only a limited selection.

***
+ + +

Ōkura (大倉) ➞ 6.5 kms. 3 hrs. 40 mins. ➞ Tō-no-dake (塔ノ岳) ➞ 3 kms. 1 hr. 15 mins. ➞ Tanzawa-yama (丹沢山) ➞ 3.5 kms. 1 hr. 30 mins. ➞ Hiru-ga-take (蛭ヶ岳) ➞ 8.5 kms. 3 hrs. 20 mins. ➞ Yake-yama (焼山) ➞ 3 kms. 1 hr. 15 mins. ➞ Nagano (長野)

Although I have described this route over Tanzawa as a two-day hike, I have completed it twice in one day, but to do this you need to be fairly fit and get a very early start. The bus from Shibusawa to Ōkura takes about 15 minutes; the start of the trail is a few minutes' walk from the bus terminus up the road after a left and a right bend. A sign points the way to the left; on the right by the left bend is a campsite by a stream. The trail from Ōkura Village to the top of Tō-no-dake is a well-trodden route, and there are often crowds of hikers at weekends and holidays. Parts of the trail are badly eroded and wooden steps have been installed along some steeper sections.

After leaving the road, the trail, at first concrete, soon becomes a dirt track as it climbs up past a hut. Several mountain huts and picnic benches are found on the way, as the trail climbs the forested ridge with a few open clearings. In late April or May, the delicate cherry blossoms of the *yamazakura* can be seen in the mixed forest. October and November sees the mountain forest ablaze with red maples. Tall, brown, feathery pampas grass (*susuki*) is a popular autumn sight. Bird boxes have been put in the forest in places to attract the varied bird species of the area.

Coming up to the peak of Tō-no-dake (1,491 m.), the forest is short and bushy, with a thick bamboo grass undergrowth. Two mountain huts are situated on the peak, which is a flat, exposed area, with wooden picnic benches, a small stone shrine, and a freshwater spring down the slope to the west. Tō-no-dake literally means Tower Peak and offers marvelous views west to the imposing cone of Fuji, east to the lower peak of Ōyama, south to the ocean, and north to the highest peaks of Tanzawa. The larger of the two huts on the summit has a small tea room, which is a pleasant place to rest in bad weather.

Going to the left of the larger hut and entering the forest is the trail to Tanzawa-yama (1,567 m.), which stays on the ridge as it first descends then climbs to the higher peak. This is an enjoyable hike through mixed forest with bamboo grass and azalea in the undergrowth. A mountain hut and picnic area are to be found on the flat summit of Tanzawa-yama, but the views are mostly obscured by the forest.

The trail to Hiru-ga-take (1,673 m.)—the highest peak in Tanzawa—descends steeply at first and then climbs the ridge to a shelter and camping area. A freshwater spring is found here down the ridge's

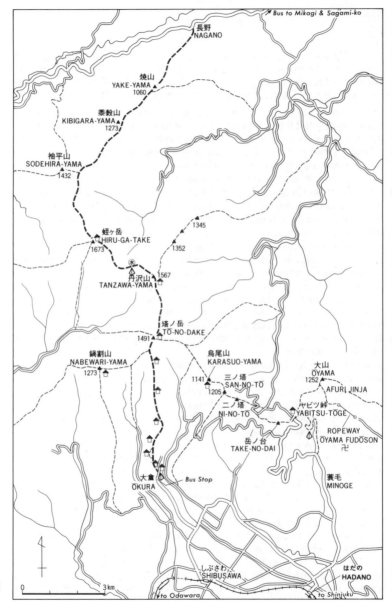

長野
NAGANO

↗ Bus to Mikagi & Sagami-ko

焼山
YAKE-YAMA
1060

黍殻山
KIBIGARA-YAMA
1273

袖平山
SODEHIRA-YAMA
1432

蛭ヶ岳
HIRU-GA-TAKE
1673

1345

1352

丹沢山
TANZAWA-YAMA
1567

塔ノ岳
TO-NO-DAKE
1491

鍋割山
NABEWARI-YAMA
1273

烏尾山
KARASUO-YAMA
1141

三ノ塔
SAN-NO-TO
1205

大山
ŌYAMA
1252

AFURI JINJA

二ノ塔
NI-NO-TO

ヤビツ峠
YABITSU-TŌGE

ROPEWAY
ŌYAMA FUDŌSON
卍

岳ノ台
TAKE-NO-DAI

蓑毛
MINOGE

大倉
OKURA

Bus Stop

しぶさわ
SHIBUSAWA

はだの
HADANO

↓ to Odawara

↓ to Shinjuku

0   3 km

north slope. Following the undulating ridge the trail leads to the summit of Hiru-ga-take with a large wooden hut sitting on the top. With the whole Tanzawa Range beneath your feet there is a good view of Fuji to the west in fine weather.

It is a long but easy ridge walk north from Hiru-ga-take to Yake-yama (1,060 m.) through a less frequented part of Tanzawa, with a better chance of spotting wildlife. You may disturb a copper pheasant, which will burst upwards with a loud noise and then glide down through the forest to lower ground, or deer may be heard moving through the bamboo grass undergrowth and occasionally making whistling calls. Yake-yama is not a peak but the end of the long ridge, and is capped with a tall fire tower lookout.

Descending steeply down a zigzag trail through natural forest you come to the village of Nagano with its thatched-roof cottages and small vegetable plots. Buses run along the main road through the village to the bus terminus at Mikagi Village 15 minutes away, from where connections are made to Sagami-ko Station, on the Chuo Line into Tokyo, taking another 15 minutes. Sagami-ko Town, situated on a dammed lake, has a youth hostel and is a good base for hiking over the lower mountains of Takao-san and Jimba-san, described in the following section.

18. Year-Round Hiking in the Kanto Mountains: Takao-san 高尾山

Travelling directly west on the Chuo Line through the urban sprawl of Tokyo, Takao-san and the neighboring mountains of the Kanto Range are the first mountains to be reached. Taking about one hour to reach from downtown Tokyo, this range of low mountains, with peaks below 1,000 meters, is easily accessible and offers year-round hiking to Tokyo's millions. It is an excellent area to get a first taste of hiking in Japan, or for more experienced hikers to keep in shape throughout the year. Hiking trails are well laid out on Takao-san, and the trail to Jimba-san is a popular one-day hike. On fine days the higher mountains of Tanzawa to the south, Okutama to the north, and Fuji-san to the southwest can be seen.

Many day-trippers from Tokyo converge on the Takao area, where there are several tourist sights as well as the well-marked nature trails. The Takao Natural Science Museum (Shizen Kagaku Hakubutsukan), situated in the village at the foot of the mountain, is a good first stop (except Mondays and national holidays). The museum contains exhibits of the fauna, flora, and geology of the area, so you will know what to look out for on a hike over these mountains. There is also a Nature Center near the top of Takao-san.

The mountains are composed mainly of Mesozoic sedimentary

133

strata, which have been folded, faulted, intruded, and metamorphosed. Forestry stands of cedar, cypress, fir, and pine cover much of the mountain, but some natural forest remains and includes beech, oak, maple, cherry, and other species. In spring the cherry trees begin to blossom from mid-April. During the summer the luxuriant green forests are an escape from the oppressive city heat. Autumn sees the transformation of the forest into a tapestry of bright colors; this change is called *kōyō* in Japanese. The clear, sunny winters afford fine views of Fuji-san, and snow does not usually fall until late February or March.

An amazing variety of wildlife can be seen in the area. One hundred bird species have been sighted here, including the resident copper pheasant (*yamadori*) and many species of flycatcher in the summer. Twenty-six species of mammal have also been recorded in the Takao-san area, ranging from small mice to squirrels, weasels, racoons, boars and deer.

Situated in a grove of tall cedars near the summit of Takao-san is the Yakuōin Temple—a Buddhist temple of the Shingon sect founded in 744. On the second Sunday in March the Buddhist priests perform a fire-walking ceremony (*Hiwatari Matsuri*) at the foot of the mountain just outside the village. Cedar boughs are set on fire in a huge bonfire, the red-hot embers are raked flat on a path several meters long, and then the priests walk across the smoldering embers barefoot. Crowds come from afar to see the sight, and the onlooker's active participation is welcomed. I was surprised to see that there were apparently no injuries inflicted on the large numbers eager to follow in the footsteps of the priests.

ACCESS

The cheapest and easiest way of reaching Takao-san from Tokyo is by taking the Keio Line from Shinjuku to Takao-san Guchi at the end of the line. This takes about one hour. Alternatively, the JR Chuo Line can be taken to Takao-san Station, from where the Keio Line runs the short distance to Takao-san Guchi.

From Takao-san Guchi Station a pedestrian path leads up to Kiyotaki Cable Car Station, where a cable car and a chairlift operate part of the way up the mountain. The road leading up to the station is lined with souvenir shops and restaurants serving such local fare as yam (*tororo*) and mountain vegetables (*sansai*).

ACCOMMODATION

There is a youth hostel at Takao-san, Takao Youth Hostel (Tel: 0426-61-0437), situated next to the museum and only five minutes' walk from the station. Several inns are also located in the village. At the other end of this hike there is a campsite in the valley at Jimba Kōgen Shita. The trail from Takao-san over the mountains to Jimba-san has plenty of small stalls selling food and drinks, but I recommend carrying your own supplies, as prices are higher on the trails.

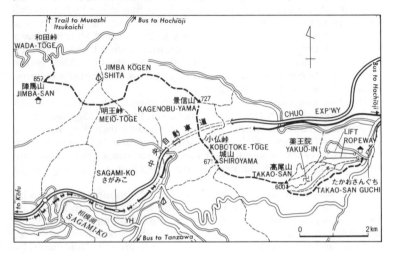

TRAILS

*
+

Takao-san Guchi (高尾山口) ⟶ 3.3 kms. 1 hr. 40 mins. ⟶ Takao-san (高尾山) ⟶ 2.5 kms. 50 mins. ⟶ Shiroyama (城山) ⟶ 2.3 kms. 50 mins. ⟶ Kagenobu-yama (景信山) ⟶ 6 kms. 2 hrs. ⟶ Jimba-san (陣馬山) ⟶ 1 km. 20 mins. ⟶ Wada-tōge (和田峠) ⟶ 3 kms. 50 mins. ⟶ Jimba Kōgen Shita (陣馬高原下)

Takao-san is an ideal area for easy one-day hikes, but as Sagami-ko and the Tanzawa Mountains are not far to the south, and the Okutama Mountains are just to the north, it is possible to make extended hikes through the area on the countless trails. Waterproofs, reasonably strong footwear, a rucksack, and a map are the only requirements.

Several routes can be taken to the top of Takao-san as alternatives to the easy way up on the cable car or chairlift. The Inari-yama Trail starts from a small bridge across the stream to the left of the cable car station, and takes a high ridge route. A steep climb up from the stream leads to a small shrine dedicated to Inari, the god of cereals, protected by guardian foxes carved in stone. However, my favorite trail is Route 6, which follows the stream most of the way up the mountain through a steep-sided valley of cedar.

Route 6 is well marked and easy to follow, with beautiful scenery and many points of interest along the way. The trail soon passes some

135

small Buddhist Jizō statues, and a bridge over the stream leads to two small caves which also contain Jizō statues. Five minutes further on and the stream cascades over Biwa-taki—a five-meter-high waterfall with a Shinto shrine beneath it. On one of my visits here, which happened to be the day of the fire-walking festival in mid-March, I saw a man and woman, clad only in thin cotton, standing beneath the icy cold falls, clapping hands and shouting incantations. This severe ascetic practice was no doubt in preparation for the opposite extreme of walking across fire later that day.

The trail continues left of the falls, following the stream through cedar forest, with many picnic spots on the way. Signboards in Japanese explain the insect life of the stream, including the large dragonflies (*tombo*) which can be seen in summer. On reaching the head of the valley, Route 6 climbs to the Inari-yama Trail. There you should turn right for the summit, which is reached after scaling a flight of steps.

From the summit of Takao-san (600.3 m.) the mountain that can be seen to the west, with the antenna, is Shiroyama (670.6 m.) It can be reached by taking the trail which goes to the left of the Visitors' Center and down some steps. The trail passes through a mixed forest of cedar, cypress, and pine, with a bamboo grass undergrowth. Dominated by the large antennaed building, the flat summit of Shiroyama is a very popular picnic site, with wooden benches and stalls selling food and drinks. A trail leads down to Lake Sagami-ko, which, from the summit, is about four kilometers away.

Continuing over Shiroyama on the trail toward Jimba-san, you descend a ridge to Kobotoke-tōge, where there are some picnic shelters. Below can be seen the highway, and the Chuo Line train tracks, both of which tunnel beneath the mountains at this pass. Climbing the ridge from the pass, the trail comes to Kagenobu-yama (727.1 m.), where there is an old wooden building serving as a food and drink shop near the summit. On Sundays, the large area of shelters and benches here is often bustling with hikers picnicking at this halfway point between Takao-san and Jimba-san.

An undulating ridge walk leads to Meiō-tōge (明王峠) along a wide, easy trail, with a shelter and small refreshment store at the pass. The trail to the south descends to Lake Sagami-ko. For Jimba-san (857 m.), stay on the ridge trail which climbs gently to the summit. At the summit you will be greeted by the sight of a large, stylized, white, concrete horse standing on the highest point of this hiking route. Shops and picnic areas are found on the surrounding grassy slopes. Cherry trees around the summit area blossom in late April and May, but I was told by a local woman, *Kono sakura wa byōki desu* —the trees no longer blossom as well as they once did.

It is a short, steep descent down to the road at Wada-tōge, where you should turn right for Jimba Kōgen Shita. Buses run from the village to the train station at Hachiōji. Just before the bus stop in the village, a road forks to the right. A campsite is situated about twenty minutes' walk up this road, which becomes a track following a stream. A trail continues up through the forest from the campsite and is an alternative route up Jimba-san.

There are some interesting and much less frequented hiking trails north of Wada-tōge which lead over the mountains to the Akikawa Valley. These quiet trails offer a contrast to the popular Takao-san to Jimba-san route.

19. A Mountaintop Shrine: Mitake-san 御岳山

On my first hike to the top of Mitake-san, climbing a trail up through the forest, I was eager to reach the famous old Shinto shrine perched on its summit, but I was not prepared to find the large village which has grown up around it. Even after several visits to the mountain I still find it amazing to walk through this village of rustic, thatched-roof cottages, minshuku, souvenir shops, and restaurants situated just below the shrine on the mountaintop. Although there is now a small road and a cable car up to the village, it must have originally been quite a feat to construct this mountain village and shrine.

Mitake Shrine is built on a flat area at the summit amidst a grove of tall cedars, and is reached after an exhausting climb up a long flight of steps from the village. On May 8 there is a festival called Hinode Matsuri (Sunrise Festival) when a parade of *omikoshi* (portable shrines) and samurai warriors can be seen at the shrine and village.

Mitake-san and the surrounding mountains, with peaks of around 1,000 meters, offer year-round hiking and it is an ideal area for one-day hiking trips from Tokyo. Lying between the Tamagawa River to the north, which supplies Tokyo with water, and the Akikawa River to the south, the mountains are covered to the highest peaks with forestry stands and natural mixed forests of cedar, cypress, maple, cherry, and azalea. Both the Tamagawa and Akikawa valleys have fine scenery, with the Tamagawa River running through a spectacular V-shaped gorge cut into Mesozoic rocks, mostly composed of Jurassic sedimentary strata. Three caves formed in Jurassic limestone are located in the Mitake-san area and are open to visitors.

ACCESS

There are a number of starting points for hiking in the Mitake-san area, but the easiest access is on the Chuo Line to Tachikawa and then the Ome Line to Mitake Station. A bus service runs from Mitake Station to Takimoto, from where the cable car runs almost to the top of Mitake-san. There is also a trail next to the cable car which takes about one hour to climb up to Mitake Village.

A longer hiking route, which is my favorite, and is described here in more detail, starts from Hinatawada Station, which is five stations before Mitake Station on the Ome Line. Crossing the bridge over the Tamagawa River, turning left and then right up a small road you come to the Yoshino Plum Groves, just ten minutes from the station. Here in late February and March, 15,000 plum trees, covering the surrounding mountain slopes, burst into white, pink, and red blossom, while a sprinkling of snow covers the peaks. In mid-March there is a plum blossom festival at the plum groves and in the village of Hinatawada, when folk dancing and folk music performances can be seen.

Another approach to Mitake-san is via the Itsukaichi Line from Tachikawa to the end of the line at Musashi Itsukaichi. A bus service runs from the station to Kamiyōzawa Village, from where a forestry track continues up the valley towards Mitake-san. This bus route is convenient for reaching the three caves in the area: Mitsugo, Ōdake and Yozawa caves. Mitsugo Cave was discovered in 1970, is the nearest to Itsukaichi, and can be reached in 15 minutes from Mitsugo Shōnyūdō Iriguchi bus stop. Ōdake Cave, named after the mountain towering above it, was discovered in 1961, and is the largest in the area. It is a thirty-minute walk up a forestry track from Ōdake-guchi bus stop. Stair-

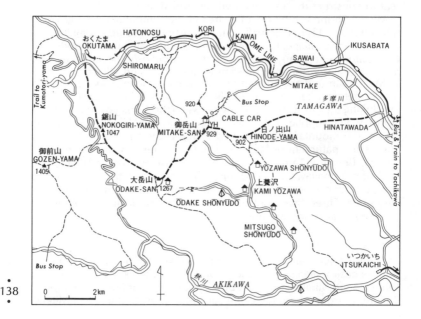

ways and lighting in the cave make it a lot more pleasant than Mitsugo Cave to explore. Yōzawa Cave, named after the village, is a 30-minute walk from the bus terminus in the village. It is a small, muddy cave, which must be explored with candles or flashlight provided at the entrance. Be prepared to get a little dirty if you explore this cave.

ACCOMMODATION

The trails in the area are not difficult, but reasonably strong boots should be worn. Waterproofs should always be carried as rainfall can occur at any time. Snowfall occurs in late February and March, but usually not enough to prevent hiking over the mountains. Summer camping is popular on the rocky bed of the Tamagawa River, and there are a few other campsites in the Tamagawa and Akikawa valleys. Mitake Youth Hostel (Tel: 0428-78-8501) is located in Mitake Village, on top of Mitake-san, between the shrine and cable car station. Minshuku and ryokan accommodation can also be found here. Shops and restaurants in Mitake Village provide food and drinks, but it is necessary to carry your own supplies on longer hikes through the area.

TRAILS

**
+++
Hinatawada （日向和田）⟶ 6.5 kms. 2 hrs. 30 mins. ⟶ Hinode-yama （日の出山）⟶ 1.6 kms. 40 mins. ⟶ Mitake-san （御岳山）⟶ 3.5 kms. 1 hr. 40 mins. ⟶ Ōdake-san （大岳山）⟶ 3 kms. 1 hr. 15 mins. ⟶ Nokogiri-yama （鋸山）⟶ 4.5 kms. 2 hrs. 30 mins. ⟶ Okutama （奥多摩）

Described here is a rather long, one-day hike from Hinatawada over Mitake-san and the neighbouring mountains, then down to Okutama at the end of the Ome Line. However, there are plenty of opportunities to shorten the hike, and descend Mitake-san via the cable car or visit the caves on the way to Itsukaichi.

After passing the Yoshino Plum Groves at Hinatawada, the track comes to a small torii gateway and signpost which marks the start of the trail to Mitake-san. The trail climbs up past a small golf course and through a mixed forest of cedar, cypress, pine, laurel, and bamboo grass. A steady climb brings you to a small shrine just to the left of the trail, and then you come out on top of the ridge. Unfortunately, the beautiful natural scenery and forest is marred by an antenna station as you follow the ridge towards Hinode-yama (Sunrise Mountain). There are good views of the mountains and valleys north and south as the easy ridge trail becomes steeper on the climb to the summit of Hinode-yama (902 m.).

The open, flat area on the summit has a picnic shelter, and groups of hikers are often found picnicking here while enjoying the view of the Okutama Mountains to the north and west, the Tanzawa Mountains to the south, and in fine weather Fuji-san to the southwest. From the summit of Hinode-yama the trail south descends to Yōzawa Cave about one kilometer away, but the main trail continues on to Mitake-san.

After hiking through natural forest it is quite a surprise to suddenly come to the large village of thatched cottages, ryokan, shops, and restaurants at Mitake-san. A narrow alley of colorful souvenir shops and restaurants leads up to a large torii gate which marks the start of the long flight of steps up to the shrine. The large, impressive shrine on the summit is made more awe-inspiring by the giant, dark cedars towering over it.

Several trails lead out of Mitake Village, either going north to the Tamagawa Valley or southwest to Kamiyama Village and the cave area. However, to the southwest two trails lead to the higher peak of Ōdake-san. One is a harder ridge route and the other a lower, easier route. Both trails join before coming to Ōdake Sansō—an old wooden mountain hut with a large, new lodge built next to it situated in the forest below the steep slope to the summit. The trail from the hut passes a shrine and small torii gate at the bottom of the steep climb. Although the peak of Ōdake-san (1,267 m.) is forested, it offers a good view southwest to Fuji and south to Tanzawa.

It is a steep descent from the peak of Ōdake-san, the highest point on this route, before the trail becomes a pleasant, easy ridge walk through stands of cypress and bamboo grass undergrowth. Passing over the peak of Nokogiri-yama, the trail descends to the Tamagawa River with some steep sections and steps placed over the rocks in places. After a long day's hike this descent can prove quite tiring to already exhausted limbs. Then at the end of the trail you come to a long flight of concrete steps which eventually emerge at a shrine overlooking the Tamagawa River. A bridge crosses the river to the nearby Okutama Station at the end of the Ome Line.

Fishing and camping are popular on the rocky river bed below, and there are a number of delightful spots for hiking down the valley. The best trail is from near Shiromaru Station following the south bank of the river to Hatonosu, where the river passes through a narrow gorge. There are several ryokan and minshuku at this popular spot. Another good section to hike is along the south bank of the river between Mitake and Sawai stations. An open-air restaurant is located on the river bank at Sawai, and there is a nearby saké brewery which can be visited. The brewery uses water from a freshwater mountain spring just behind it. I do not, however, advise drinking the samples before your hiking plans are completed, otherwise those plans may end up forgotten or at least drastically curtailed.

20. The Cloud Grabber: Kumotori-yama 雲取山

Few people realize how far the Tokyo Metropolitan District stretches; it surprises many to find that the chain of volcanic islands running hundreds of kilometers south of Tokyo out into the Pacific Ocean falls within its jurisdiction; on the main island of Honshu some remote mountain areas bordering the Kanto Plain are also included within its borders. Tokyo's highest peak, sitting right on its border with Saitama and Yamanashi prefectures to the west, soars to a height of 2,018 meters and is descriptively named "Cloud Grabber". Kumotori-yama and its surrounding mountains and valleys form part of the Chichibu-Tama National Park—the nearest national park to Tokyo and an ideal area for one-day or longer hikes in beautiful, mountain scenery.

Apart from the importance of the area for recreation, these mountains also provide Tokyo's teeming masses with water and electricity, and for this purpose the Tamagawa and Arakawa rivers have been dammed at Lake Okutama-ko and Lake Chichibu-ko respectively. Spectacular valleys and gorges are found along these rivers, and there is a scenic gorge formed in granite rock at Shōsenkyō in the southwestern corner of the park, accessible by bus from Kōfu City. The mountains of Chichibu-Tama are composed of Paleozoic and Mesozoic sedimentary strata, and are non-volcanic. Several caves have been found in the Jurassic limestones of the region, three of which, in the mountains around Kumotori-yama, are open to the public. Known as Okuchichibu, the western region of the park has the highest peaks, many over 2,000 meters, with Kimpu-san the highest. (2,595 m.) The eastern region, known as Okutama, which falls within the jurisdiction of Tokyo, has many peaks between 1,000 and 2,000 meters in height. Mitake-san (940 m.), with its mountaintop shrine, is popular with hikers, and is described in the previous section.

Year-round hiking is possible in the mountains of Okutama, but snowfall in February and March, and the rainy season in June and early July make these months less attractive. The best months are May, August, October, and November. Natural mixed forest covers the mountains to the highest peaks with such species as cedar, cypress, spruce, pine, fir, beech, maple, cherry, and plum, although many of the lower slopes are covered with commercial stands of cedar and cypress. In the undergrowth, rhododendron, azalea, and laurel bushes grow together with thick groves of bamboo grass. It is a good area for birdspotting and I have frequently surprised, and been surprised by, the copper pheasant, which suddenly bursts out of the forest undergrowth. Deer can often be heard calling and moving through the forest, and I once spotted a large macaque swinging through the trees.

An interesting diversion is a visit to the Nippara and Kurasawa caves, which can be done on an extended visit to the area or a separate day trip. Both caves can be reached by Nishi Tokyo bus from Okutama Station. Nippara Cave is a 30-minute bus ride away and is the largest cave in the Kanto Region. Electric lighting, and stairways through the cave make for easy viewing of the impressive, large caverns, with their stalactites and stalagmites. Kurasawa Cave is reached on the same bus route, but you must get off before Nippara at the Kurasawa bus stop, from where it is a 30-minute walk up a forestry track. This cave is smaller and less popular than the one at Nippara, and prospective explorers are provided with candles or flashlights at the entrance. Another cave is located near Kumotori-yama and is mentioned in the following hiking description.

ACCESS

Access to the Okutama area is best made from Central Tokyo on the Chuo Line, changing at Tachikawa to the Ome Line and going to the end of the line at Okutama Station. A few trains from Shinjuku Station go direct to Okutama. From Okutama there are a number of alternatives for hiking up Kumotori-yama. One trail starts from the town and is a long, but pleasant, ridge route via Mutsuishi-yama (Six Stone Mountain), Takanosu-yama (Hawk's Nest Mountain), and Nanatsuishi-yama (Seven Stone Mountain) to the top of Kumotori-yama, requiring two days up and down. The easiest route starts from Omatsuri, which is a 45-minute bus ride by Nishi Tokyo bus service from Okutama Station, and this is the route described here.

From Omatsuri a forestry track covers half of the distance to the top of Kumotori-yama, from where an interesting ridge trail continues northwards to Mitsumine—the location of a famous old mountain shrine. This route takes two days to complete, returning to Tokyo via Chichibu and the Seibu Line into Ikebukuro. The hike can be done the other way, or a day trip may be made to Mitsumine, by taking the Seibu Ikebukuro Line to Chichibu, changing to the Chichibu Line at Ohanabatake Station in Chichibu City, and going to the end of the line at Mitsumine-guchi, from where the bus service to Lake Chichibu-ko passes the Mitsumine Ropeway at Ōwa. The ropeway runs to the top of the ridge at Mitsumine, from where it is an easy walk to the shrine area. Mitsumine, at 1,100 meters, is 500 meters higher than Omatsuri and so there is considerably less climbing to do if you start from there, but I have always started from the Okutama side because access there is faster from Tokyo, allowing an earlier start on the trail.

ACCOMMODATION

There are many minshuku in the Okutama, Chichibu and Mitsumine areas, and Chichibu Youth Hostel (Tel: 0494-55-0056) is located in the village at Lake Chichibu below Mitsumine. On the trails there are four supervised mountain huts in the Kumotori-yama area, and one small unmanned hut on the summit. Campsites are found at Mitsumine near the top of the ropeway, and at Sanjō-no-yu Mountain Hut on the route up from Omatsuri.

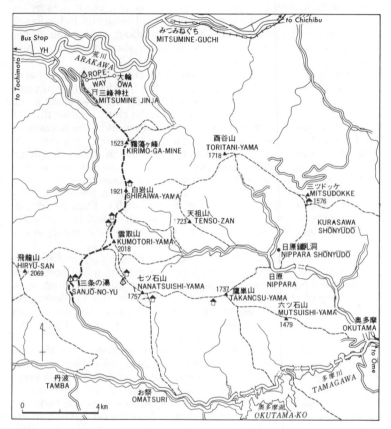

TRAILS

***
+++

Omatsuri (お祭) ⟶ 9 kms. 3 hrs. ⟶ Sanjō-no-yu (三条の湯) ⟶ 6 kms. 2 hrs. 30 mins. ⟶ Kumotori-yama (雲取山) ⟶ 3.5 kms. 1 hr. 30 mins. ⟶ Shiraiwa-yama (白岩山) ⟶ 3.5 kms. 1 hr. 40 mins. ⟶ Kirimo-ga-mine (霧藻ヶ峰) ⟶ 4 kms. 1 hr. 40 mins. ⟶ Mitsumine (三峰)

From the bus stop on the main road at Omatsuri, reached after a panoramic ride along the shoreline of Lake Okutama-ko, the forestry track opposite is signposted for Kumotori-yama. This track is motorable most of the way up to Sanjō-no-yu as it follows a beautiful forested stream valley. It takes about two hours to walk to the end of the track, from where the trail crosses a bridge and picnic area by the stream, to continue to the campsite and small mountain hut at Sanjō-no-yu. Enquiries can be made at the hut about visiting the Aoiwa stalactite cave, which is located in the valley about 45 minutes' hike away.

The trail for Kumotori-yama is the same as for the cave, but after about 20 minutes the trail divides, with the trail for Kumotori-yama climbing up the side of a ridge, and the trail for the cave leading into the valley. A small stream, the last water on this climb, crosses the trail before it climbs to the top of the ridge, and no more water is available until the huts on the other side of the peak. On reaching the main ridge to the summit, take the trail to the right which climbs steeply up the ridge through a thick bamboo grass undergrowth. This is a good place to watch out for deer. The summit appears suddenly as the trail finally climbs out of the forest to an open grassy area, where there is a small hut with a raised wooden floor large enough to sleep six people. The last time I climbed this peak the hut was occupied by a group of young Japanese hikers, and so I put up my tent on the nearby grassy area.

Morning found the summit swathed in mist and cloud, and after the unpleasant job of packing a wet tent I took the trail going north over the summit, and descended through the forest to Kumotori Sansō, passing a group of elderly hikers on their way up from the hut. Soon after the large, wooden Kumotori Sansō the trail passes Kumotori-yama Hut, which is also supervised and provides accommodation and meals.

After a short descent the trail climbs to a junction where the trail right leads down into the valley and on towards the cave at Nippara. Keeping left the trail climbs to the forested peak of Shiraiwa-yama (1,921 m.), where picnic benches are provided for tired hikers. Shiraiwa Goya, a large, wooden, unsupervised hut, is reached after descending the steep slope on the north side of the peak. Then an undulating walk along the forested ridge brings you to Shiraiwa-mae, where there are more picnic benches. Descending steeply and keeping left at a fork the trail then climbs Kirimo-ga-mine (1,523 m.)—the third main peak along this ridge to Mitsumine (Three Peak Ridge).

Continuing over the peak and keeping left at a junction, the trail is much easier and more trodden here, as it is within easy reach of the popular Mitsumine Shrine area. The trail passes a torii gate on the right marking the start of a trail to the inner shrine of Mitsumine on the peak of Myōhōga-take. Another torii gate marks the point where the trail joins the cedar- and cypress-lined avenue leading into the village and shrine at Mitsumine.

To the left of the track a Visitors' Center has a few exhibits of the local natural history and environment. The main track continues on to the campsite and ropeway station, but the large precincts of Mitsumine Shrine are entered through a large torii to the right. Set amidst an impressive forest of giant cedar, this is one of the oldest shrines in Japan for mountain worship, and it became a center for the Shugendō sect during the Kamakura period. If you happen to be there on April 8 you will see the annual shrine festival.

There is a trail leading down from the shrine area into the valley at Ōwa taking about one hour, but for the tired and weary there's the ropeway. From Ōwa buses run to Mitsumine-guchi Station. An alternative is the trail from the campsite area at Mitsumine which descends to Lake Chichibu-ko—taxis also operate on the road which winds down this way.

21. Over the Pacific Ocean-Japan Sea Watershed: Tanigawa-dake 谷川岳

Situated on the Gumma-Niigata prefectural border, the mountains of Tanigawa are infamous for claiming many lives each year. Compared to other mountains in Japan they are not high, with the highest peak at 2,025 meters and Tanigawa-dake at 1,963 meters, but the mountain slopes are very steep, and the crags precipitous. The bad, rapidly changing weather conditions, and easy accessibility result in hikers and climbers being caught unprepared in a dangerous environment.

A sharp ridge of peaks divides the rivers draining northwestwards to the Japan Sea and those draining southeastwards to the Pacific Ocean. The south and east facing slopes have precipitous rock walls, popular with rock climbers, such as those in the spectacular Ichinokura-sawa Valley, while the north- and west-facing slopes are much gentler. These latter slopes are covered with several meters of snow during the winter northwesterly monsoon with popular ski resorts centering on Yuzawa. Near the summit of Tanigawa-dake is the Tenjin-daira ski resort, popular because of its long ski season and easy accessibility via the ropeway. The Pacific-facing slopes have relatively little snow and the contrast can be quite startling on passing through the train or highway tunnel beneath these mountains from Gumma to Niigata. Snow lies year-round in sheltered valleys such as Ichinokura-sawa, and safe hiking is restricted to the period from July to the beginning of November.

Composed mainly of Paleozoic sedimentary strata, the mountains of Tanigawa form part of the Jōshin-etsu Kōgen National Park, which lies at the junction of the Chōkai, Nasu, and Fuji volcanic zones. There are approximately 70 volcanoes and 1,000 hot springs in the region, and many famous hot spring resorts are located in the valleys at the foot of the Tanigawa Mountains. The mixed forest of the lower slopes includes beech, oak, and maple, with rhododendron fairly common, while the higher slopes have an alpine vegetation of creeping pine and bamboo grass. A variety of birds and mammals may be seen, especially in the forests on the lower slopes of the mountains.

ACCESS

Frequent trains on the line between Ueno Station in Tokyo, and Niigata, pass through the long tunnel beneath the mountains. Minakami Station is the nearest stop for express trains and a gateway for several hot spring resorts in the area, but Doai Station, two stops after Minakami, is the closest and most convenient station for reaching Tanigawa-dake. Doai Station, which takes about three hours (by ordinary train) to reach from Ueno, is actually situated beneath the mountain, and the long flight of steps up from the platform through a large tunnel takes about ten minutes to the surface. A 20-minute walk up the road from the station brings you to the ropeway station. If you continue through the tunnel on an ordinary train, the first stop on the Niigata side is at Tsuchitaru Station—the end point of the hike over the watershed described here.

ACCOMMODATION

The only youth hostel in the area is Tsuchitaru Sansō Youth Hostel (Tel: 0257-87-3188), which is a five-minute walk from Tsuchitaru Station. There are two campsites: one at Futamata about five kilometers up the Tanigawa Valley from Tanigawa Onsen, and the other up the road from Doai, continuing on 20 minutes beyond the ropeway to Machiga-zawa. Both sites have limited areas of flat land, but plentiful water supply from nearby streams. Several mountain huts are found in the area, especially around Doai Station and further up the valley from there, one just below the summit of Tanigawa-dake, and one on Yomogi Pass. It is best to carry food supplies with you, as there are only a few stores in Minakami and very few places to buy food besides the mountain huts. Extra warm clothes, waterproofs, and good hiking boots are a must.

TRAILS

The Peak

****

+++

Doai (土合) ⟶ 1.5 kms. 25 mins. ⟶ Tanigawa-dake ropeway (谷川岳ロープウェイ) ⟶ 20 mins. ⟶ Tenjin-daira (天神平) ⟶ 4 kms. 3 hrs. 20 mins. ⟶ Tanigawa-dake (谷川岳) ⟶ 3.5 kms. 3 hrs. ⟶ Machiga-zawa (マチガ沢)

If you leave Tokyo on an early-morning train it is possible to climb

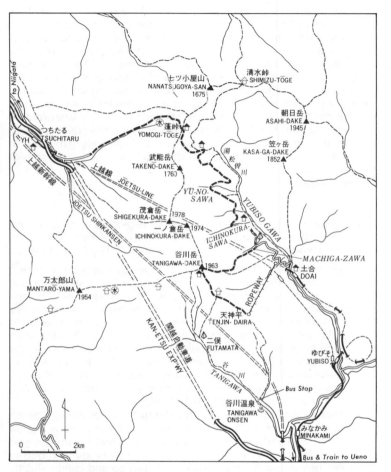

Tanigawa-dake on a day trip, and the climb is made very easy by using
the ropeway. The top station of the ropeway at Tenjin-daira is already
above 1,300 meters and in the alpine zone of creeping pine and bamboo grass. Above the ropeway and the lodge are the ski slopes and ski
lifts. The trail for Tanigawa-dake leads northwest and is fairly easy at
first up to a small hut, but then becomes a steady climb up to the
manned hut just below the peak. In early November when I climbed
the peak, the mountains above 1,200 meters already had a light covering of snow and the signboard near the summit was encrusted with ice
and icicles.

Tanigawa-dake is not the highest peak in these mountains, but there are trails going to the higher peaks along the ridges to the north and west. From the ridges the slopes drop off precipitously into the spectacular valleys of Tanigawa. Instead of returning back down the ropeway, a popular route is down the ridge to the east. This is an open, rocky ridge with some steep sections and good views across to the Tenjin-daira ski slopes. After about an hour's descent from the summit, there is a trail junction with the main trail continuing down the ridge, and the trail to the left descending to Machiga-zawa. The latter route is very steep at first, but then becomes easier as it descends into beech forest and comes out at the stream, road, and campsite. The crags in the valley, visible from the trail on the way down, are popular with rock climbers.

The Watershed

****

+++

Doai (土合) ⟶ 2.5 kms. 50 mins. ⟶ Machiga-zawa (マチガ沢) ⟶ 2 kms. 40 mins. ⟶ Ichinokura-sawa (一ノ倉沢) ⟶ 8 kms. 4 hrs. 15 mins. ⟶ Yomogi-tōge (蓬峠) ⟶ 8 kms. 3 hrs. ⟶ Tsuchitaru (土樽)

The road from Doai Station passes the ropeway station, and then a mountain center soon after, which can be used as a shelter in bad weather, before coming to the campsite at Machiga-zawa. In fine weather many sightseers drive to the end of the road at the next valley of Ichinokura-sawa for one of the best views of mountain scenery in Japan. The valley head of Ichinokura-sawa is filled with snow year-round and sheer rock walls, popular with rock climbers, rise to the ridge between Tanigawa-dake on the left and the higher peak of Ichinokura-dake on the right. This majestic scenery was set against a backdrop of clear, blue skies as I made my way along the track, leaving the cars and most of the sightseers behind.

Contouring around a ridge spur, the dirt track passes through beech forest to the next stream valley at Yū-no-sawa. Here there is a good view of the peaks and a nearby shrine and small cave. Around the next spur a trail descends to the right of the track to two mountain huts in the valley below, but the main track continues on and climbs slightly to the next stream valley at Shibakura-sawa. From here a trail which contours around the valley continues on from the end of the track and climbs gently through beech forest. At the fork, climb to the left and the trail crosses a stream before reaching a junction on a ridge. The trail descending the ridge to the right follows the main valley back down to Doai while the trail to the left climbs to Yomogi-tōge Pass. Climbing this trail you pass a tiny hut after five minutes and then bear left at a fork to climb out of the forest into thick bamboo grass. The trail crosses streams then zigzags up a slope to level off as it comes out on the watershed at the pass (1,529 m.).

Bathed in sunshine the yellow and brown painted wooden hut stood amidst snow-peppered bamboo grass with the supervisor and one or two hikers having a snack outside while enjoying the clear views of the surrounding peaks. The trail down the west side of the pass crosses a stream after ten minutes, and then there are some steep sections as the trail makes its way down to beech and silver birch forest. Keeping to the north side of a valley, the trail eventually descends to the river and levels out at a stand of cedar before coming to a dirt track. This track leads down to a paved road near the new highway, which emerges from a tunnel through the mountains (opened in 1986). The road eventually brings you out at Tsuchitaru Station after crossing a bridge over the river. Hopping on one of the infrequent local trains will take you on a ride through the long tunnel which passes beneath the watershed and mountains you have just climbed, and back to Doai or on towards Tokyo.

22. Beyond the Shrine: Nikko 日光

The mausoleum of Tokugawa Ieyasu is one of the most gorgeously decorated shrines in all of Japan. It is situated on the forested mountain slopes just above the city of Nikko, between the Rinnōji Temple and Futara-san Shrine, both of which predate it. This large temple and shrine area is bounded to the south by the Daiyagawa River, with its vermilion Shinkyō Bridge symbolizing the connecting point between the secular and spiritual worlds. Avenues leading to the shrine are lined with thousands of large cedars.

Nikko first attained recognition after Shōdō, a Buddhist priest, "opened" Futara-san—now known as Nantai-san—the high volcanic peak dominating Nikko and Lake Chūzenji-ko. He was the first man to climb to the summit, in 767, and he built Futara-san Temple on the shores of Lake Chūzenji-ko in 782. This is now the middle shrine of Futara-san, with the upper shrine on the peak, and the lower shrine next to Tōshōgū Shrine, which now overshadows it in splendor. Shōdō's statue can be seen near Rinnōji Temple nearby. Futara-san, also known as Kurokami-yama, has long been a mountain associated with Buddhism, and it was a center for the mountain climbing Shugendō sect until 1635, when the Tōshōgū Shrine was completed. Sixteen thirty-six was the turning point in Nikko's history. This was when it acquired its present name and became a popular destination for pilgrims. Nikko flourished during the Edo period, and on May 17–18 and October 16–17 each year, the Tōshōgū Shrine Festival celebrates this period with processions of people wearing Edo period costumes.

Straddling the borders of Fukushima, Tochigi, Gumma and Niigata Prefectures, Nikko National Park was established in 1934 to protect the natural beauty of the area. It is situated 140 kilometers north of Tokyo, and has the most varied features of all the parks in Japan, with high mountains, spectacular waterfalls, wide plateaus, colorful marshes, and hot spring resorts, as well as the temples and shrines. The largest and most popular area of the park centers on the small city of Nikko, but it includes the Oze area to the northwest and the Kinugawa Valley to the east.

The area is composed of metamorphosed Paleozoic strata, Tertiary and Quaternary volcanics. There are several volcanic peaks in the park, of which Nikko Shirane-san (2,577 m.) is the highest and presently dormant, although eruptions occurred during the Edo period and up to 1952. Nantai-san (2,484 m.), the second highest peak, is an extinct, conical volcano overlooking the city of Nikko and Lake Chūzenji-ko, which was formed by a lava flow blocking the upper valley.

Nikko National Park is mostly forested, with a natural mixed forest of cedar, fir, larch, silver birch, elm, and maple. It is especially popular from mid-October to November, when the kōyō (changing autumn leaves) transforms the mountains into a fiery blaze of reds, oranges and yellows. Marsh plants are found in the valley marshes and alpine flowers grow in the high mountains.

Bird life is also very rich and varied, with forest birds such as the woodpecker, jay, thrush, tit, and warbler. Summer visitors include the flycatcher, martin, robin, and cuckoo. Water birds found here include the dipper, wagtail, stonechat, and wren, as well as mallards and other ducks, which are winter visitors. Snipe and bunting are found on the more open plains.

Wildlife is fairly abundant, with deer, black bear, fox, raccoon and squirrel, as well as smaller mammals. There is a hunting season from November to February, when copper pheasants, wild duck, quail, wild boar, and rabbits are hunted. Fishing is popular in the lakes and rivers from May to September, and rainbow trout is a local delicacy.

October usually sees the first snow in the mountains, and deep snow lies until May. Nikko is a popular skiing and ice skating resort in winter. Hiking is best in July and August, but the cooler months from September to November are also good. There are many well-marked trails in the park, offering interesting hikes by the lakes, marshes, in the valleys, and to the peaks.

ACCESS

The best way of reaching Nikko from Tokyo is by the private Tobu Line from Asakusa. Express trains take 1 hour 55 minutes, and seats must be reserved. Rapid trains take two hours ten minutes and are much cheaper. If you are going to spend a few days at Nikko and intend to use the Tobu bus service, you can make great savings by buying a "Nikko Free Pass," valid for four days and allowing unlimited use of buses as far as Yumoto and Kinugawa Valley, as well as one return journey from Tokyo. The JR Nikko Line runs from Utsunomiya, but is usually less convenient and more expensive.

ACCOMMODATION

Nikko City, Chūzenji Onsen, and Yumoto have many hotels, ryokan, and minshuku. Inquiries can be made at the information offices of the Tobu Nikko and JR Nikko stations. There are two youth hostels in Nikko, both about twenty minutes' walk from either station. Nikko Youth Hostel (Tel: 0288-54-1013) and Nikko Daiyagawa Youth Hostel (Tel: 0288-54-1974). The park is also well supplied with campsites—usually only open during the months of July and August, however. Three campsites are located just north of Nikko City, two on the road to Kirifuri Kōgen, four on the shores of Lake Chūzenji-ko, one at Yumoto, and one in the valley below Tarō-san at Kōtoku. There are also a few small mountain huts in the mountains.

TRAILS

A Valley Hike

****

++

Ryūzu-no-taki (竜頭の滝) ⟶ 2 kms. 40 mins. ⟶ Senjō-ga-hara (戦場ヶ原) ⟶ 4 kms. 1 hr. 40 mins. ⟶ Yudaki (湯滝) ⟶ 2 kms. 40 mins. ⟶ Yumoto (湯元)

The very picturesque valley hike starts from the bottom of Ryūzu-no-taki, which is named after the crouching dragon shape of the falls as they cascade down a rocky course. It is near the main road and can be reached easily by bus from Nikko and Chūzenji Onsen. Near the bottom of the falls is the small Ryūzu Kannon Shrine, containing a statue of Buddha sitting on a dragon. Next to the shrine is a soba restaurant and an open-air coffee shop overlooking the beautiful double falls at the bottom of Ryūzu-no-taki. This is my favorite Nikko resting place.

The trail climbs up the east side of the falls, away from the shrine and along the course of the old road, before coming to a bridge at the main road, from where there is a good view of Lake Chūzenji-ko. From here it is a nice walk along the east bank of Yugawa River through larch forest to the southern end of Senjō-ga-hara Plain.

Wooden planks are laid out on the trail across the open, marshy plain scattered with birch trees, and there is a good view of Nantai-san and the surrounding mountains. After crossing a small bridge over the Yugawa River, which flows across the plain, the trail comes to Izumiyado-ike (泉門池)—a small pond on the northwestern edge of the plain. From here the trail crosses another bridge and follows the Yugawa River through forest to the bottom of Yudaki Falls.

A stepped trail climbs up the east side of the falls from the observation area below, and comes out at the road and Lake Yunoko. The view from the top of the spectacular Yudaki Falls, which cascade over a rocky precipice at the southern end of Lake Yunoko, takes in the entire Senjō-ga-hara Plain below and Nantai-san rising beyond it.

Yumoto hot spring resort on the northern shore of Lake Yunoko is best reached by the trail around the western shore through cedar and cypress forest. Several large lodges and ryokan are found at Yumoto, which sits at the valley head and is the terminus for buses from Nikko. A large natural hot spring pond sends steam into the air just behind the lodge area. A campsite is located on a grassy area at the bottom of the ski slopes behind the Nikko Yumoto Lodge.

A Mountain Hike
****
++++

Yumoto (湯元) —→ 4 kms. 2 hrs. 30 mins. —→ Maeshirane-san (前白根山) —→ 3 kms. 1 hr. 15 mins. —→ Shirane-san (白根山) —→ 3 kms. 1 hr. 15 mins. —→ Goshiki-yama (五色山) —→ 4.5 kms. 2 hrs. —→ Yumoto

Shirane-san (2,678 m.), is the highest peak in Nikko National Park, and offers the most scenic mountain hiking with its two picturesque mountain lakes. As its name implies, the mountain is snow-covered much of the year, because it is exposed to the winter monsoon blowing across the Japan Sea. My first attempt to climb it was in May, when the mountain was still covered in deep, melting snow, and I turned back long before the summit due to the poor hiking conditions. A second attempt in September was much more successful.

Yumoto is the best base for climbing Shirane-san, with two trails allowing a circular route to be taken. The easier trail climbs up the ski slopes next to the ski lifts and then climbs steeply through forest on a trail laced with tree roots. After reaching the top of the ridge, it is a gentler climb to the summit of Maeshirane-san (2,370 m.). From this exposed summit there is a good view of Lake Goshiki-numa nestling in an enclosed basin below the towering, rocky peak of Shirane-san.

A trail leads steeply down to this lake and another trail goes directly to the small mountain hut below Shirane-san. Either way can be taken to reach the hut, which has a raised wooden floor large enough to sleep about twenty people. From here, the trail leads up a broad valley, before climbing steeply through silver birch forest on the main slope up to the peak. Toward the top the trail levels off over several rocky peaks with alpine vegetation. The first peak has a miniature shrine on it, but this is not the summit. You must descend and climb again to the rocky summit marked by a wooden signboard. In fine weather there are views of Nantai-san to the southeast and Hiuchi-ga-take in the Oze area to the north.

Continuing north over the peak the trail goes down a gully—care should be taken here not to descend the wrong gully. Below can be seen the small, picturesque pond of Midaga-ike. The trail comes out at the pond and passes its southern end, from where one trail goes to Goshiki-numa and the other forks left to Goshiki-yama. It is an easy hike, with good views of the lake and Shirane's peak, along the ridge to the top of Goshiki-yama.

Descending from the peak along the ridge to the northeast, take the small trail to the right at the first junction. Thick bamboo grass overgrows the trail in places as it descends steeply through pine, fir and birch forest. The trail divides lower down, and both lead back into Yumoto.

23. The Marsh in the Mountains: Oze 尾瀬

Crowds of hikers and tourists descend (or ascend) on the marshes of Oze with the melting of the snow and the coming of spring in late May and early June, for the purpose of seeing the marshes burst into color with a particular marsh plant. Skunk cabbage, the unflattering English name for the plant, is known as *mizubashō* in Japanese, and while still beneath the snow this sturdy species pushes its green leaves and white or yellowish flowers up out of the marsh to cover Oze with color as soon as the snow recedes. The spectacle at Oze is so popular with the Japanese that wooden planked trails have been laid out over the marshes and these become packed solid with lines of shuffling hikers who wish to see the annual display. Unless you like being jostled along on a human conveyor belt I do not recommend visiting Oze at the height of the skunk cabbage season.

To avoid the crowds I made my trip during the Golden Week holidays at the beginning of May, when the marshes were still mostly covered with snow. Cross-country skiers were squeezing the last runs of the season out of their winter paradise, while thawing patches of marsh were growing larger each day, and the marsh flowers were already making their debut. Bright spring sunshine reflected from the snow, giving me an early summer suntan during my two-day trek across the marshes on the clearly marked, not-yet-crowded trails.

Oze is the largest mountain marsh in Japan, extending for about five kilometers east-west and two kilometers north-south. The marshy plain is situated at an altitude of about 1,400 meters on the Japan Sea side of the watershed, about 150 kilometers north of Tokyo, and forms part of Nikko National Park. The area is composed of Paleozoic sedimentary strata with Tertiary and Quaternary volcanics. The marsh was formed as a result of a lava flow from the volcanic Hiuchi-ga-take (2,360 m.), whose soaring peak dominates the marshes, blocking the upper part of the valley. There are hot springs in the area, one of which is located on the old lava flow at the northern edge of the marsh, below the western slopes of Hiuchi-ga-take. Four kilometers east of the Oze-ga-hara marshy plain and south of Hiuchi-ga-take is the subalpine marshy lake of Oze-numa at an altitude of about 1,650 meters. The edge of the marshes and lower mountain slopes are forested with silver birch, beech, and conifers, but the higher slopes and peaks are above the tree line in the alpine zone. A variety of wildlife may be seen in the area, including deer, squirrels, chipmunks, martens, and weasels.

The hiking route described here can be done on a two-day trip from Tokyo and crosses the marshes of Oze-ga-hara and Oze-numa, taking in the main sights. However, there are several hiking trails in the mountains which are less frequented, and Shibutsu-san to the west and Hiuchi-ga-take to the north can be climbed for panoramic views of the marshes. Boots should be worn, specially if you intend to climb the peaks, and waterproofs should always be carried, as rain can occur at any time from April to November, while winter conditions prevail for the other months.

ACCESS

From Tokyo the best approach is by train from Ueno Station to Numata, which takes about three hours by ordinary train. Then transfer to the bus for Tokura and Ōshimizu. The bus terminal at Ōshimizu is the end point of the hike described here, and is the best access point for Oze-numa. Tokura is the best access point for Oze-ga-hara, and from this small village a minibus service runs up to Hatomachi-tōge from where it is an easy walk down to the marshes. It is possible, but a little more difficult, to reach Oze from Niigata or Fukushima to the north, and there are also trails over the mountains from the main part of Nikko National Park to the southeast involving a one- or two-day hike.

ACCOMMODATION

Oze Tokura Youth Hostel (Tel: 0278-58-7421) is located in the village of Tokura, very near the bus stop, and several mountain huts are located in the marsh area, but these are often fully booked in summer so reservations should be made from May to September. The adventurous may prefer camping, and there are four evenly spaced campsites in the area at Yama-no-hana and Jūjiro on the marshes, on the eastern shore of Oze-numa, and a kilometer east of Ōshimizu. Meals and drinks are available at the mountain huts at the usual inflated prices, so it is best to carry your own supplies from Tokyo or Numata.

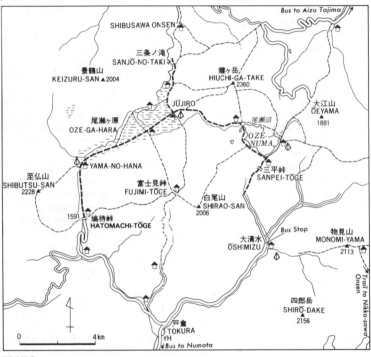

TRAILS

****
++

Hatomachi-tōge (鳩待峠) ⟶ 3.3 kms. 1 hr. 15 mins. ⟶ Yama-no-hana (山ノ鼻) ⟶ 6 kms. 2 hrs. 30 mins. ⟶ Jūjiro (十字路) ⟶ 4 kms. 1 hr. 30 mins. ⟶ Sanjō-no-taki (三條の滝) ⟶ 4 kms. 2 hrs. ⟶ Jūjiro ⟶ 4 kms. 2 hrs. 30 mins. ⟶ Oze-numa (尾瀬沼) ⟶ 9 kms. 3 hrs. 30 mins. ⟶ Ōshimizu (大清水)

It was a sunny day in early May when I arrived with a friend at Hatomachi-tōge after the 30-minute minibus ride up to the pass from the village of Tokura. We were surprised to see so many people hanging around the lodge and restaurant at the snow-covered pass; a mixture of late skiers and early hikers. Originally we had planned to take the ridge trail up from the pass to the summit of Shibutsu-san (2,228 m.), and then descend to the marsh at Yama-no-hana, but this route was very hard going through soft snow, so we opted for the easy trail directly down to the marsh. It was disappointing to miss the panoramic view of the marshes from Shibutsu-san, but a leisurely hike down through the snowy forest of beech and silver birch brought us to Yama-no-hana with plenty of time to spare.

A campsite of colorful tents was pitched on the snow-covered marsh near the five mountain huts at Yama-no-hana, at one of which we had a reservation. After checking in there was time before dinner to make a short hike around the trail loop across the western end of the marsh to get our first look at the marsh vegetation, appearing in the places where the snow had thawed out in the strong spring sunshine. The surrounding forested slopes rose to the snowy peak of Shibutsu-san to the southwest, while over the flat marshes to the northeast, across which glided one or two cross-country skiers, towered the rocky peak of Hiuchi-ga-take.

Next morning we set off on the wooden-planked trail in the direction of Hiuchi-ga-take and made the six-kilometer hike across the main part of the marshes. Hundreds of skunk cabbages were already flowering in thawed-out patches, and streams of water were flowing across the marshes and beneath the planks of the trail. Staying on the main trail we passed one wooden mountain hut on a dry part of the marsh before coming to Jūjiro, where there are several huts, a campsite, souvenir shops, and a coffee shop. This hiker's, or skier's, village is situated right on the eastern edge of the marsh where the forested slopes start rising to the peak of Hiuchi-ga-take.

After the luxury of drinking coffee in the coffee shop while gazing out over the flat, snowy marshscape, we decided to make a side excursion northward to the hot spring and waterfall before continuing on to Oze-numa. It is an easy walk along the edge of the marsh to two huts, one of which has a small bath supplied with warm spring water from beneath Hiuchi-ga-take. Lava flowing from the volcano blocked the upper valley in this area. The trail then descends steeply through forest, passing by the cascades above the waterfall, before coming to a picnic area at a spot with a good view of Sanjō-no-taki Falls. Plummeting into the deep gorge below, the roaring white water draining from the marshes makes a spectacular sight well worth the effort of side-trekking from Jūjiro.

From the hot spring, and near Jūjiro, there are two trails which climb directly up the forested slopes to the rocky alpine peak of Hiuchi-ga-take, taking about three or four hours to climb, with other trails from the peak to Oze-numa, but our plans to cross the marshes did not allow time to climb this peak. So we took the trail climbing gently through beech and silver birch forest from Jūjiro to Oze-numa. This very pleasant and easy hike brought us to a small mountain hut just before reaching the wide expanse of Lake Oze-numa, which was surrounded by forested slopes and dominated by Hiuchi-ga-take's volcanic peak to the north. There were very few hikers along the scenic trail around the western shores of the lake as we made our way to the group of huts on the southern shore.

It was already late afternoon and one or two hikers were checking into the huts as we climbed up the snow-covered trail to Sanpei-tōge. Continuing over the pass, the trail descends to a forestry track which winds its way down to Ōshimizu Village, but the trail crosses the track and cuts out a long loop to emerge back on the track at a bridge over the river in the lower valley. Crossing the bridge it is a long walk down the dirt track along the valley to Ōshimizu Village, where there is a restaurant, shop, accommodation, and the bus terminal for Numata. Opposite the restaurant and shop a bridge across the river leads to the forestry track for the campsite about one kilometer away. The next morning my friend returned by bus to Numata and back to Tokyo, while I took to the hills again on a long trek over the mountains to Yumoto and the Nikko area.

Tohoku: The Back Country

Haguro-san Pagoda (Dewa Sanzan)

The mountainous district of Northern Honshu is relatively unpopulated, less developed than the southern parts of Japan, and offers some excellent hiking amidst unspoiled natural scenery. Down the center of Tohoku runs the Ōu mountain range, which divides the district into the Pacific and Japan Sea sides. To the northeast the Kitami Mountains make Iwate Prefecture almost entirely mountainous down to the Rikuchū Coast, so that it is called the Tibet of Japan. To the west the Dewa and Echigo mountains parallel the Japan Sea coast. Most of Tohoku's mountains are of volcanic origin, with widespread Tertiary and Quaternary volcanics, and acidic to intermediate intrusive rocks. Paleozoic and Mesozoic sedimentary rocks are mainly found on the Rikuchū Coast. To the north, the lakes Towada-ko and Tazawa-ko are situated in large volcanic calderas.

The north-south orientation of the mountains causes a difference in weather during the winter monsoon between the Japan Sea and Pacific sides of Tohoku. On the Japan Sea coast and mountains winters are very long and cold, with heavy snowfalls. The Pacific coast has relatively little snow.

Most of the region is covered by deciduous broadleaf forest dominated by beech with coniferous forest on the higher slopes and alpine vegetation on the high peaks. Wildlife includes the black bear (*tsukinowaguma*), macaque monkey (*nihonzaru*) the northernmost monkey in the world, and the serow (*kamoshika*) found on the higher mountains of the Asahi Range. Smaller mammals such as squirrels, rabbits, and chipmunks are commonly seen in the region.

The main areas of interest center on the three national parks of the district. Towada-Hachimantai National Park in the north includes Lake Towada-ko caldera with the volcanic Hakkōda mountains to the north, and the Hachimantai plateau area extending to the volcanic peak of Iwate-san (2,041 m.) to the south. Rikuchū Kaigan National Park along the coast of Iwate Prefecture has an uplifted coast of cliffs to the north, and a submerged ria coast to the south. Bandai-Asahi National Park is split into three parts with the Asahi and Dewa Sanzan mountains to the north, the Iide Mountains to the southwest, and the volcanic mountains of Bandai, Azuma, and Adatara to the south. Apart from the national parks, there are several quasi-national parks and prefectural parks in the district, many of which include mountainous areas excellent for hiking. The best of these are Chōkai Quasi-National Park, Kurikoma Quasi-National Park, and Zao Quasi-National Park.

ACCESS

By Rail: The Tohoku Shinkansen runs from Ueno Station in Tokyo as far as Morioka in northern Tohoku, and is a fast, convenient way of reaching Tohoku with trains running approximately every 30 minutes between 0600 and 2030. Other main lines are the Tohoku Honsen between Sendai and Aomori, the Ōu Honsen, which runs west of the Ōu Mountains between Fukushima and Aomori, and the Uetsu Honsen along the Japan Sea coast between Niigata and Akita. Smaller lines make most of Tohoku accessible by train. Direct trains on the Tobu/ Yagan Tetsudo lines leave Asakusa for Aizu Kōgen about seven times a day. The train fare between Tokyo and Aomori taking the Shinkansen as far as Morioka is about ¥16,700 (6 hours), whereas the basic fare for local trains is about ¥10,000. The Shinkansen fare between Tokyo and Sendai is about ¥10,390 (2 hours), whereas the basic fare is about ¥5,670.

By Road: The Tohoku Expressway starting from Urawa north of Tokyo connects Tokyo and Aomori. Morioka is a six-hour drive on the Expressway from Tokyo. Many of the local and mountain roads in the district are closed during the winter. Bus services are fairly frequent during the summer and provide access to the mountain and park areas. However, schedules change with the season, and services are often suspended during the winter.

ACCOMMODATION

Tohoku is fairly well supplied with youth hostels in most of the main cities and park areas. The parks and mountains have a number of campsites, and there are mountain huts in most of the mountain parks.

Sendai, the largest city in Tohoku, has four youth hostels; Sendai Chitose Youth Hostel (Tel: 022-222-6329) is a 17-minute walk from Sendai Station; Sendai Akamon Youth Hostel (Tel: 022-264-1405) is a 40-minute walk from the station, or buses 9 and 16 can be taken from near the station; Sendai Onnai Youth Hostel (Tel: 022-234-3922) is a 20-minute walk from Kita Sendai Station; Sendai Dōchū-an Youth Hostel (Tel: 022-247-0511) is about a 10-minute walk from Nagamachi Station to the south of Sendai Station.

Three inexpensive inns in Sendai are: Sumire Ryokan, 1-30-5, Ichiban-cho, Sendai (Tel: 022-222-8100) a ten-minute walk from the station (about ¥5,500 single). Takenaka Ryokan, 2-9-23 Chuo, Sendai (Tel: 022-225-6771) twelve minutes' walk from the station (about

¥7,000 single). Japanese Inn Aisaki, 5-6 Kitame-machi, Sendai (Tel: 022-264-0700) ten minutes' walk from the station (about ¥4,500 single).

A convenient, low-priced place to stay in Morioka is Ryokan Kumagai (Tel: 0196-51-3020), located eight minutes' walk from the station. Morioka Youth Hostel (Tel: 0196-62-2220) is a 15-minute bus ride from Morioka Station. Two minutes from Aomori Station is Hotel Okuta (Tel: 0177-22-2929), an inexpensive business hotel.

24. The Explosive Killer: Bandai-san 磐梯山

After a long period of inactivity Bandai suddenly erupted on July 15, 1888, blowing off one-third of the mountain and forming a large, new crater on the north side of the volcano. In the explosions and earthquake, the landscape north of the volcano was transformed, villages were obliterated, and 477 people lost their lives. There were no lava flows from the eruption, but rocks and debris from the explosions and landslides blocked rivers and streams to create the present Ura Bandai scenery of lakes, ponds, and marshes, which is so popular with tourists. Since its explosive display one hundred years ago Bandai has settled back into inactivity again, with only a few steaming vents left in the crater.

Situated about 240 kilometers ENE of Tokyo in Fukushima Prefecture, Bandai-san forms part of the Bandai-Asahi National Park. The area's scenery, with the large Lake Inawashiro-ko to the south, is dramatic. The historic towns of Aizu Wakamatsu and Kitakata are to the southwest, and there is more volcanic scenery in the Azuma and Adatara areas to the north and east. Crowds of tourists visit Bandai and the surrounding sights at weekends and holidays from May to November, and they usually converge on the beautiful five-colored marshes of Goshiki-numa at Ura Bandai, where a well-worn trail passes the colored marshes or ponds set amidst green forest north of Bandai-san. The different colors of the ponds are due to minerals in the water from the mineral-rich volcanic rocks, and several hot spring resorts in the area utilize the natural subterranean hot spring waters.

The lower mountain slopes are forested with mixed deciduous and coniferous forests which abound in *sansai* (mountain vegetables), and in spring people may be seen collecting such delicacies as *takénoko* (bamboo shoots), *warabi* (bracken), *taranome* (angelica), and *fuki* (butterbur). Restaurants in the area often serve some of these local wild vegetables either cooked as tempura or served with noodles. The higher mountain slopes are subalpine with mountain cherry (*yamazakura*) blossoming in May and azalea flowering in May and June. Deep snow covers the area during the winter when the slopes of Bandai become a playground for skiers with one ski resort on the south and another on the north side of the mountain.

ACCESS

Frequent trains run from Ueno Station in Tokyo north via Kōriyama to Inawashiro and Aizu Wakamatsu. Some trains run direct, otherwise it is necessary to change at Kōriyama. Inawashiro Station is the best for approaching Bandai-san, with buses running from the station to Ura Bandai passing the small village at Kawakami Onsen, which is the start of the route described here, and continuing on to Goshiki-numa Iriguchi—the entrance to the trail through the five-colored marshes area. From the old castle town of Aizu Wakamatsu, less frequent bus services run along the Gold Line Toll Road west of Bandai-san to Ura Bandai, passing Bandai-machi at the highest point on the road, where there is a large car park and the start of the easiest and fastest trail leading directly up Bandai-san.

ACCOMMODATION

Two youth hostels are conveniently located to climb Bandai-san and both can be reached by bus from Inawashiro Station. Bandai Yūai Sansō Youth Hostel (Tel: 0242-62-3424) is close to the ski slopes on the southeastern slopes of Bandai-san, and Ura Bandai Youth Hostel (Tel: 0241-32-2811) is located near Goshiki-numa Iriguchi right next to the popular marsh area. Several minshuku, ryokan and hot spring resorts are found in the area, and there is one small mountain hut 200 meters below the peak of Bandai-san. Campsites are found around the shores of Lake Hibara-ko north of Bandai-san in the Ura Bandai area. Food supplies for hiking can be picked up at Inawashiro or Aizu Wakamatsu. There are stores in the small villages and resorts at Ura Bandai, but prices are higher there. It is not necessary to carry much water on the hike as there is a freshwater spring at the hut just below Bandai's peak.

TRAILS

**
+ + +

Kawakami Onsen (川上温泉) ⟶ 6.5 kms. 3 hrs. 10 mins. ⟶ Kōbōshimizu Goya (弘法清水小屋) ⟶ 0.5 kms. 30 mins. ⟶ Bandai-san (磐梯山) ⟶ 2.5 kms. 1 hr. 30 mins. ⟶ Naka-no-yu (中ノ湯) ⟶ 5.5 kms. 2 hrs. 15 mins. ⟶ Ura Bandai (裏磐梯) ⟶ 3 kms. 1 hr. ⟶ Goshiki-numa (五色沼)

Several trails climb Bandai-san, which can easily be climbed in one day, but the most interesting route is from Ura Bandai via the crater—allowing spectacular views of the crater walls below the peak and the site of the last volcanic explosion. The hike described here climbs and descends the two trails on the north side of Bandai with easy access to the popular trail through the Goshiki-numa area.

Arriving at Kawakami Onsen in the morning, after a very early start from Tokyo, two of us decided to take advantage of the good weather and make an immediate assault on Bandai-san. At first we had difficul-

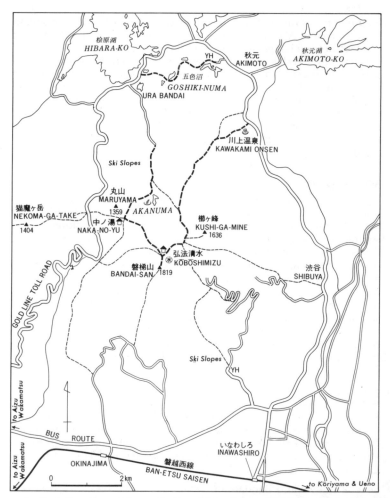

ty finding the start of the trail, but taking the small road which passes the main hotel in the village, we found a narrow trail leading off to the right and followed it up through mixed forest. After twenty minutes this trail joined another one which also climbs up from Kawakami Onsen. Continuing up through forest we came to a steep slope of loose volcanic rock which we scrambled up to emerge at the edge of the main crater. Above the flat crater floor, sparsely forested with pine and fir, rose walls of red and yellow lava and ash, with the peak of Bandai-san towering over the highest cliffs on the far side of the caldera.

Levelling off across the caldera floor the trail crosses open sandy flats. It is an eerie experience to cross the bottom of this enclosed, dish-like caldera—the site of the powerful explosion. To the west, steam vents in the lava cliffs above the small red lake of Akanuma could be seen, sending white streaks into the air—smoldering remains of the catastrophe. At a trail junction on the crater floor the trail to the right descends to the ski slopes and then down to Ura Bandai. The trail left is difficult to follow as it passes over yellow volcanic rocks, but rock cairns and paint marks lead up to the steep lava cliffs where steps have been made up to the top of the crater rim. My companion, not so used to hiking, became a little winded on this climb so I waited and enjoyed the view over the caldera we had just crossed, with the red lake of Akanuma below and the large Lake Hibara-ko stretching out in the haze to the north. To the east the craggy peak of Kushi-ga-mine (1,636 m.) pierced the sky, while to the southwest rose the main peak of Bandai-san (1,819 m.), with the hut just visible on its lower slopes.

The trail to Kōbōshimizu Hut follows the top of the ridge on the crater rim and passes a trail descending to some small, picturesque lakes to the southeast. There is a small freshwater spring on the way to the hut, but the spring at the hut is much better. A few other climbers were resting by the small hut and nearby souvenir shop as we arrived, and my companion decided to rest there while I made the steep climb to the summit and returned back to the hut. The slopes around the summit were covered in pink blossoming mountain cherry as I made my way to the rocky peak, where a group of climbers was enjoying the view from a small stone shrine on the top. To the south stretched the flat expanse of Lake Inawashiro-ko, below the peak to the east nestled small mountain lakes, and northeast jutted the tooth-like peak of Kushi-ga-mine.

Returning, I woke my companion, who was lying asleep in the sun at the hut, and we set off towards Naka-no-yu over an easy trail through bushy shrubs, including the bright pink flowering azalea, before descending steeply to the hot spring and ryokan. Just below the ryokan at Naka-no-yu a trail branches off for Bandai-machi on the Gold Line Toll Road. This is the easiest route up and down Bandai and on the wide trail down to the road people may be seen picking sansai in the forest. We took the trail which descends into the caldera and passes by the red lake of Akanuma with steam vents in the lava cliffs of its southern shore. It was then an easy walk to the top of the ski slopes and down to a large deserted ski lodge from where a dirt track runs down to the shore of Lake Hibara-ko and Ura Bandai.

Crowds of tourists were milling around the souvenir shops, restaurants, and hotels at Ura Bandai as we took the well-worn trail from there through the forest and marshes of Goshiki-numa. There are actually more than five marshes at Goshiki-numa, and some of them are more like ponds or small lakes than marshes, as the name implies. However, the subtly different shades of the marshes make for a delightful walk along the three-kilometer trail to Goshiki-numa Iriguchi. Here the largest marsh of Bishamon Numa, popular as a boating lake from spring to autumn, shimmers blue-green beneath the backdrop of Bandai's peak and the caldera whose explosion one hundred years ago created it.

25. Three Sacred Peaks: Dewa Sanzan 出羽三山

The large shrine and associated buildings amidst tall, dark cedars on the mountain of Haguro-san, one of the three peaks of Dewa, mark this as one of the most important centers for the Shugendō sect of mountain ascetics. Together with Ōmine-san on the Kii Peninsula, Haguro-san and the two higher peaks of Gassan and Yudono-san are imbued with mystery and special powers by the yamabushi and pilgrims who can be seen going through their paces over these mountains. A fascinating description of the practices still exercised by the Shugendō mountain faith priests and pilgrims can be found in Carmen Blacker's book *The Catalpa Bow*, and for a closer look at what goes on the best time to visit Haguro-san is August 24 through 30, when the annual *shugyō* or pilgrimage takes place. On a hike over these mountains in summer you will almost certainly meet groups of white-clad pilgrims, and priests in colorful costumes. A pilgrimage usually takes in all three mountains: the large shrine precincts on Haguro-san, the small shrine perched on the highest peak of Gassan (1,980 m.), and the large natural rock shrine on the northern side of Yudono-san (湯殿山), from which natural hot spring water flows.

Situated in the northern part of the Bandai-Asahi National Park, the three peaks are found in the prefecture of Yamagata but derive their name from the old northern province of Dewa. The peaks are of volcanic origin, with the highest peak of Gassan formed as a result of the activity of a now extinct shield-shaped volcano. To the south the larger mountain area of Asahi-dake (朝日岳 1,870 m.), and the higher mountains of Iide-san (飯豊山 2,128 m.), also form part of the same park and offer some remoter, exciting hiking country. These mountains are covered with virgin beech forests on their lower slopes, coniferous forests higher up, and alpine vegetation on the peaks. Gassan is famous for its alpine flora, with a variety of flowers bringing color to its slopes in late June and July. The remoter mountains to the south are better for wildlife where black bear, serow, monkey, and deer may be seen. As these mountains face the Japan Sea they get the full force of the winter northwesterly monsoon, which brings heavy snowfalls and year-round snow lying in sheltered parts of the alpine zone. Gassan is well-known for its midsummer ski slopes, where skiers may be seen practicing on short runs below its peak up to August.

ACCESS

The mountains of Dewa Sanzan are best approached from the town of Tsuruoka, situated on the main Uetsu Honsen between Niigata and Akita, from where buses operate to Haguro-san and continue up to the end of the road at the Eighth Stage of Gassan. This is the easiest way to reach the shrine at Haguro-san, and the trail from the car park at the Eighth Stage leads up to the summit of Gassan, passing the marshes of Mida-ga-hara soon after the start. Another bus service from Tsuruoka operates to Yudono-san, with the shrine and hot spring a thirty-minute walk up the road from the bus terminus. The mountains can also be approached from Yamagata City with the main road from there to Tsuruoka passing south of the mountains and bus services operating via the village of Shizu up to Ubazawa where there is a mountain chairlift and trails to Gassan. As I was travelling from Tokyo I took the latter route via Yamagata City and started hiking up Gassan from Ubazawa, then descended to the Eighth Stage and down to Haguro-san. The hiking route described here takes in the main sights except for the shrine at Yudono-san, but I think the scenic climb through flowery meadows from Ubazawa makes up for this omission or alternatively the chairlift can be taken to make the climb easier.

ACCOMMODATION

There are many mountain huts in the Shizu and Ubazawa area, and several in the mountains, which provide accommodation and meals. At Haguro-san there is minshuku and ryokan accommodation in the village of Tōge. There are no convenient campsites in these mountains, and the area is also not well supplied with youth hostels—the nearest being Tsuruoka Youth Hostel (Tel: 0235-73-3205), a fifteen-minute walk from Sanze Station, west of Tsuruoka. Food supplies for the hike should be picked up in Tsuruoka or Yamagata, although small stores and restaurants are found in the villages below the mountains. The trails are not too demanding so reasonably strong footwear is adequate, but warm clothes and waterproofs are essential as the weather can turn cold and wet even in midsummer.

TRAILS

****
++++

Ubazawa (姥沢) ⟶ 4.5 kms. 2 hrs. 50 mins. ⟶ Gassan (月山) ⟶ 5 kms. 2 hrs. 30 mins. ⟶ Mida-ga-hara (弥陀ヶ原) ⟶ bus 1 hr. ⟶ Haguro-san (羽黒山)

It was a sunny morning in August when I arrived at the Ubazawa Mountain Hut after passing the winter ski resort area at Shizu, and just up the

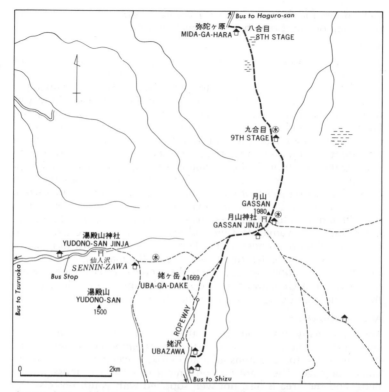

dirt track I could see the chairlift carrying hikers and skiers up the bamboo-covered slopes of Uba-ga-dake. After asking at the large hut I found the start of the trail just behind the building and set off on the climb to Gassan. Keeping to the west of a green valley the muddy trail passed through beech forest with bamboo grass undergrowth. Streams crossed the trail and many marshy areas were covered with alpine flowers as the trail climbed gently out of the forest into open alpine scenery, and the peak of Gassan rose at the head of the valley.

Coming up to the junction with the main trail from the top of the chairlift, visible on the ridge to the southwest, I joined the crowds of hikers and skiers making their way up to a large year-round snow patch. Here skiers practiced down 100-meter runs as mist rose and blew over the cold snow. Reaching the ridge above the snow slopes, the trail west leads to Uba-ga-dake and Yudono-san, but the trail east climbs a steep rocky slope up to a mountain hut. On their way down from the summit I met a small group of pilgrims who must have

166

climbed over from Haguro-san. Climbing past the hut I came out on a flat summit with many rock cairns, but this was not the top of Gassan which I could see a little further on, topped by its shrine. A ten-minute walk brought me to the shrine after passing another mountain hut where food and drinks were being sold. The wooden shrine of Gassan is built on a huge pile of rocks sitting on top of the conical peak, and at the entrance sat a priest collecting a ¥300 entrance fee. A similarly extortionate practice can be encountered at Tateyama. Although it was August the wind was cold on the summit and groups of hikers huddled for warmth in the hut while others took in the views to Uba-ga-dake and Yudono-san.

Going around the back of the shrine below the eastern side of the summit rock pile, the trail is very rocky as it descends through open alpine scenery with the picturesque Omowashi-hara plateau dotted with small ponds to the east. The trail descends gently to the mountain hut at the Ninth Stage, and continues down to an area of small ponds and marshes at Mida-ga-hara. Here wooden planked trails have been laid out around the plateau to allow viewing of the marsh plants and alpine flowers in this wide, open area. Descending from the marshes, the trail passes a small shrine, mountain hut, and restaurant before coming out at the car park at the Eighth Stage where there is a large rest house, shop and restaurant.

The bus from the Eighth Stage of Gassan winds its way down the road to Haguro-san, which is rather a ridge than a mountain, and you can either get off near the shrine at the top, where the bus stops at a large hotel, or at Tōge Village at the bottom of the hill. As I was to stay at a ryokan in Tōge I got off there, and later made the long climb up the 2,446 stone steps through the cedar forest to the large thatched shrine on the top. A large concrete torii, the largest in Tohoku, marks the start of the climb from the village. It is an interesting climb through the dark forest of ancient cedar with a large, old pagoda, shrine buildings and stone statues along the way. Groups of pilgrims wearing straw sandals and hats, and carrying wooden staffs, were being led by the more colorful yamabushi or mountain priests as I made my way up to the impressive shrine on the summit. In Tōge the many rest houses for pilgrims were alive with voices of suppressed excitement, and I came away with the impression that Japan's mountain faith is far from dead.

26. A Plateau and a Fuji: Hachimantai and Iwate-san
八幡平/岩手山

Forming the southern part of the Towada-Hachimantai National Park, the plateau and peaks from Hachimantai to Iwate-san offer some exciting hiking through beautiful volcanic scenery. The conical stratovolcano of Iwate-san, which looms over the city of Morioka and the surrounding area of Iwate Prefecture, is known as Tohoku's Fuji and, at 2,041 meters, is Northern Tohoku's highest peak. Many volcanic features may be seen in the area, including the lava flow at Yakibashiri on the eastern slopes of Iwate-san, the deep crater on its summit, the crater lakes at Hachimantai, steaming vents and bubbling mud pools at Tōshichi Onsen, and countless hot spring resorts. Japan's first geothermal power plant was built in 1966 at Matsukawa Onsen in the valley northwest of Iwate-san.

The mountains are mostly forested with conifers such as pine, spruce, and fir, with alpine vegetation growing on the higher slopes. Many small ponds and marshes in the mountains, especially in the Hachimantai area, offer wonderful scenery with a rich variety of flora. Wildlife which may be seen on a hike through the area includes deer, fox, chipmunks, squirrels, and black bear in the remoter parts. Winters are long in these mountains, and the road to Hachimantai is closed from November to April, when the lower slopes become a skier's playground. The best time for hiking is July and August, when the snow has gone and alpine flowers adorn the mountaintop marshes.

ACCESS

It is possible to climb Iwate-san in one day from Morioka by taking the bus up the slopes to the chairlifts, which climb Ōkura-san from the hot spring, campground, and ski slopes at the Iwate-san Roku Kokumin Kyūkamura. Hachimantai can also be visited for a one-day hike around its scenic trails by taking a bus up to Mikaeri-tōge via the Aspete Line toll road. These buses can be taken from three stations: Morioka, Ōbuke (the nearest convenient station on the Hanawa Line), and Lake Tazawa-ko (the bus from the town runs via the lake). On my visit to the mountains in August I approached from Lake Tazawa-ko, where I had spent a pleasant day on the shores of Japan's deepest and second most transparent lake after Lake Mashū-ko in Hokkaido. I took the bus up to the pass at Hachimantai and hiked from there across the long ridge of peaks to Iwate-san, descending the steep volcanic ash slopes on the northeastern side to the lava flow of Yakibashiri. Hence the route described here, which requires two days, takes in both popular mountain areas as well as the much less frequented, but scenic, ridge of peaks between.

ACCOMMODATION

There are four youth hostels in the area: Morioka Youth Hostel (Tel: 0196-62-2220) is 15 minutes by bus from Morioka Station; Shizukuishi Youth Hostel (Tel: 0196-93-2854) is 20 minutes by bus from Shizukuishi Station below the southern slopes of Iwate-san; Tazawa-ko Youth Hostel (Tel: 0187-43-1281), near the lake, is 15 minutes by bus from the station; and Hachimantai Youth Hostel (Tel: 0195-78-2031) is

50 minutes by bus from Ōbuke Station. The towns and villages in the area have plentiful minshuku, ryokan and hotel accommodation, and there are a few unsupervised huts in the mountains providing shelter, with one supervised hut on the higher slopes of Iwate-san. Campsites are found around the lower slopes of the mountains at the chairlift southwest of Iwate-san, Yakibashiri, Matsukawa Onsen, and near the southeastern shore of Lake Tazawa-ko. Food supplies for the hike should be carried from Morioka, Ōbuke or Lake Tazawa-ko, but water supplies are fairly plentiful in the mountains. The trails are not too demanding, except for the steep ash slopes on Iwate-san, but strong boots should be worn, and, as most of the hike is above 1,400 meters, extra warm clothes are needed, together with the essential water-proofs.

TRAILS

★★★★
++++
Hachimantai (八幡平) —→ 2 kms. 30 mins. —→ Tōshichi Onsen (藤七温泉) —→ 4 kms. 1 hr. 25 mins. —→ Morobi-dake (諸檜岳) —→ 3 kms. 1 hr. 15 mins. —→ Kensomori (嶮岨森) —→ 3 kms. 1 hr. 15 mins. —→ Ōfuka-dake (大深岳) —→ 5 kms. 2 hrs. —→ Mitsuishi-yama (三ッ石山) —→ 5 kms. 2 hrs. 20 mins. —→ Ōkura-yama (大倉山) —→ 7 kms. 3 hrs. —→ Iwate-san Goya (岩手山小屋) —→ 1 km. 40 mins. —→ Iwate-san (岩手山) —→ 6 kms. 2 hrs. 30 mins. —→ Yakibashiri (焼走り)

Getting off the bus at Mikaeri-tōge after the two-hour ride from Lake Tazawa-ko, I was greeted by crowds of tourists milling around the car parks, shops, and restaurants at this pass on the Akita-Iwate boundary. To the north, a concrete trail climbs through pine forest to the flat summit of Hachimantai, passing the small lakes of Gama-numa and Hachiman-numa. Wooden planked trails are laid out around the marshes, which are covered in colorful flowers during summer. On a bright summer day the peak of Iwate-san could be seen from this mountaintop marsh with a long ridge of peaks connecting the two.

After the one-hour circuit hike around the marshes of Hachimantai I took the small road down from the pass to the ryokan at Tōshichi Onsen. In the gully above this rustic, old, wooden hot spring resort, natural springs can be seen bubbling and steaming out of the ground. You can bathe in the green-colored natural spring waters in the wooden bath house adjacent to the ryokan, where a large wooden phallus stands at one end of the large bath. Further down the road is the larger Hōrai-sō Kokumin Shukusha providing accommodation, and a nature trail through the forest to a small pond.

Early next morning I set out at dawn, as I intended to make a two-day hike—to the summit of Iwate-san and down the other side—in one day. Picking my way up the eroded gully of steaming vents and bub-

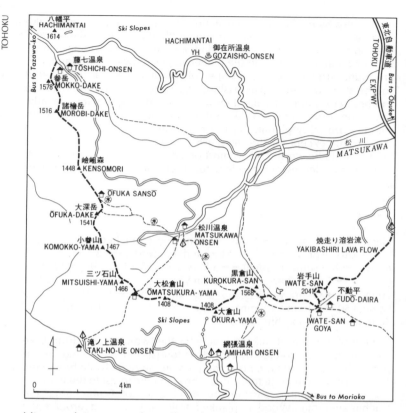

bling mud, I came to the trail on the ridge which leads from a bend in
the road between the pass and the hot spring resort. Following the trail
through bamboo grass and creeping pine, and skirting to the east of
Mokko-dake (畚岳 1,578 m.), it was an easy hike to the flat top of
Morobi-dake. Relatively few people venture this far from the popular
Hachimantai area, and I met only one or two hikers during the morning I hiked along the ridge of open scenery. Descending through bamboo grass, the trail passes two small marshy ponds before climbing
over a hill of laurel bushes and flowers, and then up a steep ridge to
the creeping pine-covered peak of Kensomori (1,448 m.). Below and
to the east lies a large pond amidst the forest as the trail continues on
the ridge through deep bamboo grass and Sakhalin fir. Just after passing a small muddy pond or marsh there is the unsupervised, wooden
mountain hut of Ōfuka Sansō which provides basic accommodation
and shelter.

Climbing from the hut you soon come to a trail on the left which leads to a freshwater spring 200 meters away, but the main trail climbs to the top of the ridge where another trail left leads down to Matsukawa Onsen. The peak of Ōfuka-dake (1,541 m.) is soon reached, and then the trail descends to a pass before climbing steeply to Komokko-dake (1,467 m.). Climbing over a lower peak the trail then descends to a marshy area before another climb to the top of Mitsuishi-yama (1,466 m.) or Three Stone Mountain. Another large marshy area is reached at the pass on the other side of the mountain, with the unsupervised Mitsuishi Sansō situated right on top of the marsh. Trails descend to campsites in the valleys on both sides of the pass, but the ridge trail climbs over Ōmatsukura-san (大松倉山 1,408 m.), and continues along an undulating ridge to the trail junction for the chairlift. Here I met several hikers on their way to and from the chairlift, which climbs from the hot spring resort, campsite and ski slopes at Iwate-san Roku Kokumin Kyūkamura. This is a popular route to the top of Iwate-san.

A steep flight of steps climbs to the summit of Ōkura-yama (1,408 m.), and then the trail descends to a forest of fir and pine, with a freshwater spring down to the north of the trail. The trail is laid with planks as it climbs onto a ridge and then descends slightly before contouring south of Kurokura-yama (it is not necessary to take the trail over the peak). After climbing a steep slope a junction is reached with a choice of routes to the top of Iwate-san—the ridge route or the valley route. The valley route looked easier on the map, so I opted for this one and went down the trail on the left, descending to an area of yellowish-white volcanic rock indicating recent activity. Several hikers were exploring this interesting place as I followed the right bank of the stream in the valley. After crossing the stream, the trail becomes very steep with some rock climbing sections, and then follows the bed of a small stream up to Fudō-daira (不動平). This section was more difficult and took longer than I had planned, and so I was glad when I reached the trail junction and stone hut at this flat, rocky area below the cone of Iwate-san.

Clouds had built up during the afternoon, and the summit of Iwate-san was covered in fog, which occasionally blew away to reveal the bare volcanic ash slopes rising to the crater rim at the summit. Inside the stone hut a group of Boy Scouts had already called it a day and were sleeping in their sleeping bags on the floor. About fifteen minutes away down the slopes of Iwate-san there is a larger, supervised hut providing better accommodation. I set off through the drifting fog and cloud, up the steep cone of Iwate-san, and was hit by strong winds as I came onto the summit rim. I could not see the bottom of the crater as I made my way to the left around the exposed rim to the rocky summit, which was marked by stone Buddhist statues. No one else was braving the cloud and wind on this desolate volcanic peak, and there were no views, so I quickly proceeded around the northern rim and found the poorly marked trail which descends the Fuji-like ash slopes.

Digging my heels in, I slid down the loose slope taking care not to lose the trail, and eventually came out of the fog and cloud. The trail goes off at an angle to the slope, cutting across to the east, and becomes wider and easier to follow as it reaches the first scanty vegetation and then comes into the forest. Descending steeply, the trail comes out at the top of the Yakibashiri lava flow—a desert of black, jagged rock covering the lower slopes. Keeping to the northern edge of the lava flow, the trail is rocky and laced with tree roots as it continues through forest. At the bottom of the lava flow the trail comes out at a car park, and it is a short walk along a level track below the frozen lava to the campsite at Yakibashiri.

Sunset came just as I was putting my tent up in the forested campsite, and a few other campers were cooking on the barbecue grills provided. Next morning it was a nine-kilometer walk down the road to Ōbuke Station, as the bus service to Yakibashiri only operates at weekends and holidays. However, I did not mind the pleasant downhill walk through farmland to the small town of Ōbuke. It gave me time to look back at the looming specter of Tōhoku's Fuji, partly hidden in clouds, and savor my victory over its imposing might.

27. Cold Mountains, Beautiful Valley, Expansive Lake: Hakkōda 八甲田

Mention the Hakkōda Mountains to a Japanese person, and the chances are they will tell you the tragic story of Corporal Gotō and his men. On January 23 1902, Corporal Gotō and his regiment of 210 men set out from their base in Aomori City to climb over the snow-covered Hakkōda Mountains as training for possible combat in Siberia prior to the Russo-Japanese War of 1904. A severe blizzard hit the men on the first day out, and on the fourth day rescuers found Gotō and 17 survivors looking more like frozen statues than living men. Of these, only Gotō and 10 men survived the ordeal, and most of these survivors lost arms or legs due to frostbite.

This story should not put you off a trip to these scenic mountains, and although it is only a very brave and adventurous soul who would venture here in winter, the summer presents a spectacular contrast. Lush green forests and marshes on the lower slopes give way to alpine flora at about 1,300 meters, with the highest volcanic peak of Ōdake standing at 1,585 meters. The Hakkōda Mountains were formed by volcanic activity, and large craters are found on the highest peaks, but these are not active at present. Below the peaks are several hot spring resorts, and mixed bathing is enjoyed at Sukayu Onsen whose natural hot spring waters were visited long before the inn complex was built. Tsuta Onsen is an old, wooden mountain inn built in 1908, which perfectly blends in with the surrounding forest and ponds—the place to come for a taste of old Japan. Both of these hot spring resorts are located on the road which passes over the mountains between Aomori City and Lake Towada-ko. This road is closed and snowbound from mid-November to mid-April, but in mid-February it is cleared from Aomori City up to the ropeway, which is used by skiers.

The Oirase Valley is one of the prettiest valleys in Japan, with lush greenery in summer and colorful golds and reds in fall. Flowing out of the northeastern corner of Lake Towada-ko at Nenokuchi, the stream passes through a narrow, thickly forested valley of steep cliffs, and is full of rapids, miniature waterfalls, and mossy boulders. This picturesque valley is spoilt by the winding road and heavy tourist traffic which passes through it in summer and fall, but the scenery is so good that it is well worthwhile to take the path along the valley between Ishigedo and Nenokuchi.

Lake Towada-ko, the third largest lake in Japan, is the largest tourist attraction in the northern part of the Towada-Hachimantai National Park, which also includes the Oirase Valley and the Hakkōda Mountains. It is a caldera lake surrounded by natural coniferous forest, with sightseeing boats plying its waters and campgrounds on its shores catering to the hordes of tourists for whom this is a must on any tour of Tohoku. The tourist town of Yasumiya on its southern shore is nothing but hotels, souvenir shops, and restaurants, with the Towada Science Museum housing displays of the local geology, flora and fauna.

ACCESS

To reach Lake Towada-ko and the Hakkōda Mountains, bus services operate from Aomori City to the north or Towada Minami to the south, both of which are served by JR trains. From Aomori Station the bus climbs the Hakkōda Mountains to the ropeway which scales the 1,324 meter Tamoyachi-dake—a good place to start a hike over the mountains. Sukayu is reached fifteen minutes after the ropeway, and from mid-April to mid-November the bus continues over the mountains to Tsuta Onsen, and then through the Oirase Valley to Nenokuchi. To hike through the valley you should get off the bus at Ishigedo (石ヶ戸) and walk to Nenokuchi (子ノ口). This is about nine kilometers and takes about three hours to hike. Buses operate around the eastern side of Lake Towada-ko between Nenokuchi and Yasumiya, and from there to Towada Minami Station. These bus services also operate in the opposite direction.

ACCOMMODATION

The Towada area is well supplied with youth hostels: Oirase Youth Hostel (Tel: 0176-74-2031) is a ten-minute walk from Yake-yama bus stop in the Oirase Valley; Hakubutsukan Youth Hostel (Tel: 0176-75-2002) is a two-minute walk from the bus terminal in Yasumiya; Towada Youth Hostel (Tel: 0176-75-2603) is a five-minute bus ride south of Yasumiya; Kuromori-sō Youth Hostel (Tel: 0186-37-2144) is a 17-minute bus ride from Towada Minami Station on the route to Lake Towada-ko—get off at the Ōyu Onsen bus stop from where it is a two-minute walk. Campsites are found at several locations around the shores of Lake Towada-ko, and there is a very convenient campsite near Sukayu Onsen which can be used as a base for climbing the Hakkōda Mountains. Two other campsites are found in the mountains to the south of the road, and there are three simple mountain huts in the area of Ōdake—the highest peak of Hakkōda-san. Hotels and ryokan are especially plentiful around Lake Towada-ko and cheaper minshuku may also be found here.

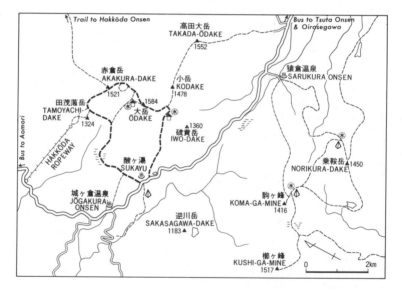

TRAILS

***

+++

Sukayu (酸ヶ湯) ⟶ 6.5 kms. 3 hrs. ⟶ Akakura-dake (赤倉岳) ⟶ 2 kms. 1 hr. 15 mins. ⟶ Ōdake (大岳) ⟶ 4 kms. 1 hr. 50 mins. ⟶ Sukayu (酸ヶ湯)

Good boots and warm clothes are needed for hiking in the Hakkōda Mountains, but walking along the Oirase Valley and around Lake

Towada-ko requires no special equipment. It is a good idea to carry food supplies for camping and hiking from Aomori or Towada Minami as prices around Lake Towada-ko are inflated. The following is a description of a one-day hike over Hakkōda's highest peak using a circular route from Sukayu. There are several other possibilities for one-day or longer hikes over these mountains, but this route offers good scenery and many points of interest.

Early one morning I took the trail that climbs steeply up on the left side of the inn complex. The path soon enters a mixed forest with an undergrowth of bamboo grass. The trail is laid with wooden planks as it climbs gently and crosses dry stream beds before coming out at a flat, marshy area. Continuing along the planked trail you reach a beautiful area of small ponds with interesting marsh and alpine plants. A small wooden hut is located in the forest about 100 meters from the trail here. Rising abruptly from the flat, open, marshy area, the trail climbs steeply up wooden steps through fir forest with views of the marshes below. At a trail junction the main trail continues directly up through forest and bamboo grass to Ōdake Hut, and is the shortest route to the summit. I took the trail left (north) which contours around to the ridge and trail from the ropeway and Tamoyachi-dake. The ropeway climbs Tamoyachi-dake from the road a few kilometers from Sukayu Onsen in the Aomori direction. On joining this ridge trail I met other hikers who had used the ropeway to reach these higher peaks with less effort and in a shorter time. Climbing the ridge the trail leaves the forest and comes out on the top of Akakura-dake (1,521 m.) which is marked by a small shrine on its summit.

Passing the shrine and crossing an open, level, and rocky alpine area, the trail comes to a large crater. There were no signs of activity in this deep, rocky hole on top of Hakkōda, which can be circum-navigated via the trail around its rim. The shortest route to the south side of the crater is to the left (east), and then the trail descends rocky alpine slopes to Ōdake Hut. This small, wooden, unsupervised hut has no facilities, but offers shelter, and water is found at a spring just down the trail from the hut. Climbing directly up from the hut the trail leads to the exposed, rocky summit of Ōdake (1,585 m.)—the highest peak of Hakkōda-san, situated on the rim of a crater, and marked by a small shrine.

The trail descends a steep, rocky slope from the summit and comes to a junction where the trail left goes over the other peaks of Hakkōda, and the trail right descends back down to Sukayu. This trail passes a freshwater spring and a small mountain hut before descending the rocky trail through mixed forest and bamboo grass to Sukayu. Steep in places, the going becomes easier as you approach Sukayu, and you can look forward to soaking tired limbs in the natural hot spring waters supplied by the volcanoes whose peaks you have just conquered.

Hokkaido: The North Country

Akan Fuji from Meakan-dake

Yezo (or Ezo), the old name for the northern island of Japan, is the last refuge of the Ainu people, who were slowly pushed northward by the advancing Japanese. It was not actively settled by the Japanese until the end of the last century and beginning of this one, when the island was given the name Hokkaido. Due to its late development, there are still many unspoilt areas on the island, which is the second largest in the Japanese archipelago, constituting one-fifth of its area but only one-twentieth of its population. Hokkaido's big attraction is its wide, open spaces, rare in the rest of Japan, and during its short summers it is an ideal place for campers, hikers, and nature lovers.

The mountain ranges generally form two chains running north-south. To the west the Teshio Range in the north runs into the Yūbari Range in the south, and down the center of the island there is the Kitami Range in the north and the Hidaka Range in the south. These mountain ranges are mainly composed of sedimentary rocks dating from the Paleozoic to the Quaternary, but apart from these ranges there are other mountainous areas formed by Tertiary and Quaternary volcanics.

The Daisetsu-zan Mountains, the highest in Hokkaido, are situated in the center of the island and are of volcanic origin. They are located at the end of the Chishima Volcanic Zone, which runs eastward from these mountains to the active Lake Akan-ko area, northeast of which are the large calderas of Kussharo and Mashū, containing large caldera lakes. The Chishima Volcanic Zone runs northeastward from this area to the Shiretoko Peninsula, formed by a chain of volcanoes, and on through the Kuril Island chain to Kamchatka and Siberia. The southwestern part of Hokkaido falls in the Nasu Volcanic Zone, which runs northward through Tohoku. This is also an area of volcanic mountains and caldera lakes.

Hokkaido's climate and flora resemble that of Canada or Northern Europe. Winters are long and cold, with a mean February temperature in Sapporo of −4.4°C and temperatures as low as −30°C inland.

Snow falls mainly on the mountains facing the Japan Sea during the winter northwesterly monsoon. However, Hokkaido is dry relative to the rest of Japan, with no distinct rainy season, and typhoons rarely reach this far north. Summers are cool and short, lasting little more than the month of August, although some years there may hardly be a summer at all. The mean August temperature in Sapporo is 22.8°C.

Forest covers more than seventy percent of Hokkaido and is of subarctic type dominated by spruce, fir, birch, and oak. The alpine zone is reached at about 1,000 meters, much lower than in the rest of Japan. Here alpine plants and flowers grow in abundance. Hokkaido is on the migration route of many birds, especially the Japanese crane and swans which come from Siberia to spend the winter in Hokkaido. November to March is the season to observe these birds in the eastern part of Hokkaido. Some animals are only to be found in Hokkaido, for example the brown bear (*higuma*), which may be seen in the remoter mountain regions, and the crying hare or Asiatic pika (*naki usagi*), which is a rare species found only in the northern, western, and central parts of Hokkaido. The deer, fox, squirrel and chipmunk have subspecies which differ from those of the southern parts of Japan. These and other small mammals are quite abundant in Hokkaido.

The main areas of interest in Hokkaido are the following six national parks: Daisetsu-zan National Park in the center of the island, Akan National Park to the east, Shiretoko National Park, which covers most of the peninsula jutting out into the Okhotsk Sea, Shikotsu-Tōya National Park in the southwest, and Rishiri-Rebun-Sarobetsu National Park in the north. This last national park includes a coastal marsh and two islands. Kushiro National Park is Hokkaido's sixth and Japan's 28th, and probably last, national park, which was designated in 1987 on an area of coastal marsh east of the city of Kushiro. Apart from these areas of outstanding beauty there are four quasi-national parks; Ōnuma Quasi-National Park in the southwest, Niseko-Shakotan-Otaru Coast Quasi-National Park in the west, Abashiri Quasi-National Park on the northeast coast, and Hidaka Mountain Range and Cape Erimo Quasi-National Park in the south center of the island, which is a large, remote area of high mountains offering some exciting hiking possibilities. There are also several smaller prefectural parks, and the Tanchōzuru Natural Park at Akan about 20 kilometers northwest of Kushiro.

ACCESS

By Air: Regular domestic flights are operated to Hokkaido from major cities by three airlines: Japan Air Lines (JAL), All Nippon Airways (ANA), and Japan Air System (JAS). There are about 25 daily flights from Tokyo's Narita or Haneda airports to Sapporo's Chitose Airport, with a flying time of 1 hour 25 minutes; one way fare costs ¥23,850 and round-trip ¥43,100. Chitose Airport is connected with downtown Sapporo by JR express train (35 mins. ¥720) or by bus (1 hr. ¥930).

By Rail: JR operates frequent services between Tokyo and Hokkaido, and since the spring of 1988 the Seikan Tunnel between Honshu and Hokkaido provides direct access. The Tohoku Shinkansen (super express) runs as far as Morioka, and if this is taken the fastest travelling time from Tokyo to Sapporo is about 13 hours, costing about ¥20,500 one way with express surcharges. The basic fare without taking express trains is about ¥12,800. To Hakodate travel time is about nine hours by Shinkansen and express costing about ¥17,150 and the basic fare is about ¥10,800.

By Sea: The Kinkai Yusen Ferry Co. operates a twice-weekly service from Tokyo to Kushiro taking 33 hours. Two ferry companies also operate a service from Tokyo to Tomakomai, and ferries can also be taken from Nagoya, Sendai, and Hachinohe to Hokkaido. Ferry fares are cheaper than train fares, especially for reaching the eastern side of Hokkaido. Latest timetables and fares should be checked at TIC.

ACCOMMODATION

Hokkaido is well provided with campsites at the national parks and main places of interest. Youth hostels are found in most of the main towns and tourist centers. Hakodate has one youth hostel, Hakodate Youth Guest House (Tel: 0138-26-7892) which is reached by tram 2 from Hakodate Station, and is three minutes' walk from the Hōrai-cho tram stop.

Sapporo has three youth hostels: Sapporo House Youth Hostel (Tel: 011-726-4235) is seven minutes' walk from Sapporo Station, Sapporo Miyagaoka Youth Hostel (Tel: 011-611-9016) and Sapporo Lions Youth Hostel (Tel: 011-611-4709). Inexpensive accommodation is found at Sōen Green Hotel, Nishi 14-chome, Kita 6-jo, Chuo-ku, Sapporo (Tel: 011-231-1661). This is seven minutes by bus from Sapporo Station or ten minutes from Sōen Station. Many places in Hokkaido have cheap accommodation during the summer months of July and August to cater to the large influx of young travellers from the south. Some of these places are called Rider's Houses (*mitsubachi*) and provide basic accommodation for motorbike riders, but other travellers can also stay. Facilities are simple and communal.

28. Caldera Lakes and Active Volcanoes: Lake Shikotsu-ko 支笏湖

Of the six national parks in Hokkaido the Shikotsu-Tōya National Park is the southernmost, the nearest to Sapporo, and the easiest to reach. The park is rich in volcanic scenery and sights, with the two large caldera lakes of Shikotsu-ko and Tōya-ko, several volcanic peaks, some of which are active, and many hot spring resorts, the most famous of which is Noboribetsu Onsen. With so much to offer it is no wonder that the park attracts crowds of tourists, but the best scenery is found off the roads, on the many hiking trails around the lakes, and up to the volcanic peaks.

The most attractive area in the park for hiking, and the base for the hike described here, is Lake Shikotsu-ko, which is Japan's northern-most ice-free lake in winter. It is a geological y recent caldera lake, formed by the subsidence of the land between the surrounding volcanic peaks of Eniwa-dake (1,320 m.), Fuppushi-dake (1,103 m.), and Tarumae-san (1,038 m.). Eniwa-dake to the north of the lake is the highest peak, and rises steeply from the deep blue waters, showing some signs of activity. To the south of the lake, Fuppushi-dake is now dormant, but adjoining it to the southeast Tarumae-san is still active, and the most interesting. There have been about 70 eruptions recorded since 1667, with large eruptions in that year and 1739 creating the present cone and crater. An eruption in 1909 resulted in the formation of a lava dome within the crater, one of the best ex-amples of a lava dome in Japan, and steam still ssues from vents in the crater.

About 40 kilometers southwest of Lake Shikotsu-ko, the circular Lake Tōya-ko, with four forested islands in its center is a very popular tourist and hot spring resort. South of the lake the active Usu-zan fre-quently erupts, with the last major eruptions in 1910, 1944 and 1977. The last eruption in 1977 destroyed the cable car up the volcano, but it is a testament to the indomitable Japanese faith in nature that they reopened it in 1982. In 1943 a series of earthquakes hit the area, culminating in the 1944 eruption when the new lava dome mountain of Showa Shinzan was born on the eastern slopes of Usu-zan. This is now designated as a Special Natural Monument, and the natural history of this volcanic activity can be seen in displays at the Volcanic Science Museum on the southern shore of Lake Tōya-ko.

There is said to be an overpopulation of deer on the central islands of Lake Tōya-ko, and they can sometimes be seen swimming across the lake. The largest island of Ōshima may be visited by boat, where you can see displays of the lake's history, fauna, and flora in the Forest Museum. From the lake the conical peak of Yōtei-zan (1,893 m.) can be seen to the north rising above the forested caldera walls which sur-round the lake. Yōtei-zan is the highest peak in the park, and its extinct stratovolcano is a major landmark which, because of its similarity to Fuji-san, is also known as Ezo Fuji.

The Shikotsu-Tōya National Park is covered with virgin forests which give way to rocky alpine slopes on the higher peaks. Wildlife includes the brown bear, Ezo deer, northern fox, squirrel, chipmunk, and weasel, mostly found in the forests, and there is a variety of birdlife in the forests and on the lakes. The main hike I describe here is a climb over Tarumae-san from Lake Shikotsu-ko, which I think is the most interesting in the park, but the peaks of Yōtei-zan, Eniwa-dake, and Fuppushi-dake may also be climbed, and offer good hiking.

ACCESS

Lake Shikotsu-ko is easily accessible by regular bus services from Sapporo (1 hr. 20 mins.) and Chitose Airport (40 mins.), which stop at the trail entrance for Eniwa-dake before reaching the lake at Poropinai Campsite, and going around the shore to Shikotsu Kohan. Bus services also run from here to Tomakomai on the coast, around the lake to Morappu, and to the Seventh Stage of Tarumae-san. Lake Tōya-ko can also be reached by bus services from Sapporo, and from Tōya Station on the JR Muroran Line. Yōtei-zan can be reached from Kutchan Station on the main JR line between Hakodate and Sapporo, from where a bus runs to the trail entrance on the west side of the mountain. However, transport within the park between Lakes Shikotsu-ko and Tōya-ko, and Yōtei-zan is not good.

ACCOMMODATION

There is a youth hostel near Shōwa Shinzan at Lake Tōya-ko: Showa Shinzan Youth Hostel (Tel: 01427-5-2283). Another hostel, Usu Kankōkan (Tel: 0142-38-2411), is located near Usu-zan on the coast seven minutes' walk from Usu Station. There is also a convenient youth hostel three minutes' walk from the bus terminal at Shikotsu Kohan: Shikotsu-ko Youth Hostel (Tel: 0123-25-2311). At Morappu on the eastern shore of Lake Shikotsu-ko there is a cheap place to stay at Tarumae-sō (Tel: 0123-25-2902), which has a small store on the ground floor. Minshuku are fairly plentiful in the park area.

Camping is popular around the lakes, with four campsites on the shores of Lake Shikotsu-ko. The Morappu campsite is convenient for climbing Tarumae-san, Poropinai is convenient for climbing Eniwa-dake, and there is one campsite each at Okotan and Bifue on the western shores of the lake. Three campsites are also found around the shores of Lake Tōya-ko, and there is a campsite below the northern slopes of Yōtei-zan. When camping it is best to bring all food supplies from a large town, as there are few stores in the park area.

TRAILS

★★★★
+++
Shishamonai （シシャモナイ）⟶ 6 kms. 2 hrs. ⟶ Tarumae-san (west rim) （樽前山(西峰)）⟶ 2 kms. 40 mins. ⟶ east rim （東峰）⟶ 1.5 kms. 40 mins. ⟶ 7th Stage Hut （七合目ヒュッテ）⟶ 8 kms. 2 hrs. ⟶ Morappu Campsite （モラップキャンプ場）

Easy hiking trails follow the shores of Lake Shikotsu-ko between Poropinai and Bifue in the west, and between Shikotsu Kohan and Morappu in the east. The trail entrance for Eniwa-dake is about one kilometer up the road from Poropinai, and is clearly signposted. About three hours are needed to climb to the summit along an easy trail at first, which becomes steeper and climbs out of the forest at 800 meters onto rocky, alpine slopes. (The same trail must be taken down.) From the peak there are panoramic views of Lake Shikotsu-ko and Lake Okotampe-ko below, west to Yōtei-zan, and on a fine day east to the Hidaka Range. Active vents may be seen in the crater on the east side of the peak. The climb up Yōtei-zan requires about four hours, and goes up through forest which gives way to rocky, alpine slopes with alpine flowers on the higher section of the climb. Several trails climb this Fuji-like pyroclastic cone, and so a different route may be taken back down.

Tarumae-san may be climbed by taking the bus up to the Seventh Stage, located at the tree line, and making a 40-minute hike up to the

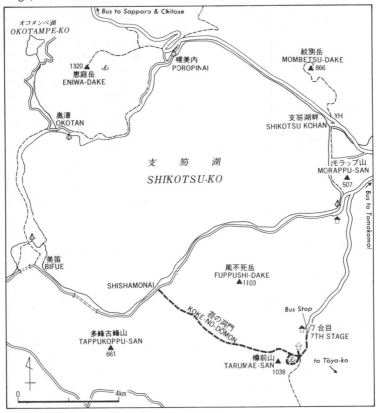

crater rim. However, a more interesting route starts from Lake Shikotsu-ko at Shishamonai, and climbs to the western rim before taking the popular tourist route down. The starting point at Shishamonai is about nine kilometers around the southern shore of the lake from Morappu, and is reached by road, but there are no buses this way, so it's either a two-hour walk, a hitch, or a taxi.

From the car park at Shishamonai the trail enters a narrow gorge called Koke-no-dōmon (苔の洞門), or Moss Gorge, and follows it for about four kilometers. The name of this narrow cleft, cut into the volcanic rock on the lower slopes of the mountain, is soon explained by the green velvet covering on the vertical walls of the gorge. There are apparently thirty different species of moss growing here, in what must be the ideal moist, sheltered conditions for moss to grow.

Leaving most of the tourists behind, the trail climbs gently up out of the gorge, and then out of the forest onto the dark, volcanic ash slopes of Tarumae-san, with Fuppushi-dake rising steeply to the north. The trail becomes steep as it makes its way to the barren western rim of the crater, from where there is an awe-inspiring view of the central lava dome of Tarumae-san. Going to the left (north), circle around the north side of the dome across a desolate moonscape, and make your way to the peak on the eastern rim, where the escape hut is located. You are now on the main tourist route from the Seventh Stage Hut below. On the eastern side of the central lava dome is an active vent, which can be reached by a circular trail across the crater floor to get a closer look at the action, and steaming, sulphurous fumes.

Returning to the eastern rim, the trail down to the Seventh Stage Hut and car park descends the outer, volcanic ash cone of the volcano. White azaleas grow on the slopes above the tree line, where the hut is located. Buses run down the road from the hut to Shikotsu Kohan. Otherwise it is an eight-kilometer walk down through the forest to Morappu, or 12 kilometers to Shikotsu Kohan.

29. Fire and Fury over Furano: Tokachi-dake 十勝岳

The picture-postcard scenery of the Furano Basin in Central Hokkaido, with its wide, open fields, and Western-style farmhouses, has become the image most Japanese associate with Hokkaido. Its rich, fertile, volcanic soils promote vegetable cultivation, and it is famous for its specialty, Furano wine.

Hemmed in by the Yūbari Mountains to the west, the Hidaka Mountains to the southeast, and the Daisetsu Mountains to the northeast, the Furano Basin is watched over by the peak of Tokachi-dake, which is located in the southwestern part of Daisetsu-zan National Park. This active volcano, whose steam pours out in copious quantities, is visible from most of the plain below on a fine day. The tranquility of the peaceful farming communities lying beneath its peak was shattered when large eruptions in 1926 and 1962 wrought death, destruction, and crop damage with its fiery fury.

Tokachi-dake's simmering peak is an exciting one-day climb, with two marvelous hot spring resorts on its lower slopes at Tokachi-dake Onsen and Shirogane Onsen, where the hike described here starts and ends. More adventurous hikers can make much longer expeditions into Daisetsu-zan National Park, with a four-day hike going northeast along a ridge of peaks to Asahi-dake, through excellent alpine scenery (see the next section, "Over the Roof of Hokkaido").

ACCESS

Access to Tokachi-dake is made via the JR Furano Line, which runs between Furano and Asahikawa. Bus services operate from Kami Furano Station to Tokachi-dake Onsen (45 mins.), and from Biei Station to Shirogane Onsen (35 mins.)

ACCOMMODATION

Two youth hostels are located in the area. One is near ski slopes, ten minutes' bus ride from Furano Station: Furano White Youth Hostel (Tel: 0167-23-4807). The other is a two-minute walk from the bus terminus at Shirogane Onsen: Shirogane Center Youth Hostel (Tel: 0166-94-3131). There is plentiful accommodation in the town of Furano, and a few ryokan near the stations at Kami Furano and Biei. At Shirogane there is also a large, modern hotel and an old, rustic hot spring ryokan. At Tokachi-dake Onsen the wooden mountain hut at the end of the road is perched above a stream valley, and has a very scenic rotenburo as well as indoor baths. A large mountain hut is one kilometer further down the road.

A well-laid-out campsite is located one kilometer from the bus terminus at Shirogane Onsen, passing a volcano research station on the way. Camping is also popular at two mountain huts in the high mountains, one about two kilometers along the ridge southwest of Tokachi-dake's peak, and the other at Biei Fuji about eight kilometers along the mountain trail to the northeast of the peak. Both of these are small, unmanned mountain huts, and there is another below Tokachi-dake's steaming crater, which is a little larger.

TRAILS

****
++++
Tokachi-dake Onsen (十勝岳温泉) ⟶ 6.5 kms. 5 hrs. ⟶ Tokachi-dake (十勝岳) (2,077 m.) ⟶ 7.5 kms. 3 hrs. 45 mins. ⟶ Shirogane Onsen (白金温泉)

The narrow, winding road climbs above 1,200 meters to the car park and wooden mountain hut at Tokachi-dake Onsen, where the hot

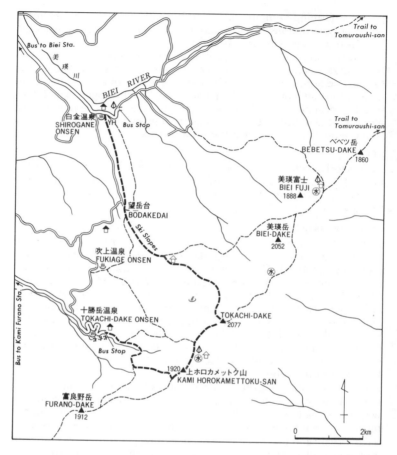

spring baths are well worth a dip. From the bus terminus outside the hut, a wide trail continues up the valley through bushy forest and creeping pine, with a trail off to the left taking a more difficult route to Tokachi-dake. About one and a half kilometers from the hut there is a stream valley of yellow and white rocks showing signs of recent activity. The trail crosses this valley and climbs up through creeping pine to another trail junction after one kilometer. On this stretch I met a small northern fox cub diving in and out of the bushy creeping pine, but I caught no sight of its mother. Going left at the junction, the climb becomes steeper as it climbs up a ridge, and then a rocky gully, which leads to the summit ridge. A gale was blowing as I came out onto this ridge, and I sheltered behind rocks before continuing on the trail north-eastward.

Contouring around the eastern side of a peak the trail descends slightly to a low point in the ridge, from where a trail leads down to the east to a small, wooden hut, and camp area a few minutes away. The trail to the peak continues to the north along the ridge, and the rocky peak of Tokachi-dake with the steep trail leading up to it can be seen ahead, with steam rising from behind the ridge west of the peak. After scrambling up the rocks to the summit you are rewarded with a panoramic 360° view of nearby desolate volcanic scenery and distant peaks. To the northwest is the main crater and active area of Tokachi-dake, belching forth its white vapors. To the northeast, across a flat plain of dark volcanic ash, rises the craggy peak of Biei-dake (美瑛岳 2,052 m.), with a trail going that way, and leading to the central peaks of Daisetsu-zan National Park. On a fine day the Hidaka Mountains may be visible to the south.

Leaving the summit, with a few other hikers eating their lunch amidst the rocks, I took the steep, rocky trail northwest leading down towards the steaming vent. A previous trail went around to the left (southwest), very close to the crater, but this trail was impassable, and completely obscured in clouds of steam billowing out of the crater. Another trail goes down a steep slope of dark volcanic ash to the right, and comes onto a wide, flat ridge. It is then an easy walk over barren, volcanic ash, with the active vent to the left, and a dead crater on the right. The trail then descends more steeply, and comes to the escape hut, a stone structure which provides shelter and accommodation but is not manned, and is primarily for use if the volcano erupts.

Directly below the hut are the ski slopes, and the wide trail makes its way over volcanic rock down to Bōdakedai (望岳台), where there is a restaurant and car park at the end of the road from Shirogane Onsen. However, it is best to take the trail east of the road, which takes about one hour down to the village, and comes out opposite the youth hostel, with the campsite about ten minutes walk along the road to the right. There is a small store and a restaurant at Shirogane Onsen, and a natural hot spring bath may be had at the old inn to wash away the volcanic dust from the peaks.

30. Over the Roof of Hokkaido: Daisetsu-zan 大雪山

Daisetsu-zan National Park contains three volcanic mountain groups: to the north of the plateau the Daisetsu-zan Group includes Asahi-dake (2,290 m.), Hokkaido's highest peak; to the southwest the Tokachi Group is dominated by the smoking Tokachi-dake (2,077 m.), an active volcano; and to the east the Shikaribetsu Group is dominated by Ishikari-dake (1,962 m.). The central mountainous area between these groups of peaks is untouched by all but the most intrepid hikers, and dominated by the prominent peak of Tomuraushi-yama. (2,141 m.)

At the foot of the Daisetsu-zan Mountains, deep gorges have been cut by the headwaters of the Ishikarigawa River, which flows into the Japan Sea. Sōunkyō Gorge in the northwestern part of the park is the largest gorge in Japan, extending for about 20 kilometers, with columnar jointed volcanic lava cliffs more than 150 meters high in places. On the western side of the Daisetsu-zan Mountains another magnificent gorge called Tenninkyō cuts its way beneath Hokkaido's highest peaks. Mountain streams cascade down from the plateau and alpine valleys into these gorges creating spectacular waterfalls. Many hot spring resorts are also to be found in these gorges and around the periphery of the park where natural hot spring waters from the volcanic depths of the mountains are tapped.

Daisetsu-zan National Park is forested with conifers including Yezo spruce (*Ezomatsu*) and Sakhalin fir (*todomatsu*) up to about 1,500 meters, where the forests give way to alpine vegetation in the high mountains. This is one of the best areas in Japan for alpine flowers, with about 200 species of alpine plants, including many local varieties, growing in luxuriance during the short summers. The area is also blessed with abundant wildlife. The Hokkaido brown bear (*higuma*) may be seen in the remoter parts away from the main tourist routes. More commonly seen are the Hokkaido deer (*Ezo shika*), northern fox (*kita kitsune*), Hokkaido squirrel (*Ezo risu*), and Hokkaido chipmunk (*Ezoshima risu*). The fox may be seen either at the foot of the mountains or in the high alpine zone, but rarely in the forests between. In the alpine zone the chipmunk may be seen scurrying amongst the creeping pine (*haimatsu*) which grows along the ground in the high mountains. The crying hare or Asiatic pika (*naki usagi*) is a rare species which may also be found in these mountains, notably near the hut below Hakuun-dake.

Some of the birds to watch out for in the forests are the giant woodpecker (*kumagera*), ruby throat (*nogoma*), and Japanese accentor (*kayakuguri*). The rare pine grosbeak (*ginzammashiko*) may be seen in the high mountains amongst the creeping pine, where its crossed bill is used for opening pine cones. Crows (*karasu*) and the occasional eagle frequent the high peaks.

Winters are long and severe in these mountains, lasting from November to April, with about four meters of snow lying on the ground during March and April. Daisetsu-zan is a popular ski resort with a long season, hikers not usually venturing to the peaks until June, with year-round snow remaining in sheltered gullies of the alpine zone. July, when most of the alpine flowers burst into color, is usually the best month for hiking and climbing. There is a good chance of fine weather in August, but some years Hokkaido hardly has a summer at all and the weather may be cold and wet in the mountains. Autumn follows quickly in September, when the leaves turn red and the first snow already begins to fall on the peaks.

Daisetsu-zan National Park offers some excellent hiking opportunities during the short summer season, when one-day hikes or longer, several-day expeditions may be made into the mountains, valleys and gorges along a network of well-marked trails. The most popular area for hiking is in the Daisetsu-zan group of volcanic peaks between the Sōunkyō and Asahi-dake ropeways. This route goes over Hokkaido's highest peak of Asahi-dake in a traverse of the mountains. The hike described here can easily be done in one day if you are reasonably fit, but if you wish to return to the same starting point and not carry all of your things with you then the climb to Hokkaido's highest peak is much shorter from the Asahi-dake Ropeway. For those of a more adventurous bent I can recommend taking the trail south from the peak of Hokkai-dake and making a three- or four-day hike, passing Tomuraushi-yama and following the ridge of peaks to Tokachi-dake.

The small resort village of Sōunkyō, nestled beneath the towering crags and forested slopes of the gorge, and above the rushing Ishikarigawa River, is crowded with hotels, ryokan, minshuku, restaurants and souvenir shops (sounds familiar?). Just up the road from the bus station can be seen the ropeway, and the campsite is about one kilometer up the main road through the gorge and entered by a small road on the left.

During the summer there are regular evening performances at an outdoor theater in the village of Sōunkyō of traditional singing, dancing and religious rites by the local Ainu residents, mainly for the benefit of hordes of Japanese tourists from the south. While in Sōunkyō it is worthwhile making the eight-kilometer trip through the gorge. You can take a bus or hire a bicycle, but walking allows a more leisurely view of the gorge and its spectacular cliffs and waterfalls, and takes about two hours one way.

ACCESS

Access to Daisetsu-zan is best made via Asahikawa City, which is 1 hour 45 minutes by JR express train from Sapporo. Regular bus services operate from there to Tenninkyō (1 hr. 30 mins.), Asahi-dake Ropeway (2 hrs.), and Sōunkyō (2 hrs.). To reach Sōunkyō, however, it is best to take the train to Kamikawa Station, and go by bus from there (35 mins.). Another bus service operates from Rubeshibe to Sōunkyō (2 hrs.), passing through the Sōunkyō Gorge on a main route through the center of Hokkaido. Sōunkyō is the most popular tourist resort in Daisetsu-zan National Park. The two ropeway services on Daisetsu-zan from Sōunkyō and Asahi-dake Onsen operate for most of the year, being used by skiers in winter and hikers in summer, and provide fast and easy access to the alpine peaks.

ACCOMMODATION

Several campsites are found at convenient locations in the resorts at Sōunkyō and Yukomambetsu Onsen, in the mountains at Kurodake Stone Hut, Hakuun-dake Hut, just below the peak east of Asahi-dake, and at many other locations in the mountains to the south, including a popular site below the peak of Tomuraushi-yama. There is a plentiful supply of fresh stream water in the mountains, so it is not necessary to carry large quantities.

The mountain huts provide simple accommodation and sometimes meals. Booking is not required, but the huts may be quite crowded in July and August. There are three convenient youth hostels, which should be booked in advance to be sure of a place. Two of them are a few minutes' walk from the bus station in Sōunkyō: Sōunkyō Youth Hostel (Tel: 01658-5-3418) and Ginsenkaku Youth Hostel (Tel: 01658-5-3003). The other is at Yukomambetsu Onsen, about ten minutes' walk from the bottom of the Asahi-dake Ropeway and opposite the campsite entrance. It is Daisetsu-zan Shirakaba-sō Youth Hostel (Tel: 0166-97-2246).

TRAILS

*****
++++
Sōunkyō Lift （層雲峡リフト）→ 1.8 kms. 1 hr. → Kurodake （黒岳） (1,984 m.) → 1 km. 25 mins. → Kurodake Stone Hut （黒岳石室）→ 2.8 kms. 1 hr. 15 mins. → Hokkai-dake （北海岳） (2,149 m.) → 4.2 kms. 2 hrs. → Asahi-dake （旭岳） (2,290 m.) → 2 kms. 1 hr. 15 mins. → Asahi-dake Ropeway （旭岳ロープウェイ）

Strong boots, extra warm clothes, and waterproofs are needed for climbing over the roof of Hokkaido, where the weather can be very cold, even in midsummer. If the weather looks bad from the resorts in the gorges it is sure to be worse in the peaks, and it is better to wait for good weather before venturing to the high alpine zone.

The ropeway operates from 0600 to 1900 in the summer season, allowing an early start. It is not cheap, and so the ten-percent discount for youth hostellers is most welcome. Whisking you up to 1,300 meters over steep forested slopes of spruce, pine, and fir, the ropeway saves a gruelling two-hour climb through the forest on the old, now little-used, trail. From the top station it is a two-minute walk to the chair lift which takes you up to just over 1,500 meters, with a trail to the north taking about 45 minutes to climb.

Coming out of the top lift station the trail to Kurodake goes to the right of a small restaurant and is a steep, rocky, zigzag climb to the sum-

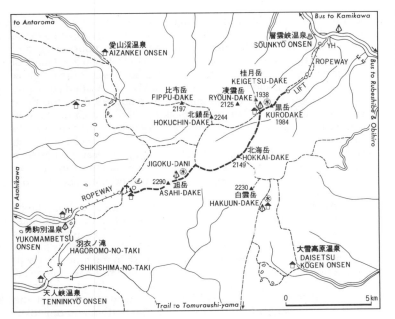

To Antaroma

愛山渓温泉
AIZANKEI ONSEN

層雲峡温泉
SŌUNKYŌ ONSEN

Bus to Kamikawa

YH

ROPEWAY

Bus to Rubeshibe & Obihiro

桂月岳
KEIGETSU-DAKE

比布岳
FIPPU-DAKE
2197

凌雲岳
RYŌUN-DAKE
2125

1938

黒岳
KURODAKE
1984

LIFT

北鎮岳
HOKUCHIN-DAKE 2244

北海岳
HOKKAI-DAKE
2149

To Asahikawa

JIGOKU-DANI
2290 旭岳
ASAHI-DAKE

ROPEWAY

YH

2230
白雲岳
HAKUUN-DAKE

勇駒別温泉
YUKOMAMBETSU
ONSEN
羽衣ノ滝
HAGOROMO-NO-TAKI

SHIKISHIMA-NO-TAKI

大雪高原温泉
DAISETSU
KŌGEN ONSEN

天人峡温泉
TENNINKYŌ ONSEN

Trail to Tomuraushi-yama

0   5 km

mit. Soon, leaving the forest and climbing alpine slopes of colorful flowers there are views back down to Sōunkyō and the deep gorge. On the rocky summit of Kurodake there is a tiny shrine and a watchman's hut, and I was surprised to see a fox roaming around looking for food left by hikers. To the south and west rise the highest peaks in Hokkaido in a rugged, alpine landscape blotched with patches of white snow. From the summit the rocky trail is clearly marked by rope and yellow paint down to Kurodake Stone Hut just below 1,900 meters. This simple, quaint hut provides accommodation and food, with a campsite 200 meters to the north next to a snow patch which provides meltwater.

Temperatures are much colder in these alpine peaks than in the bottom of the gorges, and several well-clad campers were busy around the campsite. From the hut there are two possible trails to Asahi-dake, but the trail to the south going over Hokkai-dake is the most scenic. First passing through creeping pine, you come to an area carpeted with colorful alpine flowers and cross two streams. Following the bank of the second stream, and passing snow patches, the trail climbs towards some crags, passing below them and coming out onto a ridge which leads to the exposed, rocky peak of Hokkai-dake.

To the northwest can be seen an enclosed basin of yellowish-white rock containing some active hot springs. To the south rises the craggy peak of Hakuun-dake (白雲岳 2,230 m.) with the trail on the ridge to the southeast leading to Hakuun-dake Hut about one hour away, and from there to the less-frequented central area of Daisetsu-zan National Park. For the trail to Asahi-dake take the ridge southwest from the peak with the enclosed basin to the north and a view of Asahi-dake's gray peak to the southwest. There are many alpine flowers along this ridge route as you come to a flat-topped peak marked by a cairn at a trail junction. The trail north circles the enclosed basin and returns to Kurodake Stone Hut, but for Asahi-dake take the trail southwest. Descending through a bare, rocky landscape, the trail comes to a campsite on a saddle below a large snow patch on the main slope to the peak. Few campers venture to camp in this desolate spot at Hokkaido's highest campsite.

Crossing the small stream from the melting snow, the trail climbs very steeply up loose scree or over snow to the summit of Asahi-dake. In fine weather there is a 360° panoramic view of Daisetsu-zan's peaks from this highest point in Hokkaido, and below to the west is Jigoku-dani (地獄谷) or Hell's Valley—a craggy deep gash in the mountain with steaming hot volcanic fumes rising from the bottom. I have been surprised at the number of people, and even young children, who reach this high peak in summer, most of them climbing up the ridge from the Asahi-dake Ropeway, which can be seen at the bottom end of Jigoku-dani. The climb up the ridge south of Jigoku-dani takes about two hours, but the descent takes about one hour, and although very steep and rocky, it is not particularly difficult.

As you descend the ridge the steaming vents of Jigoku-dani come into closer view and can be heard hissing out their potent sulphurous vapors, which hang heavy in the air and lungs. At the bottom of the ridge the trail comes to the tiny Asahi-dake Stone Hut next to a small volcanic lake. Several trails are marked by ropes over the area, and two more volcanic lakes are located further down the mountainside. The towering peak of Asahi-dake rising above the steaming Jigoku-dani dominates this beautiful area above the top station of the Asahi-dake Ropeway.

The ropeway whisks you back down from the alpine roof of Hokkaido in two stages over the dark, coniferous forest to the resort of Yukomambetsu Onsen below. There are several lodges, a youth hostel and campsite just down the road from the lower ropeway station, and a Visitors' Center with exhibits of the local flora and fauna. Buses run to Tenninkyō Onsen and the city of Asahikawa. However, there is a trail from the campsite taking about two hours through the forest to Tenninkyō Onsen, with a spectacular view of Tenninkyō Gorge before the steep descent to the resort. The head of the road up this narrow gorge is crowded with large, modern, concrete hotels, but it is worth taking the 30-minute hike up the gorge from the resort to see the splendid Hagoromo-no-taki Falls and the smaller Shikijima-no-taki Falls at the end of the trail.

Many of the hotels and lodges at Tenninkyō Onsen and Yukomambetsu allow visitors to use their hot spring baths, which are supplied with natural hot spring water tapped from beneath the Daisetsu-zan Mountains and piped to the baths.

31. Mountain Island: Rishiri-san 利尻山

Born from volcanic activity out of the seabed, the circular island of Rishiri (183 sq. kms.) is a miniature representation of the whole Japanese archipelago. Rishiri-san (1,719 m.), an extinct volcano whose central, hard, rock core forms its finely shaped peak, rises majestically out of the northern Japan Sea about 20 kilometers west of the northern extremity of Hokkaido. Fishing villages line its coast, from which forests climb its slopes to the alpine flora on the higher mountain. Its soaring peak is the highest in Northern Hokkaido, and is very alluring to Japanese hikers and climbers, who travel far just for the chance to climb this remote island peak.

However, the rewards of a visit to Rishiri are much greater than the bagging of another mountain peak. Quaint fishing villages around the rocky coast offer fresh seafood, with a chance to see seals, especially at Senhōshi Misaki (仙法志岬) on the south coast, and there are the two beautiful lakes of Hime-numa (姫沼) and Otadomari-numa (オタドマリ沼) not far from the coast. A road (53 kms.) circles the island with a bus service operating in both directions, and bicycles are for hire, making a circular tour of the island easily possible in one day, against the backdrop of its ever-present central peak. Few roads venture inland up the mountain slopes, leaving the central part of the island a hiker's or climber's domain, with three trails to the enticing peak starting from the harbor villages of Oshidomari, Kutsugata, and Oniwaki (now closed on the highest section due to danger from erosion). The route I have chosen takes the popular trail to the summit from Oshidomari, and then descends the trail to Kutsugata. This hike can be done in one day, but many climbers stay the night at the small Rishiri-dake Yamagoya, so they can be on the summit early the next morning.

Ten kilometers northwest of Rishiri can be seen Japan's northernmost island of Rebun (82 sq. kms.), which is relatively flat and elongated. It is called "the island of flowers" because over 300 species of alpine plants, some of which are endemic to the island, grow on its alpine plateau. Fishing villages are strung out along the east coast, but the west coast is a less inhabited, wild, rugged coast of rocky cliffs, with the west coast trail offering spectacular hiking on this island. Rebun's highest peak of Rebun-dake (礼文岳 490 m.) is much lower than Rishiri's peak, and can be climbed in two hours on a trail from the village of Nairo (内路) on the east coast.

Rishiri and Rebun islands form part of Japan's northernmost national park, Rishiri-Rebun-Sarobetsu National Park, which also includes the marshy Sarobetsu Plain, famous for its flowers, on the mainland of Hokkaido facing the islands. Wakkanai, Japan's northernmost port and train station, is the main access point for reaching the park and islands, and a 75-minute bus ride from Cape Sōya—Japan's northernmost point. On a very fine day the Soviet island of Sakhalin (Karafuto in Japanese) can be seen about 100 kilometers to the north.

Winters are very long, cold and snowy in this northern extremity of Japan, with snow remaining in sheltered gullies on Rishiri's peak year-round. Hiking on the islands, and viewing the colorful alpine flowers, is restricted to the months from June to September, but even the summer months of July and August can be very cold and wet, especially on Rishiri's peak, and so plenty of warm clothes are essential.

ACCESS

Wakkanai is linked by JR lines with the rest of Hokkaido, and from Wakkanai Station it is a five-minute walk to the ferry terminal from where the Higashi Nihonkai Ferry Company operates ferries to Rishiri and Rebun islands. Ferry services operate several times a day in the summer months between Wakkanai, Oshidomari on Rishiri, and Kafuka on Rebun, with less-frequent services to Kutsugata on Rishiri, and Funadomari on Rebun. The ferry takes about two hours from Wakkanai to Oshidomari, two hours thirty minutes to Kafuka, and about one hour between Oshidomari and Kafuka. There is also a ferry service to Rishiri and Rebun from the port of Otaru west of Sapporo, but this service does not run daily. Bus services operate on the main roads of both islands, and bicycles can also be hired. From Wakkanai bus services also operate to the Sarobetsu Plain, and to Cape Sōya, from the terminal near the station.

ACCOMMODATION

Youth hostels are well represented, with two in Wakkanai, two on Rishiri, and three on Rebun. In Wakkanai, the Wakkanai Moshiripa Youth Hostel (Tel: 0162-24-0180) is a five-minute walk from the station, and Wakkanai Youth Hostel (Tel: 0162-23-7162) is a ten-minute walk from Minami Wakkanai Station. Rishiri Green Hill Youth Hostel (Tel: 01638-2-2507) is 20 minutes' walk from the ferry terminal, and Rishiri Youth Hostel, only open in July and August, (Tel: 01638-4-2523) is ten minutes' walk south of Kutsugata. On Rebun, the Rebun Youth Hostel (Tel: 01638-6-1608) is a 15-minute walk from Kafuka Ferry Terminal, Momoiwa-sō Youth Hostel (Tel: 01638-6-1421/1390), in a very scenic location on the west side of the island, is 15 minutes by bus and then ten minutes on foot from Kafuka Ferry Terminal, and Rebuntō

Funadomari Youth Hostel (Tel: 01638-7-2717) is a 20-minute walk from the Funadomari Ferry Terminal on the north of the island. There is also plenty of minshuku accommodation on the islands.

There are three campsites on Rishiri, the most popular and convenient one for climbing the peak being about 50 minutes' walk up a narrow road from Oshidomari. Chalets are also for rent. The campsite at Kutsugata is next to the small lighthouse on the coast, and very near the ferry terminal. A quiet campsite is located near the museum in Oniwaki at the start of the trail on the southeast side of the mountain. On Rebun there is only one campsite on the shore of a lake behind the sports center in Funadomari. This is the most northerly campsite in Japan.

Food stores are found in the main ports on the islands, so it is not necessary to carry supplies for camping. On the climb up Rishiri-san, water is available only at the natural spring near the campsite at the start of the hike, and so a sufficient supply for the climb should be carried from there.

TRAILS

* * * * *
+ + + +
Oshidomari (鴛泊) ⟶ 3.5 kms. 1 hr. ⟶ Rishiri-hokuroku Campsite (利尻北麓野営場) ⟶ 5 kms. 3 hrs. ⟶ Rishiri Goya (利尻小屋) ⟶ 2 kms. 1 hr. 50 mins. ⟶ Rishiri-san (利尻山) ⟶ 3 kms 2 hrs. ⟶ Goya (小屋) ⟶ 7 kms. 2 hrs. 30 mins. ⟶ Kutsugata (沓形)

Clouds covered the peak of Rishiri-san on my arrival by ferry one day in August, and as I wanted to see the views on the climb I decided to stay on the coast and wait for good weather. However, clouds turned to rain in what turned out to be a bad summer in Hokkaido, and I spent three days making a circuit of the island before blue skies appeared. Most climbers leave early in the morning from the campsite up the road out of Oshidomari, and fill their water bottles with fresh spring water at Kanrosensui (甘露泉水) on the trail just after leaving the camp. The trail climbs up through forest, and soon passes a junction, where the trail to the left leads to the small peak of Ponyama and the lake of Hime-numa.

Staying on the main trail to the right, it is a fairly easy, pleasant hike through shady forest, with bamboo grass undergrowth, but it becomes steeper with some very slippery sections after rain. As the trail climbs the ridge you come into creeping pine vegetation before coming out on a shoulder where the small, wooden hut is located. From this vantage point on the ridge, there is a superb view of Rishiri's peak towering above, with a snowy gully in the valley below. A blanket of white cloud below obscured my view of Rishiri's coastline, and across the sea to Rebun and the mainland. A few hikers were resting inside the

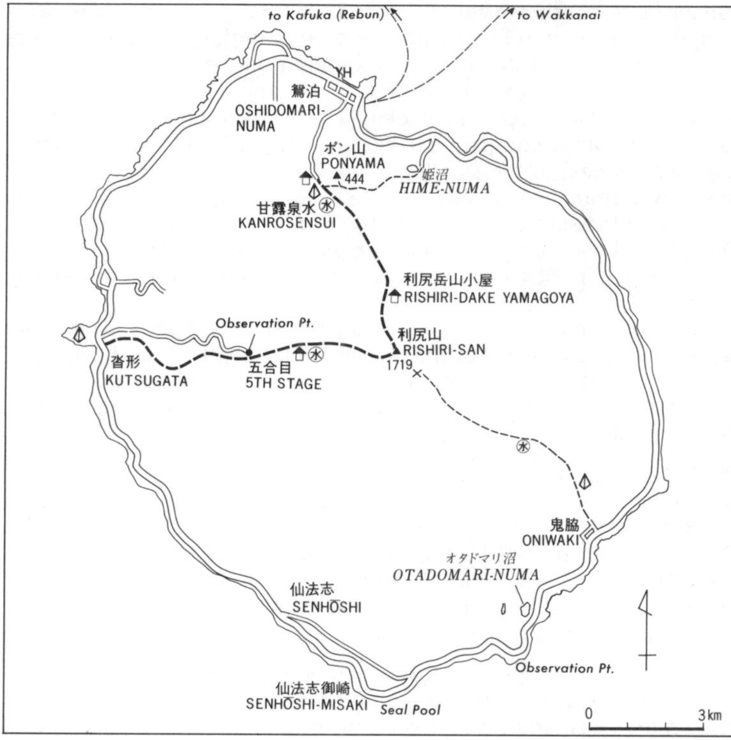
to Kafuka (Rebun)
to Wakkanai
YH
鴛泊
OSHIDOMARI-NUMA
ポン山
PONYAMA
444
姫沼
HIME-NUMA
甘露泉水
KANROSENSUI
利尻岳山小屋
RISHIRI-DAKE YAMAGOYA
Observation Pt.
利尻山
RISHIRI-SAN
1719
沓形
KUTSUGATA
五合目
5TH STAGE
鬼脇
ONIWAKI
オタドマリ沼
OTADOMARI-NUMA
仙法志
SENHŌSHI
Observation Pt.
仙法志御崎
SENHŌSHI-MISAKI
Seal Pool
0
3km

hut, while others were enjoying the views outside, and on the trail up the ridge to the peak a few specks indicated the presence of climbers on the rocky slopes. The ridge is very easy going at first after leaving the hut, but then becomes a very steep scramble up loose rocks with a sharp drop into a valley to the west. A signpost marks the trail to the right which leads down to Kutsugata, but the summit is a further 30-minute climb up the ridge from here. On the summit you are presented with a flat, table-like area, with a small Shinto shrine in the middle. It was a fine, sunny morning when I reached this peak, and many other successful climbers were sitting in the sun eating early lunches. The green slopes around the peak were speckled with bright colors, and I spent more than an hour photographing alpine flowers, including the white edelweiss, and peering down into precipitous ravines. Breaks in the layer of white, fluffy cloud below gave a few glimpses of Rishiri's coast, but Rebun remained concealed, as did the mainland, and there was no chance of seeing Sakhalin far to the north.

Pulling myself away from the summit I made my way back down to the trail junction for Kutsugata. This trail cuts below the ridge, and leads onto another ridge to the west of the peak. There are some difficult sections to traverse on the upper part of the trail, but then it descends the ridge through creeping pine vegetation. The trail eases off before coming to a small, unmanned hut, and continues down a relatively gentle slope through bamboo grass and then into the forest. At a trail junction, the trail right leads to a road and observation point, from where the port of Kutsugata, situated on a small peninsula, is visible below. The road leads down into Kutsugata, or alternatively you can continue down on the trail, which goes to the left at the junction and descends through forest to the port.

Both Rishiri Youth Hostel (turn left) and Kutsugata Campsite (turn right) are within ten minutes' walk after reaching the main road, or a bus can be taken back to Oshidomari. Many climbers go up and down the same route from Oshidomari to Rishiri's peak, as this requires less planning and is the easiest way to conquer Rishiri-san. If you encounter bad weather on the mountain it is recommended to take the same route back down. My conclusion after the climb to the top of this mountain island in the north was that it was well worth waiting three days to climb it in fine weather.

32. Climbing an Active Volcano: Meakan-dake
(雌阿寒岳)

Steam and sulphurous vapors were shooting and hissing out of the vent, and billowing hundreds of meters into the clear blue sky, as three adventurous volcanologists warily crept to the edge of the several-meter-wide hole in the mountain to suspend measuring instruments into its infernal depths. The raging volcanic vent in the crater of Meakan-dake was an awesome sight from the peak on the crater rim, and terrifying when approached at closer quarters on the crater floor, where the hissing sound and overpowering sulphur fumes were stronger. Coming fresh out of the bowels of the earth, the breath of Hades, which was coming from the same source of energy that had created the mountain, was now relatively tame and issuing its high-pressure steam in a constant, controlled manner into the cool mountain air. I had seen this steam rising from the volcanic peak the day before from 20 kilometers away as I approached Lake Akan-ko by bus from Teshikaga, and now I had reached its mountaintop source, which had been turned into an open-air natural scientific laboratory for probing the earth's secrets.

Meakan-dake is the highest peak and the only active volcano in Akan National Park in Eastern Hokkaido, which is almost entirely formed by volcanic features. According to its name and legend Meakan-dake is the female volcano, whereas to the east, across from Lake Akan-ko, rises the male volcano—the dormant Oakan-dake. Just south of Meakan-dake and fused to its slopes is the conical cinder cone of Akan Fuji only slightly lower and so forming twin peaks.

Apart from these volcanic peaks, Akan National Park is famous for its many lakes which are also the result of volcanic activity. Between the peaks of Meakan-dake and Oakan-dake lies Lake Akan-ko, after which the park is named. On the southern shores of this lake, at Akan Kohan, hot steam issues forth from natural hot springs, which rise from the muddy shore and bubble up into the lake. The lake was formed by volcanic activity as eruptions and lava flows from the now dormant Oakan-dake blocked the river valleys. However, Lake Akan-ko is most famous for its *marimo*, a rare green ball weed or algae which grows up to 20 centimeters in diameter, and is designated as a special natural monument. Due to photosynthesis, marimo balls rise to the surface of the lake in the early morning and sink to the bottom at night. The northern part of the lake, where there is a research station, is the best place to see them, that is, apart from the souvenir shops in Akan Kohan, and boat trips may be taken on the lake to view the algae.

To the north of the park Lake Kussharo-ko is the largest caldera lake in the world, and to the east Lake Mashū-ko lies in a parasitic caldera. Lake Mashū-ko is completely enclosed by 200-meter-high rock walls, has no inlet or outlet, and is often obscured by dense mist or fog. This mysterious lake was called "lake of the devil" by the Ainu, and its water is amongst the most transparent in the world.

The scenic Akan Transverse Road from Teshikaga to Akan Kohan has two lookout points. Sōgakudai commands a magnificent view of the volcanoes—Meakan-dake and Oakan-dake, while Sōkodai allows a glimpse of the two small lakes east of Oakan-dake—Penketō and Panketō.

Natural virgin forests cover Akan National Park's volcanic scenery with Yezo spruce, Sakhalin fir, Japanese beech, and silver birch, with rhododendron, azalea, and bamboo grass in the undergrowth. Wildlife abounds in the park and includes the brown bear, northern fox, deer and squirrels, as well as a variety of birdlife.

A relatively large population of Ainu live within the park area, and Ainu villages are located at Akan Kohan, and the southeastern corner of Lake Kussharo-ko, where there is an Ainu museum. Ainu music, singing, and dancing may be seen at these places, especially during summer evenings, but the performances have become very tourist-oriented and commercial.

Akan Kohan is a popular hot spring resort full of hotels and souvenir shops, but it is the best base for climbing the volcanoes. Kawayu, on the northeastern shores of Lake Kussharo-ko, is also a popular hot spring resort, and both have Visitors' Centers, with informative displays explaining the natural history of the area.

The best hiking in the park is on Meakan-dake, the highest peak, which is climbed by three different trails, and is a one-day hike up and down. There is also one trail to the top of Oakan-dake, which can be climbed easily in one day from Akan Kohan. The hike I describe here climbs Meakan-dake from Akan Kohan, goes over the peak and crater at the top, and down the west side to the beautiful Lake Onnetō.

ACCESS

Access to the area is best made on the JR Semmo Line which runs between Kushiro and Abashiri and goes through the park. Teshikaga is the station to get off at for the bus to Akan Kohan. Buses are necessary for reaching the main points of interest in the park, and a sightseeing bus service operates between Akan Kohan, Teshikaga, Kawayu, and Bihoro in either direction during the summer. The route between Teshikaga and Akan Kohan provides good views of Lake Akan-ko and its volcanoes. Lake Mashū-ko can be viewed from two observation points on the route between Teshikaga and Kawayu. Regular bus services to Akan Kohan also operate during the summer from Kushiro, Obihiro, and Bihoro. Local bus services include the one between Akan Kohan and Lake Onnetō, which is useful to return to Akan Kohan at the end of the hike over Meakan-dake.

ACCOMMODATION

The area is well supplied with youth hostels and minshuku. Akan Angel Youth Hostel (Tel: 0154-67-2309), located near the lake and campsite, is a 12-minute walk from Akan Kohan Bus Terminal. Ryogoku Minshuku (Tel: 0154-67-2773) is a few minutes' walk from the bus terminal. On the western side of Meakan-dake, about two kilometers from Lake Onnetō near the end of the hike described here, is Nonaka Onsen Youth Hostel (Tel: 01562-9-7454). A ten-minute bus ride from Teshikaga Station is Mashū-ko Youth Hostel (Tel: 01548-2-3098). Nomura Kawayu Youth Hostel (Tel: 01548-3-2037) is a 15-minute walk from Kawayu Station. Minshuku Nibushinosato (Tel: 01548-3-2294), located by Lake Kussharo-ko, is a ten-minute bus ride from the same station, around which there are many minshuku.

There are two convenient campsites for the hike described here: Akan Kohan Campsite is very close to the Ainu village and Lake Akanko, and was my starting point, and the other is at the southern end of Lake Onnetō in beautiful forest scenery near the end of the hike, just before coming to the lake. There is also a mountain hut at this location, but there are no mountain huts on the volcanoes. Two campsites are located on the shores of Lake Kussharo-ko at Kawayu and the Wakoto Peninsula to the south. Barbecue grills and firewood are available at the campsites, and it is best to bring food supplies from a large city such as Kushiro or Obihiro. The campsites have water supplies, but there is little fresh water on the hike, so plenty should be carried.

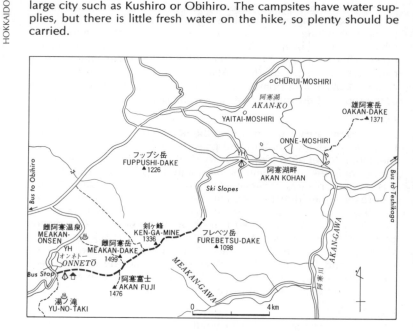

TRAILS

****

++++

Akan Kohan (阿寒湖畔) ⟶ 12.5 kms. 4 hrs. 15 mins. ⟶ Meakan-dake (雌阿寒岳) (1,499 m.) ⟶ 4.2 kms. 2 hrs. 30 mins. ⟶ Onnetō (温根沼)

Setting out early the next morning from the campsite, 200 meters on the main road west out of Akan Kohan brought me to the Meakan-dake trail entrance marked by a signboard. Turning left off the road, the forestry track is drivable for about five kilometers, and was easy walking through silver birch forest swathed in mist. (Paralleling a stream on the right there are other forestry tracks turning off, but continuing along the main track and not crossing the stream it soon winds up through the forest.) After climbing, the track returns to the stream and comes to a major junction more than one hour's hike from the road. The main track goes left, but the trail to Meakan-dake goes right, and there is a small box with a book for hikers to enter their name and intended route.

The trail crosses a small bridge over the stream after five minutes, and care should be taken here to follow the signposted trail as forestry tracks go left and right. This is a good place to look out for deer as you pass through a forest of Sakhalin fir, spruce and red spruce. After a few minutes the trail leaves the wide track and is signposted off to the right; the narrow trail here is marked by red arrow markers and red paint on the trees. Climbing through pine forest with bamboo grass undergrowth, a more open area of creeping pine is reached as the trail goes up the left side of a small valley. Signs of recent hot spring activity were visible in the yellow and white rocks of the valley.

At a fork the trail is signposted right and soon the rocky peak of Ken-ga-mine (1,336 m.) looms ahead. Climbing up to the ridge behind this peak the trail leaves the bushy vegetation and enters a rocky moonscape of volcanic ash. From the ridge the peaks of Meakan-dake and Akan Fuji are visible to the southwest, and on the far northwest side of the ridge a large volcanic vent belches forth steam. There are old mine workings nearby but they must have been abandoned due to the volcanic activity.

It is an exposed ridge hike going southwest on the ridge of yellowish volcanic rock until it joins the main slope up to the crater rim of Meakan-dake. A steep climb bearing right brings you onto the crater rim with the peak of Meakan-dake around the rim to the right. From the rim the billowing steam from the vent on the south side, and the barren cone of Akan Fuji beyond, with the whitish or yellow rocks and white steam set against a deep blue sky, presented a surreal land-scape. The northern part of the crater is much deeper, and the red lake marked on my map had dried up, but the higher crater floor to the southeast contains a small green pond. One or two other hikers had made their way up the steep shorter trail from Meakan Onsen to the west, and were catching their breath on the summit before it was taken from them again by the view.

Going around the crater rim on the eastern side it is possible to de-scend to the crater floor for a closer view of the green pond and the ac-tive, steaming vent where I met the team of Japanese volcanologists. Care should be taken to note the wind direction when hiking into the crater, or on the trail passing the vent, as the sulphur fumes can be dangerous and badly affect your breathing. The trail descends south of the vent and a small trail can be seen climbing the barren, rocky, sym-metrical cone of Akan Fuji. The climb or scramble to the top takes about 30 minutes.

The trail down to Lake Onnetō is steep and rocky until it comes to creeping pine, then pine forest, and there is a panoramic view of Lake Onnetō below before entering the shade of spruce, fir, and pine forest. Continuing down steeply through forest, the trail eventually emerges at a campsite and a large mountain hut at the southern end of the lake. The track from the hut joins the road which goes around the western shore of the lake. To the south there is a trail to the scenic Yu-no-taki

Waterfall, which is worth exploring if you are staying at Onnetō. From
the road along the western shore the view across the lake to the twin
peaks of Meakan-dake and Akan Fuji is splendid. Buses run to Akan
Kohan or it is a three-kilometer walk to Meakan Onsen and the
Nonaka Onsen Youth Hostel, which the bus passes, from where the
direct trail to the peak of Meakan-dake is signposted 100 meters north
of the hostel.

33. Hiking the End of the Earth: Shiretoko (知床)

Rising majestically from 200-meter-high sea cliffs, over which waterfalls cascade into the Okhotsk Sea, the ridge of volcanic peaks un-
dulate along the peninsula, and then descend to Shiretoko Misaki at its
northeastern extremity. A boat trip from the fishing port of Utoro,
situated halfway along the northwestern coast of the 65-kilometer-long
Shiretoko Peninsula, provides scenic views of the wild, dynamic
coastline fringing this finger of land jutting out into the cold sea off the
northeastern coast of Hokkaido. Most of the peninsula is covered by
the Shiretoko National Park, one of the wildest and remotest regions of
Japan. The Ainu name for this sea-bound mountain wilderness is apt—
''the end of the earth.''

In recent years the remoteness of this peninsula has been lessened
somewhat by the building of the Utoro-Rausu road across the peninsula in 1980. Smaller roads follow the coasts, providing access to the
main tourist attractions. The Shiretoko Five Lakes sit on a forested
plateau above the sea cliffs, with a two-kilometer-long trail around the
lakes whose waters reflect the backdrop of volcanic peaks. Further
along the peninsula the Kamuiwakka Falls, supplied with hot spring
water from the active Iwo-san, cascade down a steep, rocky valley
from an active area on the lower slopes of the mountain. The hot
water pools along its course are popular for outdoor bathing, with the
steaming water finally falling over the sea cliffs into the cold Okhotsk
Sea. Other hot springs on the peninsula include the rotenburo at
Iwaobetsu Onsen and Rausu Onsen, and the hotel resort area of Utoro
Onsen.

Despite the crowds of tourists at the height of the summer season,
the short hike around the five lakes is very scenic, and worth braving
the hordes of southerners. The most popular route for hikers in the
mountains is the climb up Rausu-dake, the highest peak on the peninsula, from Iwaobetsu Onsen, or alternatively the longer route from
Rausu Onsen. A climb to this peak and across the peninsula makes a
good one-day hike. More spectacular, longer, and much less trodden
is the route along the ridge of peaks, the backbone of the peninsula,
from Rausu-dake to Iwo-san, and descending to the Kamuiwakka Falls
through the active area of Iwo-san. This is the hike described here,

which usually takes two days to complete, requiring one night of camping in the mountains.

The Shiretoko Peninsula is formed by a chain of volcanic peaks which are part of the Kuril-Chishima Volcanic Zone stretching along the Kuril Islands to the Kamchatka Peninsula in Eastern Siberia. Rausu-dake, the highest peak on Shiretoko, is formed by a lava dome, and is not active at present, but Iwo-san, whose name means sulphur, is an active stratovolcano with volcanic vents on its northwestern slopes. Further along the peninsula is the lower peak of Shiretoko-san (1,254 m.). From the peaks, and the southeastern side of the Shiretoko Peninsula, can be seen the elongated Kunashiri Island to the east, with the higher conical volcanic peak of Chacha-dake (1,822 m.) at its northern end. This island is part of the disputed Northern Territories, a group of islands which were taken from Japan by the Soviets in 1945, and which the Japanese would like to see returned.

Winters are long and summers are very short on Shiretoko, where the cold Oyashio Current washes the shores of the peninsula, which becomes ice-bound in winter. The cold ocean often causes the formation of fog around the coast, especially the southeastern coast, but the area has relatively low precipitation. Hiking trips are restricted to the June-September period, with snow in the mountains for the rest of the year, and a few snow patches remain year-round on Rausu-dake.

The mountain slopes of the peninsula are forested up to about 1,000 meters with spruce, Sakhalin fir, beech, Japanese oak, and silver birch, with rhododendron and bamboo grass in the undergrowth. Above 1,000 meters the mountains have an alpine vegetation with creeping pine, and a profusion of alpine flowers bursting into color in the short summers. Unique to Iwo-san is a small, white violet (*Shiretoko sumire*). Wildlife on the peninsula includes the brown bear, deer, fox, squirrel and chipmunk. The sea cliffs abound in sea birds, including the white-tailed sea eagle, sooty guillemot, and Temminck's cormorant.

ACCESS

Shari, located on the JR train line between Kushiro and Abashiri, is the most convenient gateway to Shiretoko, with regular bus services to Utoro. Bus services also run from the train station at Nemuro-Shibetsu to Rausu, but are less frequent. During the summer months the ports of Utoro and Rausu are linked by a bus service which crosses the peninsula on the road over Shiretoko Pass, from where there is a good view of Rausu-dake. A bus service for tourists in the summer starts from Utoro and goes to Shiretoko Five Lakes and Kamuiwakka Falls, passing Iwaobetsu Youth Hostel and the track for Iwaobetsu Onsen, to which there is only one bus a day.

ACCOMMODATION

Four youth hostels are located on the peninsula. On the hill above the port of Utoro is Shiretoko Youth Hostel (Tel: 01522-4-2034). Iwaobe-tsu Youth Hostel (Tel: 01522-4-2311) is near a salmon hatchery about 20 minutes by bus from Utoro, on the road to the five lakes. Rausu Youth Hostel (Tel: 01538-7-2145) is located in the port town of Rausu. Shari Youth Hostel (Tel: 01522-3-2220) is a five-minute walk from Shari Station. Several minshuku are also found in Utoro and Rausu.

There are several campsites in Shiretoko. Large, official campsites are located next to the youth hostel in Utoro, on the hill overlooking Rausu Port, and at Rausu Onsen at the start of the trail up Rausu-dake, across the road and river from which there is a natural outdoor hot spring bath (*rotenburo*). Camping is also allowed behind the hotel at Iwaobetsu Onsen, where there is another rotenburo. Iwaobetsu Onsen is at the end of a four-kilometer-long dirt road starting near Iwaobetsu Youth Hostel, and is at the start of the trail up Rausu-dake. There is also a mountain hut behind the hotel here at the start of the trail, but there are no other mountain huts in the mountains of Shiretoko. If you spend a night in the mountains it is necessary to camp, and there are several good sites, but few with water. On this hike the best place to camp is at a site between the peaks of Mitsumine and Sashirui-dake, where there is a small spring. Water is available on the climb up Rausu-dake, but there is none on the climb over Iwo-san.

TRAILS

* * * * *
+ + + + +

Iwaobetsu Onsen (岩尾別温泉) —→ 7.2 kms. 4 hrs. —→ Rausu-dake (羅臼岳) (1,660 m.) —→ 2.5 kms. 1 hr. 25 mins. —→ Mitsumine Camp (三峰キャンプ) —→ 8 kms. 5 hrs. —→ Iwo-san (硫黄山) (1,562 m.) —→ 5.5 kms. 3 hrs. 45 mins. —→ Kamuiwakka-no-taki Falls (カムイワッカの滝) —→ 10 kms. 3 hrs (bus 30 mins.) —→ Shiretoko Five Lakes (知床五湖)

It was a cool, clear morning, with steam rising from the hot spring pools of the rotenburo, as I struck camp and set off up the trail to Rausu-dake from the small wooden mountain hut behind the large hotel at Iwaobetsu Onsen. The trail climbed steadily through mixed forest before coming to a spring called Yosankissui (弥三吉水) at an altitude of about 800 meters, after a two-hour hike. From the flat area next to the freshwater spring there are good views down to the Shiretoko Five Lakes, sitting on the wide ledge above the sea, and up to the peaks of Rausu-dake above and Iwo-san to the northeast. Camping is possible in this spot, where chipmunks may be seen scampering in the surrounding forest.

The trail continues over a gentler slope covered with silver birch forest, and then zigzags up a steeper slope to another freshwater spring after about fifty minutes. This spring is called Ginreisui (銀冷水), and also has a flat dirt area for camping. Soon leaving the forest, the

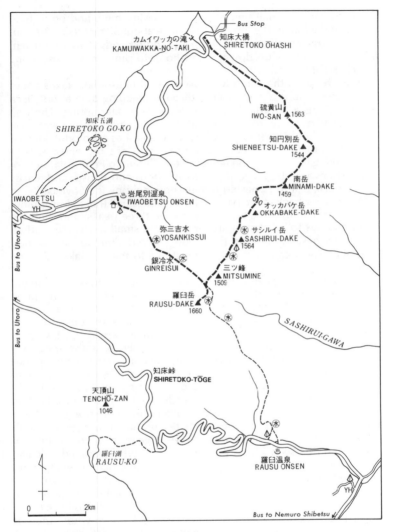

trail follows the bottom of a dry gully, and becomes rocky and steeper
as you climb up to the top of the pass. Alpine flowers and creeping
pine cover the ground in this alpine zone above about 1,200 meters.
The pass between the lava dome peak of Rausu-dake and the triple
peaks of Mitsumine is called Rausu-daira, and is a large flat area of

creeping pine. A small trail goes north to Mitsumine and on to Iwo-san, with the trail to the top of Rausu-dake about 50 meters further on. The main trail continues over the pass and descends to Rausu Onsen, taking about four hours down, or five hours to climb from Rausu along a very beautiful trail.

From the pass, the climb to the summit of Rausu-dake takes about 50 minutes, and is a gentle climb through creeping pine at first, to a small rock cave covered in moss with a freshwater spring. The trail becomes very rocky from here, with the route marked by paint, as it climbs over boulders amongst which grow splashes of colorful flowers. Coming onto the exposed, rocky peak, you are presented with a breathtaking view along the length of the Shiretoko Peninsula, to Iwo-san and beyond, below to the ports of Utoro and Rausu, and across the Okhotsk Sea to Kunashiri Island—now held by the Soviets.

Descending back to the pass and taking the small trail to Mitsumine, it is a short climb to the area between the three peaks, and then the trail descends to a flat camping area near a small freshwater spring. This is the best campsite in the mountains of Shiretoko, surrounded with alpine scenery, and with views down to the five lakes and the coast.

Climbing from the camp area the trail goes over a minor peak on the west side of Sashirui-dake (サシルイ岳), from where a small pond can be seen on the pass below. The trail descends to this pond, and is rocky and steep at first, before going through low bushes and creeping pine down a gully filled with snow. The snowmelt here is the last fresh water on the hike over the mountains. At the pass the trail goes through bushy vegetation and then turns left and comes to the pond.

From the marshy area by the pond the trail climbs the next peak of Okkabake-dake (オッカバケ岳), going over a minor peak to the north-west of the main peak, the trail descends again to two ponds, passing around the western shore of the first, larger one before rising slightly to the second smaller pond, which was dry on my visit. A gentle climb from the ponds soon brings you onto the ridge from where the peak of Iwo-san can be seen across a steep valley of white, eroded volcanic rock. Turning right and going eastwards the trail is difficult going here, as it climbs over dense creeping pine to the peak of Minami-dake (南岳). Staying close to the ridge it undulates to a flat, marshy area before going east of the ridge on a level section. The trail then climbs back to the ridge below the rocky peak of Shirenbetsu-dake from where there is an awe-inspiring view across precipitous volcanic ash slopes to the peaks of Iwo-san.

I would not like to do the next section in bad weather as it cuts beneath the rocky peak and goes north on a narrow, exposed ridge of yellowish-white volcanic ash, passing between pinnacles before coming to vegetated slopes again. Here the trail goes down to the right of the ridge and climbs a steep gully, then goes right through creeping pine to the first (lowest) of the three peaks of Iwo-san. The two higher peaks can be seen towering above, with a flat area between them. Making your way down to this flat area is a little difficult, going down a rocky slope of dense creeping pine, and then heading towards the eastern side of the highest peak to the north. The trail then goes down the ridge to the east where a sign marks the rocky route down into a gully to the north. This section on top of Iwo-san is difficult, the trail is not clearly marked, and there are many steep, rocky gullies eroded into the volcanic rock. On my hike from Rausu-dake I met no one until I luckily saw another hiker who had just climbed Iwo-san from Kamuiwakka-no-taki Falls, and he was able to point out the trail down.

Descending into a rocky gully the trail follows it for about one kilometer until a rope marks off the point where the trail leaves the gully and climbs to a ridge on the left (southwest). After climbing through forest the trail descends through creeping pine and bamboo grass before coming out in an open, desolate area of steaming, volcanic vents. The trail is marked by red paint on the rocks here as it goes left of the ridge, and through the hot spring area above a stream valley to the south. The hot spring waters which boil up out of the white and yellow rocks flow down into the valley, and supply the Kamuiwakka-no-taki Falls, popular with bathers who climb up the valley from the road way down below.

Leaving the active area the trail enters a silver birch forest, and it is an easy hike down to the dirt road. A wooden signboard marks the trail entrance at the road, making it easy to find if coming in the other direction. Turning left on the road it is about half a kilometer to the Kamuiwakka-no-taki Falls, whose hot waters cascade down the rocky valley floor before plunging into the sea. This is an excellent place to soak in one of the pools, and relax after the tiring climb over Iwo-san.

It is about ten kilometers from here to Shiretoko Five Lakes, or about 14 kilometers to Iwaobetsu Youth Hostel along a dirt road through forest, but a bus service now runs along this road to Utoro.

ABOUT THE AUTHOR

Paul Hunt graduated from London University with a degree in Geography. He worked as a meteorologist at Birmingham University for two years, and also taught in a Master of Science meteorology course.

Mr. Hunt first came to Japan in 1978, to work with a team exploring for oil in the Japan Sea. He returned in 1979 and lived in Japan for five years, hiking the length and breadth of the country. He has also travelled extensively in Asia and Africa, and is now working as a freelance travel writer based in Japan.

日本ハイキングガイド
HIKING IN JAPAN

1988年8月15日　第1刷発行
1998年8月20日　第9刷発行

著　者　　ポール・ハント

発行者　　野間佐和子

発行所　　講談社インターナショナル株式会社
　　　　　〒112-8652 東京都文京区音羽 1-17-14
　　　　　電話：03-3944-6493

印刷所　　株式会社　平河工業社

製本所　　株式会社　堅省堂

GATEWAY TO JAPAN   3rd Edition
June Kinoshita and Nicholas Palevsky

The premier guide to Japan, offering a comprehensive survey of every region of the country, complete with historical and cultural notes.

Paperback; 808 pp; 128 x 188 mm; ISBN 4-7700-2018-X

NEW JAPAN SOLO   Expanded Fourth Edition
Eiji Kanno and Constance O'Keefe

From two experienced travel professionals, a dependable, easy-to-use companion for all visitors to Japan, and of special appeal to the first-time visitor.

Paperback; 528 pp; 128 x 188 mm; ISBN 4-7700-2187-9

JAPAN: BUDGET TRAVEL GUIDE   Updated
Ian L. McQueen

The classic guide to getting there and enjoying it more – with minimum hassle and expense. Perfect for the independent traveler.

Paperback; 658 pp; 128 x 188 mm; ISBN 4-7700-2047-3

DAY WALKS NEAR TOKYO   Revised Edition
Gary D'A. Walters

One-day treks of scenic beauty and cultural interest in the Tokyo area. Features 25 different walks and includes detailed maps.

Paperback; 160 pp; 128 mm x 182 mm; isbn 4-7700-1620-4

A GUIDE TO JAPANESE HOT SPRINGS
Anne Hotta with Yoko Ishiguro

Over 160 hot springs throughout Japan, from rock-lined river pools to mountaintop hot tubs. Clear maps and recommended accommodations.

Paperback; 284 pp; 128 x 182 mm; ISBN 4-7700-1220-9

SKI JAPAN!
T. R. Reid

A fact-packed, entertaining guide to one of the most exciting ski meccas in the world. Details to over 320 ski areas, including over 20 world-class resorts and the sites of the '72 and '98 Olympics.

Paperback; 336 pp; 128 x 182 mm; ISBN 4-7700-1680-8

Tectonics, Mountain Ranges, and Active Volcanoes (Erupted since 1850)

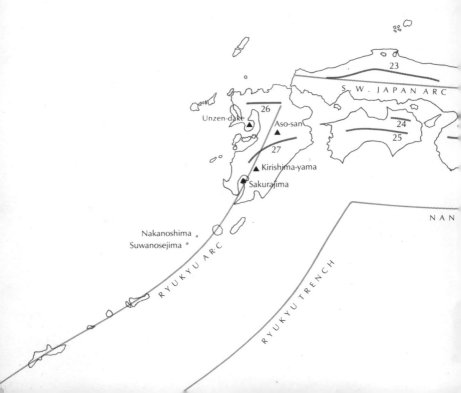